WITHDRAWN

D1651858

STUDENT RELIGION DURING FIFTY YEARS

Programs and Policies of the Intercollegiate Y. M. C. A.

By

WILLIAM H. MORGAN

WITH A FOREWORD

By

HARRISON SACKETT ELLIOTT

Submitted to the Department of Educational Research under the Faculty of Philosophy of Columbia University in partial fulfilment of the requirements for the degree of Doctor of Philosophy

ASSOCIATION PRESS

1 9 3 5

NEW YORK :: 347 MADISON AVENUE

BV
1170
M68
1935a

Copyright, 1935, by
WM. H. MORGAN

PRINTED IN THE UNITED STATES OF AMERICA

ACKNOWLEDGMENTS

THE author wishes to acknowledge his indebtedness to various persons who have coöperated to make this study possible. First of all are the members of his Dissertation Committee—Professors Harrison S. Elliott, George S. Counts, Floyd B. O'Rear, and Arthur L. Swift. For their unstinted help through their suggestions, their encouragement, and their criticisms the author is grateful. He is especially indebted to the chairman, Professor Elliott, who first inspired the thought of such a study and whose criticisms have enabled the author to bring it to a close in the form presented herewith.

To Mr. David R. Porter and Mr. Jesse R. Wilson, executives respectively of the National Student Movement, Y.M.C.A., and of the Student Volunteer Movement, as well as their associates, in making available essential materials, and to others who have contributed information through letters and interviews the author is deeply indebted. He wishes to acknowledge his obligation to his wife, Mildred Inskeep Morgan, whose help in countless ways has contributed to the completion of the study. He is indebted to Mr. S. M. Keeny for his criticism of the literary form, as well as to the following who have read parts or all of the manuscript: Dean A. J. Brumbaugh, Miss Leslie Blanchard, Mr. David R. Porter, Mr. Claud Nelson, Miss Winnifred Wygal, Professor M. Willard Lampe, Miss Margaret Logan Clark, Miss Sarah Beach, and Professor Ernest W. Warrington. He is grateful also to the various authors whose writings are quoted, and to the publishing houses and periodicals which have generously granted permission to use selections from their publications.

FOREWORD

ONE of the best ways to gain understanding of present-day problems and to find help for their solution is to study them in relation to their origin and development. Mr. Morgan's book is just this type of historical study of the major problems in connection with one of the most significant modern religious movements in the United States, the Student Young Men's Christian Association. His history of this Men's Student Christian Movement is not a mere chronology of events; instead, he has organized his material around the major issues faced in this Movement in the fifty-three years of its history up to 1930, and he has shown the developments which have come in meeting these issues in four major periods of its history. Since these problems are similar to those arising at the same time in the general Young Men's Christian Association and in denominational and other religious agencies, the book will prove of interest and significance to all religious workers who wish to face their present problems with the insight which comes from seeing them in their historical perspective. Further, this student agency has been so closely related with the general Young Men's Christian Association, of which it is a part, with the Young Women's Christian Association, and with the various denominations, that a record of its history necessarily involves interests and activities of more general concern.

The Student Young Men's Christian Association has been so bound up with the life of the campus that the book merits its title, *Student Religion During Fifty Years,* and it is consequently of importance to all those who are concerned with the religious life of students. The discussion of the relation of the Student Men's and Women's Associations, the Student Volunteer Movement, the denomi-

national agencies, and the college administrations, in their efforts to
influence the religious development of students, is an important part
of the volume. But the very fact that the Student Young Men's Christian Association is a student organization has resulted in its having
a profound influence upon social-religious activities far beyond the
college campus. Consequently, the book describes points of emphasis and method within the student organizations which were
carried by graduates into other agencies. There is discussion of
the pioneer endeavor carried on by the Student Young Men's Christian Association in such widely accepted forms of work as the
organization of small groups on a social basis, the employment of
discussion method, the development of student initiative and organizational self-determination, the utilization of a life-situation and
problem approach to program development, the efforts to correlate
the various lines of study and other activities in a unified program,
methods of life-work guidance and of sex education, selection and
training of volunteer workers, and conferences for inspiration and
training.

A survey of some of the issues in the Student Young Men's
Christian Association on which Mr. Morgan reviews the experience
of that agency will show the pertinence of the material to the problems now being faced by social and religious workers. These include: personal and public evangelism; study programs in the Bible,
missions and social questions; personal work and counseling; foreign-missionary interests; ways of developing religious experience;
service activities on the campus and in the community; inter-racial
problems; and the relation of students to campus life and to economic and other social questions beyond the campus. A major
issue in these areas is given full consideration: namely, that between
an "evangelistic and recruiting" method and an "educational and
counseling" approach. Efforts to make the Student Association an
all-campus influence are described, and the merits of this plan as
compared with developing it as a smaller, thoroughly committed,

and active group of students are considered. The Student Association has been so closely allied with the Student Volunteer Movement that the history of the efforts to interest and enlist students in foreign missions occupies a prominent place in the volume. Especially significant is the discussion of the issue around the relative attention students should give to campus problems and to the wider social issues as they manifest themselves on the campus, as compared with their attention to economic, inter-racial, and international questions beyond the campus. There is a review of the influence of the newer developments in psychology, education, and mental hygiene upon the program.

This book is commended to religious and social workers because of their interest in the college field and particularly because of the contribution it will make to their thinking. So many individuals now engaged in various aspects of the world's work were influenced by the Student Movement in their undergraduate days that the book will also be of interest to the general reader.

HARRISON S. ELLIOTT.

NOVEMBER 20, 1934.

CONTENTS

PREFACE

THIS study undertakes to bring out critically into relief some of the major program emphases and organizational policies of the Intercollegiate Y.M.C.A., i.e., the national organization now known as the National Student Movement of the Y.M.C.A. It seeks to follow these developments and the principles employed in connection with them from the inception of the intercollegiate phase of Y.M.C.A. work in 1877 to 1930, suggesting at the conclusion some of the continuing issues. Every institution, however, is a product of the social *milieu* in which it is developed. The Intercollegiate Y.M.C.A. is a product of the American society. Accordingly, an effort has been made to relate the program developments to the changing social situations.

The study in no sense claims to be exhaustive; it is intended as a preliminary step which it is hoped will facilitate further specialized study of specific phases of the programs and policies of the organization.

The Intercollegiate Y.M.C.A. includes sections for professional and preparatory school students and has a relation to work with other departments of the Y.M.C.A. for American racial and cultural minorities and foreign students. Moreover, Canadian students were for a long time included in the same general organization. This study, however, is concerned primarily with the programs and policies of the movement in relation to the undergraduates in the colleges and universities of the United States, exclusive of such specialized groups.

The focus of attention is directed to the work under a national committee with headquarters in New York which is charged with the development of the activities throughout the country. The study seeks, however, to take account of developments in the Y.M.C.A. work with students as viewed from a local campus or a state or a section of the country when these become a part of the national consciousness.

In developing the study the author has drawn upon such documentary material as the year books of the Y.M.C.A., containing official legislation and reports of the international and national conventions; the magazine of the Intercollegiate Y.M.C.A., that of the Student Volunteer Movement, and that of the World's Student Christian Federation; textbooks of the Intercollegiate Y.M.C.A. and of the Student Volunteer Movement on Bible study, foreign missions, race relations, industry, international questions, etc.; reports of the members of the staff of the Intercollegiate Y.M.C.A., of assemblies of these and other secretaries working with students, and of the annual reports of the organization to the World's Student Christian Federation; as well as miscellaneous collections of pamphlets and reports dealing with various phases of the work. The author has supplemented these documents with statistical data (from the year books and other sources), and with information gained through interviews and correspondence with a limited number of persons who have had a relation to the organization. In addition, the author has drawn upon his own experience with the organization as a student and as one of its staff members for several years afterwards.

A survey has been made of the materials in order to bring into relief the major developments in programs and policies, main emphases, problems, and changes, throughout the years. An analysis of these trends has then been attempted in order to locate some of the issues facing the movement today.

STUDENT RELIGION
DURING FIFTY YEARS

Part One: BACKGROUND

Chapter I. INTRODUCTION

The Religious Background of the Intercollegiate Y.M.C.A.

Prominent in the religious *milieu* in which the Intercollegiate Y.M.C.A. was started was the emphasis upon revivalism, developed in America for winning people to the Church, and led in the closing third of the nineteenth century by Dwight L. Moody.[1] Started by Jonathan Edwards as a "new and highly emotional reaction" in New England in the fourth decade of the eighteenth century, the first movement of this sort soon spread to other parts of the colonies and became known as the "Great Awakening."[2] Many others followed, including the revival of the Wesleys and Whitefield in the closing years of the eighteenth and the opening years of the nineteenth century.[3]

The force of such movements is illustrated in a revival at Yale in 1802, which is reported to have resulted in the conversion of one-third of the student body. Similar religious awakenings took place at Williams and other eastern colleges, as well as among the general populace in the East, in the middle Atlantic states, and in the South.[4] Nor did the West escape. In the life on the frontier, fervent religious meetings developed into what came to be called "camp meetings."[5] From this period also date the beginnings of American missionary activity, which went beyond the western fron-

[1] Sweet, W. W., *The Story of Religions in America*, pp. 7, 8.
[2] *Ibid.*, p. 97.
[3] *Ibid.*, p. 326.
[4] *Ibid.*, p. 326.
[5] *Ibid.*, p. 329.

1

tier and included work with American Indians and with the "heathen" in foreign lands.[6] Approaching more definitely the period which primarily concerns us, we shall note the new role being assumed by laymen, the rise of Mr. Moody, and the prevailing religious ideas and forces at the time in which he started his work. Beginning with the Great Awakening of 1732, the leadership was in the hands of the clergy; but the need of great numbers of preachers called out many who were not trained in the ministry. "The place of the layman was most distinctly recognized in the Methodist bodies, but practically all American Protestantism made a place and a large place for him . . . ." [7] The significance of the lay influence is seen strikingly in the development of the Sunday-school movement. In 1737, John Wesley "had already established Sunday-schools on the missionary journey to America." [8] In 1782 the movement was organized and made interdenominational by the work of Robert Raikes. "As it made its way everywhere in reorganized Protestantism, it enormously increased the activity of the lay elements of the churches, and the general theory was that every converted boy and girl . . . . could trust God's Spirit to guide them in instructing. . . . This was the firm and humble faith of all conventicle piety, in which the infallible Bible made all men and women equal so long as they had the Holy Spirit to lead them into all truth . . . ." [9]

The early and middle nineteenth century brought rapid changes in the economic life of the people. "An industrial revolution was under way comparable to that which had taken place in England a century before." New peoples were pouring into the country. The common people had been elevated to power, a fact symbolized by the election of Andrew Jackson as President of the United States. "Opportunity was the key word of this new era. . . . An individ-

[6] *Ibid.,* p. 351.
[7] Hall, T. C., *The Religious Background of American Culture,* pp. 240 ff.
[8] *Ibid.,* p. 243.
[9] *Ibid.,* p. 243.

ualistic attitude dominated the people, while emotionalism everywhere prevailed." [10]   Such individualism and optimism led to wild
speculation, which brought on the panic of 1857.   This precipitated
another great revival which swept over the country.

The dominant religious note of the time was restricted almost
exclusively to emphasis upon individual salvation. Of the work in
the Sunday-schools at the time, it is reported that the "Reverend
Stephen H. Tyng, rector of St. George's Church, New York, writing
in 1860, and looking back over forty years of experience, said,
'You will see that . . . . the purpose of Sunday-school teaching
is . . . . the actual conversion of children to God.' " [11]   In a
paper which was read before the General Sunday School Convention held in London in 1862, Charles Reed expressed the purpose
of Sunday-school work as follows: "For a religious education to be
worth the name it must . . . . first see that the Spirit is safe for
heaven, and then let us teach how to spend the intervening time on
earth." [12]

It was within such religious emphases that Mr. Dwight L. Moody
began to express his own program. Born in a Unitarian family in
Northfield, Massachusetts, in 1837, he came to feel more at home
in a Congregational church. One day in 1856, while wrapping up
a package of shoes in connection with his work as a clerk in a shoe
store, his Congregational "Sunday-school teacher . . . . dropped in
on him and in a few earnest words urged him to give his allegiance
to Jesus Christ. . . . 'I will,' he replied." [13]   He became at once
active in prayer meetings and Sunday-school work. The same year
he moved to Chicago, and became a wholesaler of shoes. "The
nation-wide revival of 1857 . . . . infused in him the zeal that
flamed into the mastering passion of his life and it gave the first defi-

---

[10] Sweet, W. W., *op. cit.*, pp. 374 ff.
[11] Brown, A. A., *A History of Religious Education in Recent Times*,
p. 63.
[12] *Ibid.*, p. 74.
[13] Loud, G. C., *Evangelized America*, p. 237.

nite direction toward the career for which he was heading." [14]   During the Civil War he "could be seen, night after night, at Camp Douglas, 'going from tent to tent, striving to bring the soldiers under the influence of divine grace.' " [15]

In the post-war period also such an emphasis upon personal religion as Mr. Moody represented was the dominant note of the time.   True, Horace Bushnell, a Congregational minister at Hartford, Connecticut, was inspiring a new religious thought and experience; in contrast to revivalism, which insisted upon a conscious emotional experience, Bushnell urged "that the child should grow up a Christian and never know himself as being otherwise." But this point of view was not widely accepted.[16]   Some were disturbed with a great influx of Irish and German immigrants between 1865 and 1884 and the consequent tendency to forsake the Puritan Sabbath.[17]   Again, others were concerned with the problem created by the doctrine of evolution, proposed by Charles Darwin, because it seemed to conflict with the biblical account of creation.[18]   Although the Civil War minimized theological differences in the face of militant politics"; heightened religious feeling; called out charity on a wide scale; and caused increased giving to "home" and "foreign" missions; nevertheless one may say that at the end of the War "the great churches in the United States were thoroughly orthodox and conservative." [19]

Discussing the post-war religious emphases and their reflection in Mr. Moody's work, Professor Shailer Mathews says,

"The eighteenth century saw not only the rise of democracy among English-speaking peoples and, with modifications, in France, but it also saw the marked individualization of religion.   The church

[14] *Ibid.,* p. 237.
[15] Seldes, G., *The Stammering Century,* p. 136.
[16] Sweet, W. W., *op. cit.,* p. 491.
[17] *Ibid., p.* 479.
[18] *Ibid.,* p. 492.
[19] *Ibid.,* pp. 467, 491.

accepted the economic and social *status quo,* and devoted itself to the saving of souls. Where, as in the case of slavery, an attempt was made by Christians to effect social change, there followed a cleavage among the nonconformist churches, like the Presbyterians, Methodists, and Baptists. Each of the two main divisions thus formed tended to maintain the social *status quo;* churches in the North, where there were no slaves, favored anti-slavery, and churches in the South, where slavery existed, championed it. And slavery was as much an economic as a political issue. After the Civil War, the period of revivalism begun by Finney developed under the leadership of Dwight L. Moody and laid emphasis almost exclusively upon individual salvation. The doctrines stressed were chiefly those of the substitutionary atonement and the necessity of rebirth. The ethical connotation which the Christian life bore was hardly more than conventional morality. Little attempt was made in the name of religion to change the economic or social *status quo,* although decided emphasis was given to missionary activities in non-Christian lands . . . ." [20]

Mr. Moody helped to establish the Y.M.C.A. in Chicago, and was for a long time its active head. He soon also became a conspicuous figure in the national conventions of the Associations.[21] Through his work in the Y.M.C.A. and as an evangelist, he was destined, as we shall see, to wield a strong influence with students related to the Y.M.C.A.

ORGANIZATIONAL BACKGROUND OF THE INTERCOLLEGIATE Y.M.C.A.

The Intercollegiate Y.M.C.A. developed in a lay movement which started in another country, among "dissenting circles in the North of England and the South of Scotland, where industry and business were calling young men away from their country

[20] *Religious Thought in the Last Quarter Century,* edited by Gerald B. Smith, pp. 229 ff.
[21] Morse, R. C., *History of the North American Young Men's Christian Associations,* p. 122.

homes to the city with its temptations." [22]   The moving spirit
in the parent organization was an apprentice in a dry goods
establishment in Bridgewater, England, who had been brought
under religious influences and was converted and who soon began
to seek for his associates the same experience.   It was this desire
which inspired the development in London in 1844 of the Association, which gave as its object, "the improvement of the spiritual
condition of young men in the drapery and other trades."   Membership was for "any person who gives decided evidence of his conversion to God." [23]   This evangelistic emphasis began to express
itself more and more, however, through attractive rooms where young
men could meet for social purposes, and for reading and lectures.
Soon employed officers began to appear in the Association, the first
one under the title of "a missionary secretary." [24]   The work soon
became established in other cities in Great Britain and on the Continent.   In 1851 two organizations were formed in America—the
first at Montreal, and the other at Boston.[25]   The work spread rapidly.   In 1854 thirty-seven young men, delegates from nineteen
Associations, met in Buffalo and a Confederation of "independent,
equal, but coöperating Associations" was formed with plans for an
annual convention and an Executive or Central Committee, later
called the "International Committee." [26]   The movement soon expanded also into various branches for work with special groups.   In
1858 a student association was formed at the University of Virginia,
followed very soon afterwards by another at the University of Michigan.[27]   No special effort, however, was made for the development
of work with students until later.   Mr. Robert Weidensall, the first

[22] Hall, T. C., *op. cit.*, p. 247.
[23] Morse, R. C., *op. cit.*, p. 3.
[24] *Ibid.*, pp. 3 ff.
[25] *Ibid.*, p. 15.
[26] *Ibid.*, p. 31.
[27] Shedd, C. P., "The Origin and Development of the Student Young
Men's Christian Association Movement in North America," pp. 36 ff.   (Unpublished study.)

secretary of the International Committee, said that the student "department of Association work barely received its first favorable public recognition in 1870." [28] That year the International Convention held at Indianapolis adopted a resolution, presented by Professor A. K. Spence of the University of Michigan, urging "that Christian Associations be planted wherever practicable in our academies, colleges, and universities, and that we urge especially such Societies already existing that they seek to extend their work in this important field." [29] The next year the Associations of the State University and Olivet College, the only college associations in Michigan at that time, sent delegates to the state convention. Definite steps were taken in the convention to form Associations in other colleges of the state.[30] Subsequent national conventions emphasized the importance of work with students.[31] Students also manifested an interest in having the work extended into educational institutions. Mr. Weidensall, reporting on a trip into the South in 1872, said that the president of the Association at the University of Virginia "is very anxious to have an organization in all southern institutions of learning. I advised him to correspond with the Association in Michigan and Cornell Universities." [32]

There was no relation between these student associations as such, however, until 1877, when an intercollegiate department of the International Committee was formed. This was brought about by developments in which students and professors of Princeton University took the initiative. One of their number, Luther D. Wishard, had been a student at Hanover College, Indiana; his father had attended the International Convention at Indianapolis in 1870, and he, himself, was a delegate in 1872 to a similar convention in Lowell, Massachusetts. Wishard entered Princeton Uni-

[28] Weidensall, Robert, *Early History of the College Work of Young Men's Christian Associations*, p. 102.
[29] *Report of the International Convention of the Y.M.C.A.*, 1870, p. 64.
[30] Weidensall, Robert, *op. cit.*, p. 34.
[31] Morse, Richard C., *My Life with Young Men*, p. 142.
[32] Weidensall, Robert, *op. cit.*, p. 60.

versity in the fall of 1875 and, along with others, was instrumental in having the "Philadelphian Society," a religious society of the University, require its members to be members of an "evangelical" [33] church in order that it might affiliate with the Y.M.C.A.

A religious "revival" in Princeton in 1876, led by Dwight L. Moody and William M. Taylor, stirred the students to visit neighboring colleges in an effort to extend its influence to other students. A member of the International Committee of the Y.M.C.A. suggested that a place would be made for the discussion of student work, if desired, in the approaching international convention.

The students began to feel that what Princeton ought "to do in nearby colleges, other institutions also ought to do" and that if "such work were to extend and abide there must be organization and coöperation through permanent union." [34]   Not all the students, however, were inclined to join with the Y.M.C.A. Mr. Wishard continues:

"Some were disposed to stand for an exclusively student movement which might be called an Intercollegiate Christian Union;

[33] The basis of membership in the Y.M.C.A. at the time was known as "evangelical," which required essentially that controlling membership be restricted to those who were members of "churches held to be evangelical," i.e. those churches "which, maintaining the Holy Scriptures to be the only infallible rule of faith and practice, do believe in the Lord Jesus Christ (the only begotten of the Father, King of Kings, and Lord of Lords, in whom dwelleth the fullness of the Godhead bodily, and who was made sin for us, though knowing no sin, bearing our sins in his own body on the tree) as the only name under heaven given among men whereby we must be saved from everlasting punishment and to eternal life." Morse, R. C., *History of the North American Young Men's Christian Associations,* p. 279.

Robert Weidensall found that this basis of membership was a deterrent to the extension of the work among students. "A much larger number of College Associations," he said, "could have been formed before the Louisville Convention in 1877. To my certain knowledge, the doors of the colleges and universities were open to the formation of Association work a considerable time before that date in the West and South. . . . The chief objection seemed to be the evangelical basis of active membership . . . ." Weidensall, Robert, *op. cit.,* p. 113.

[34] Wishard, L. D., *Beginnings of the Students' Era in Christian History,* pp. 25, 29, 53, 55 ff.

but this I insisted would defeat two ends. First, it would deprive the colleges of the stimulus to be derived from the touch of practical Christian business men; second, it would deprive city Associations of the steady inflow of men from the colleges who would naturally pass from one department of the Brotherhood to another and who might render invaluable help to young business men from whom they were temporarily separated by college walls but with whom and for whom they were destined to live and to do the greater part of their life work." [35]

The Philadelphian Society sent out a circular inviting colleges to send delegates to the Convention at Louisville, June, 1877. Twenty-five delegates from twenty-one colleges and universities in thirteen different states came together at Louisville at the time of the convention for an intercollegiate student conference. They requested the convention to promote an intercollegiate Y.M.C.A. movement and to employ a secretary for that purpose. The convention granted their request and engaged Mr. Wishard as the employed worker.[36]

[35] *Ibid.*, p. 62.
[36] *Ibid.*, pp. 69 ff.

PART TWO: EARLY PROGRAM EMPHASES
1877-1890

Chapter II. EARLY OBJECTIVES AND EMPHASES

THE newly-formed organization reflected in its purpose the dominant religious emphases of the time. It declared its objectives to be the promotion, in addition to Bible study, of such things as the following:

1. Devotional meetings conducted by the students.
2. "Individual Work," i.e., personally inviting others to become Christians.
3. Religious work in the neighborhood—in Sunday-schools, prayer meetings, services in hospitals, almshouses, and jails.
4. Missionary meetings.
5. An association room, attractive, neatly-carpeted, supplied with papers and magazines, as well as "a neat cabinet organ and a good supply of hymn books." [1]
6. "Intercollegiate Christian sympathy." [2]

At first the promoters of the organization expected to achieve such objectives by means of correspondence, conventions, exchange visits by students, the use of an existing religious publication (*The Watchman*), and supervision by a "corresponding secretary." [3] Although the work was soon to claim all of his time, Mr. Wishard

[1] Of such a room Mr. Wishard said very soon afterwards, "It is the students' home, where they always meet to read, sing, and pray. About it are clustered many precious memories of times of refreshing, when one and another of our companions" are "born into the Kingdom of God." Wishard, L. D., *The College Bulletin,* Vol. 1, No. 4, 1879, p. 1.

[2] *Ibid.,* p. 1.

[3] Wishard, L. D., *op. cit.,* p. 71.

started in September, 1877, to give part of his time as the "corresponding secretary." [4] He was quite an influential force in determining the character of the organization, a fact which was due not alone to his official relationship to it, but to his own experience expressed through an unusually energetic, dynamic personality.[5] Mr. Wishard has enabled us to catch something of the sense of compulsion which he felt growing out of his early experiences. Through his father, who attended the International Convention of the Y.M.C.A. in 1870, he says he was first "interested in the Y.M.C.A. and first impressed with its power." [6] Strongly influencing his interests was the attitude of his mother also. Writing of her death, which took place in 1868, he said:

"It just happened . . . . if anything happens . . . . that the night before her home-going she gave expression to a desire, which had evidently deepened into a life hope, namely, that my life be devoted to the ministry. While the program of my Christian work has been such as she could not then have forecast, I have never doubted that the spirit of my mother's last expressed wish concerning me has been fulfilled . . . ." [7]

When Mr. Wishard accepted the position with the Intercollegiate Y.M.C.A. he looked upon it as only temporary, for he was anxious to become a foreign missionary. After counseling, however, with a number of older friends (most of whom advised his remaining in America for the new student work), he discussed the matter finally with the Chairman of the International Committee. He tells of the developments following that interview which led to his continuing with the college work.

"I did not reach a clear decision until the following noonday and that found me in Fulton Street Prayer Meeting, to which I had sent a request for prayer for divine guidance. My request was

---

[4] *Ibid.*, pp., 77, 82.
[5] Interview Document, No. 18.
[6] *Ibid.*, p. 25.
[7] *Ibid.*, p. 23.

read at the meeting and prayer was offered, followed by the singing of Ray Palmer's immortal hymn, 'My faith looks up to thee.'
As they sang the lines, 'O may I from this day be wholly Thine,'
I walked out of the room assured that I was destined for a period
of years to remain in America for the sake of foreign missions." [8]

A small monthly magazine was started by the Intercollegiate
Y.M.C.A. a year after the beginning of the organization. At first
called *The College Bulletin,* it was succeeded by *The Intercollegian,*
which was in turn succeeded by *The North American Student,* and
that in turn by *The Intercollegian.* The first editorial in the first
number of *The College Bulletin,*[9] says that the only subscription
price asked "is sympathy with the college work and a renewed consecration on the part of students for the salvation of their class-
mates and friends in college." Another statement in the same paper
says that the movement had grown out of three convictions:
(1) "the salvation of students; (2) the salvation of students while
in college; (3) the value of united work and united prayer." [10]

One of the means for putting these convictions into effect was
suggested by Mr. Wishard in his annual report for 1884:

"The Committee on Membership privately assigns each unconverted student to some Christian who prays for him, invites him
frequently to the meetings, and whenever possible speaks a word
which is calculated to help him settle the great question of life." [11]

BIBLE STUDY FOR PERSONAL WORK

Central in the means employed by the Intercollegiate Y.M.C.A.
to accomplish its objectives was Bible study. At the very first meeting in Louisville, when the intercollegiate movement was organized,
the students indicated that "diligent study of the Word of God,"
along with prayer, personal work, and a well-organized Association

[8] *Ibid.,* p. 86.
[9] November, 1878.
[10] *The Y.M.C.A. Year Book,* 1884, p. 77.
[11] *Ibid.,* p. 77.

was essential to success.[12]   An immediate incentive for such an emphasis was indicated in a statement by Mr. Wishard concerning the convention which authorized the intercollegiate work:

"The deepest, most abiding impression made on me by the leading men . . . . was their exceptional familiarity with the Scriptures, their reliance upon the word of God as an infallible rule of faith and practice, and their dependence upon it as an inspired manual on Christian living and Christian service, a proper acquaintance with which makes the Man of God perfect and thoroughly furnished unto all good works." [13]

Mr. Wishard urged Bible study as one of the most important things for the new converts:

"They ought to be nourished with the Word.   For this reason there should be an Association Bible class.   Nothing else can take the place of this.   I Peter ii:2." [14]

Special emphasis was placed upon the study of the Bible in order to "render students familiar with the use of the Word in dealing with the unconverted." [15]   An excerpt from a report of an annual conference of the New England College Associations, which met with the Society of Christian Brethren of Harvard University, February 20 to 22, 1885, indicates the force of this emphasis.

"The Amherst Association reported twenty groups of students, with about five in each, which meet once a week to study the Word, with the view of ascertaining its answers to the various objections offered for not accepting Christ.   They do a great deal of individual work between the meetings, which suggests topics for this study. Yale reported a similar system." [16]

[12] *The College Bulletin,* Vol. I, No. 2, Dec., 1878, p. 2.
[13] Wishard, L. D., *op. cit.,* pp. 109 ff.
[14] *The College Bulletin,* Vol. II, No. 7, Mar., 1880, p. 3.
[15] *The College Bulletin,* Vol. V., No. 1, Oct., 1882, p. 3.
[16] *The College Bulletin,* Vol. VII, No. 5, Mar., 1885, p. 18.

In order to provide for "students an opportunity for such study of the Word as will promote their own spiritual life and render them wise in winning souls," leaders of the Intercollegiate Y.M.C.A. recommended the following methods:

(1) "Book-by-book study"—studying each book of the Bible separately.
(2) "Biographical method"—analyzing the characters of the Bible in order to learn the secret of their power.
(3) "The topical method." [17]

The last-named method was emphasized and developed in a special course prepared by the leaders—Mr. Wishard and Mr. C. K. Ober, who had been added to the staff in January, 1885, for student work, as well as Mr. R. C. Morse and Mr. H. E. Brown, other Y.M.C.A. secretaries. This course, developed in a topical-outline form and published in 1886 as a pamphlet entitled *Outlines of Bible Study for the Bible Training Class,* contains thirty-three lessons. The first five are devoted to introductory studies of the Bible itself, considering its titles, authorship, theme, and divisions.[18]

The theme developed is that the Bible, an inspired book, foretells of Christ's coming; that Christ is the theme of the Bible.

The remaining twenty-eight studies are devoted to "Fundamental Truth"—on God (What does God say in his Word concerning Himself?) ; on "Sin"; on "Christ"; on "Christ our Saviour"; on "the Holy Spirit"; on "Repentance and Confession of

---

[17] *The College Bulletin,* Vol. III, No. 4, Feb., 1885, p. 14.
[18] The first lesson, for example, appears in this form:
"How shall I study the Bible?
    As all sufficient and conclusive.
        Is. 8:20, Mark 12:24-27 . . . .
        To find Christ . . . . John 5:39."

The outlines appear in essentially the same form for the group members and the leaders, except that very few of the biblical references are given in the students' outlines.

Sin"; on "Faith"; "Forgiveness"; "Regeneration"; "Justification";
and "Christian Living." [19]

Interspersed through the studies are opportunities for the consideration of individual cases, including the following types:

I. "The Ignorant—of the plan of Salvation, of the Nature
and Importance of Repentance and of Faith; of the
evidence of Conversion.

II. "The Doubting, of the existence of God, of the Inspiration of the Bible; of the Deity of Christ; of the Reality
of Future Punishment; of the Reality of Conversion,"
etc.

III. "The Self-satisfied," etc.

IV. "The Complaining."

V. "The Fearful."

VI. "Those Lacking Conviction."

VII. "The Discouraged."

VIII. "The Wilful."

IX. "Those Lacking Decision."

X. "Backsliders."

XI. "Those Weak in the Faith."

XII. "Young Converts."

The outlines provide for reports of workers in dealing with individual cases. "Bible drill" is urged because it "is the business of
the training class to find and consider carefully these appropriate
messages of God, and to hold them ready for use." A number of
lessons are devoted to review and examination.

Alternative forms of pledges of regular attendance are suggested.

[19] An idea of the treatment of each of these topics may be gained
from the outline of the last-named—"Christian Living":

I. "Confession of Christ. Luke 12:8, 9; Rom. 10:9, 10.

II. "Communion. Matt. 28:20; John 15:5; Phil. 4:13; Heb. 12:1, 2.
By prayer . . . . .John 16:23, 24; Jas. 1:5.
Bible Study . . . . .Josh. 1:8; John 15:7; i Tim. 3:16, 17.

III. "Consecration. Rom. 12:1."

Both are exacting, especially so for work which was purely voluntary. One concludes: "Absence from the class twice in succession, excepting for any of the above reasons [sickness, absence from the city, or pressing business], which shall be given in writing to the secretary, will be considered equal to resignation." The other pledge form suggests the following: "We agree to study diligently, devoting not less than three hours each week to preparation for the the study in the class." [20]

To provide for direction of the class it was urged that a mature man be secured as teacher, but one who is "most apt to teach—not to talk," one who will "teach men to work as well as fill them with information"; or that a member be chosen from the group and carry on the work with members gathered "around a table." [21] The recognized value of the informal, democratic, group spirit and activity, as well as the opportunity for self-expression which this engendered, is significant. "It would be," say the authors, "a . . . . serious mistake for any persons . . . . to pursue such a course of study as this without putting the results of their study into actual and immediate use. We learn how to walk by walking, and so we learn how to do personal work by doing it . . . ." The class was accordingly urged to study actual instead of imaginary cases.[22]

The same general plan was developed in succeeding studies. In the January, March, May, and June, 1889, numbers of *The Intercollegian* (which succeeded *The College Bulletin*) studies appeared in the form intended for members of the group under the title, "Topical Studies and Plans of Work for Bible Training Classes." [23] Special forms were prepared for leaders. Characteristic features of each lesson may be illustrated by the following excerpt:

[20] Leader's edition, *Outlines of Bible Study for the Training Class*, p. 15 (Pamphlet).
[21] *Ibid.*, Member's edition, p. 16.
[22] *Ibid.*, Leader's edition, p. 11.
[23] *The Intercollegian*, Vol. XI, No. 3, p. 8; No. 4, p. 7; No. 5, p. 10. This form is for members of the class.

I. Topical Bible Study . . . .
    "A. The man who is not a Christian—
        1. What testimony shall we accept as reliable con-
           cerning him?
           a. What about the man's opinion regarding
              himself? Jer. 17:9; Isa. 44:20.
           b. Is the judgment of other men likely to be
              correct and unbiased concerning him?
              I Sam. 16:7.
           c. What testimony have we which is both un-
              prejudiced and infallible on this and
              other kindred questions? Heb. 44:12;
              Ps. 19:7-8." [24]

The following "Hints on Bible Drill" reveal the significance attached to the biblical material:

"Have the Bibles closed during this part of the exercise. Take up each point in the topic, calling upon some member to repeat one or more passages from the Bible, which will clearly establish it. Let another member give the exact location of the passage quoted. . . . The leader must insist upon ready answers and rapidity of quotation. Do not wait upon a man. The object of this Bible Drill is to cultivate accuracy and readiness in the use of the Scriptures. Every successful personal worker must have these qualities; must be ready for emergencies. . . . Cover the lesson in the required time. . . . Absolutely insist on asking all the questions yourself during the larger part of the hour. Leave a few moments at the close for others to ask questions." [25]

A typical incentive to growth is that through the work students were urged to qualify to become leaders. Even those who felt that they might fail were urged to try before "giving up. One great object of this system is to develop leaders." This emphasis on training students to do "personal work," i.e., "to lead men one by one

---

[24] Leader's edition, *Topical Studies and Plans of Work for Bible Training Classes*, p. 11.
  [25] *Ibid.*, pp. 6 ff.

to commit their lives to Jesus Christ as their Lord and Savior" [26] called out a similar text soon afterwards.[27]   Other texts prepared by the Association for the same purpose have appeared from time to time since then.

RESTRICTION OF MEMBERSHIP TO MEN

It is necessary to note developments also in this early period which resulted in restricting membership in the Intercollegiate Y.M.C.A. to men.   For a long time in the general Y.M.C.A. it had been a question of whether membership should be restricted to young men only.   As late as 1881, the question was still being discussed.   In a convention that year at Cleveland, the general secretary of the Toronto Association urged Bible study classes exclusively for young men on the ground, .

"that there are in the Word of God many passages which were designedly addressed to and ought to be enforced upon the minds of young men only."   Also, "a company of young men sitting together are more easily drawn out to ask questions, to give expression to their thoughts or desires than if there were a mixed company . . . ." [28]

Long before that a resolution had been passed in a previous convention restricting voting membership and office holding to men.[29] That point of view was strongly emphasized in the East.   In the West, however, such a restriction as to membership was regarded rather lightly, and in some cases actually ignored.   Mr. Wishard had his first contacts with the Y.M.C.A. in the West and was not informed of developments which were taken seriously in the East. Moreover, education in the West was co-educational in a degree

---

[26] *The Intercollegian,* Vol. XII, No. 4, Jan., 1890, p. 62.
[27] McConaughy, James, *Christ Among Men.*
[28] *Report of the International Convention of the Y.M.C.A.,* 1881, p. 55.
[29] Morse, R. C., *op. cit.,* pp. 120, 279 ff.

not existing in the East.[30] Women began to enter the University of Michigan in 1870 and from that time they were admitted as members of the Association there seven years before the Intercollegiate Y.M.C.A. was formed.[31] Moreover, there was some criticism by faculties of plans to divide the corporate life of the institution for religious work.[32] It became evident to Mr. Wishard that no Association could be organized in the western colleges which did not include women as well, and some seventy-five mixed Associations were formed. Finally, however, the presence of young women in a state convention in the West was reported to the International Committee and soon Mr. Wishard was obliged to seek a way of releasing the women. In 1883, he found a leader of the Y.W.C.A. who, at a state convention of the Y.M.C.A., urged separate Associations in colleges. To her statement that "only a girl can reach the heart of a girl!" were added these more convincing arguments agreed upon by herself and Mr. Wishard:

"First, the mixed association really ignored the identity of young women by its very name, 'Young Men's Christian Association' and as a matter of fact, the young women occupied a very subordinate place in the offices and on committees and in promoting intercollegiate relations." In the second place, ... "the existence of two organizations working side by side would induce a friendly emulation which would considerably increase the results of organized work." . . . . In the third place, the women "could enjoy all the advantages which they had derived from united work because they could have joint meetings whenever they desired. . . . Finally, ... young women had a mission to young women through the country, just as the young men had a duty to perform to young men, and this mission and duty could be discharged far more effectively by entering during college life into helpful relations with young women beyond the boundary of that life. . . ."[33]

30 Wishard, L. D., *op. cit.,* p. 138.
31 Letter Document, No. 7.
32 For one instance where the faculty blocked the development of the Y.M.C.A. for this reason, see Ober, C. K., *Luther D. Wishard,* p. 104.
33 Wishard, L. D., *op. cit.,* pp. 138 ff.

Mr. Wishard performed his work so well that between 1883 and 1886 in some eighty to ninety institutions women students were organized into separate Associations, yet with the same purpose, the same sort of constitution, and similar methods of work.[34]

BEGINNING OF SUMMER CONFERENCES

A significant means for training students for the work was started in 1886 through summer "Bible Schools," later called "camps," and in turn "conferences."

The needs of the intercollegiate work had already called out special gatherings to deal with its problems. The summer conference was an enlargement, both in the length of time and in the number of delegates, of these special conferences.

". . . . We felt . . . . that we had not attained the necessary method for properly promoting the missionary life or any other department of the college association. The state conferences were all short and with few exceptions were not sufficiently large to insure the power and enthusiasm of numbers. . . ." [35]

The first summer conference, although authorized by the committee directing the Intercollegiate Y.M.C.A., was called in the name of Mr. Moody and was held July 7–August 2, 1886 on his estate at Mount Hermon, Massachusetts. It was attended by 251 students from 22 states and Canada. Happenings in the daily program included the following:

8:00 A.M.   Students assembled "for an hour's vigorous discussion of some phase of college association work. . . ."

9:00–10:00   Recreation.

10:00–12:00   The period was presided over by Mr. Moody. It was spent in "taking careful notes of the addresses

[34] Ober, C. K., *op. cit.*, pp. 66 f.
[35] Wishard, L. D., *op. cit.*, p. 103.

of the speakers, including Dr. Moody's pointed comments upon Bible study and practical work. The themes considered cover the great fundamental truths of the inspiration of the Word, redemption, and Christian growth. . . .

"The afternoons were spent in recreation, on the ball and tennis grounds, swimming, boating, and hill climbing.

"The days were closed with choral singing . . . . and room prayer meetings." [36]

A marked feature of the program consisted of missionary meetings. Indeed, the developments in missionary emphasis assumed such proportions that a special chapter will be devoted to that phase.

The second summer conference was held at Northfield, only a short distance from the gathering of the year before, with a similar program. A visitor at the conference wrote that every morning at six o'clock Mr. Moody met a group of early risers and gave them hints on Bible study, methods of work, and questions of conscience; at 8:30 A.M. a meeting was conducted by Mr. Wishard and Mr. Ober, with the help of the other leaders, on methods of Y.M.C.A. work. "At least four hours each day were spent in listening to addresses and discussions of signal value." Characteristic happenings in meetings of this type are indicated:

"At ten in the morning or eight in the evening, Mr. Moody began promptly by announcing a familiar hymn. Various exercises followed, including audible and silent prayer, frequent hymn singing, and perhaps a solo by Mr. Sankey. . . . Before introducing the first speaker Mr. Moody would drill the students in the contents of some one chapter of the Gospel of John, asking them to mention, without looking at their Bibles, the salient points of the chapter, their favorite verses, and the verses likely to be of service in dealing with inquirers. . . . After another hymn he would introduce one

[36] *College Y.M.C.A. Souvenir*, Summer School for Bible Study, July, 1886.

of the leading speakers, whose discourse would continue nearly
. . . . an hour. The people then . . . . sang some appropriate
hymn. The second speaker would likewise occupy nearly an hour.
. . . Mr. Moody's frequent exclamations, 'Hear, hear,' 'Good,' accentuated the best points of the principal lectures." [37]

Among the speakers was Professor Henry Drummond, professor
of natural science in the Free Church College in Glasgow, who
spoke on such subjects as the following: "How to Learn How to
Learn"; "The Kingdom"; "Sanctification, or How to View the
Bible"; "Narrative of Evangelical Work at Edinburgh University";
"Doubt"; "Love." [38]   Other annual summer conferences of varying
lengths followed at Northfield. The first, in 1886, lasted twenty-
six days; that of 1887, twelve days; of 1888, fifteen days; of 1889,
eleven days; of 1890, thirteen days. In the beginning years the
program remained essentially the same from year to year. Of the
conference in 1891, a reporter wrote of one of the morning sessions
when President Harper of the University of Chicago had spoken:

"The morning session was a typical Northfield meeting, thought-
ful, studious, then enthusiastic, and closing with a fervent prayer
for President Harper and a burst of applause for Stagg when he
announced the ball games in the afternoon." [39]

Other conferences of approximately the same length of time and
with essentially the same sort of program were soon started in other
parts of the country. Mr. Moody had been implored to start another conference at Lake Geneva, Wisconsin, or to move the Northfield Conference to that place; but he found that impossible, and
so the additional conferences were held under the auspices of the
Intercollegiate Y.M.C.A. entirely.[40] The first of the additional conferences was held at Lake Geneva in the summer of 1890, and an

[37] Shanks, T. J., *A College of Colleges*, pp. 19 ff.
[38] *Ibid.*
[39] *Young Men's Era*, Vol. 17, No. 29, July 16, 1891, p. 471.
[40] *The Intercollegian*, Vol. 11, No. 4, Mar., 1889, p. 5.

annual gathering has been held there ever since. Another was held the same year at Chautauqua, New York. In 1892, the first conference for southern students was held at Knoxville, Tennessee.[41] We must now turn, however, to the missionary emphasis, which assumed from the very beginning a large share of attention in the summer conferences.

[41] *The Intercollegian,* Vol. 13, No. 1, pp. 9 ff.

Chapter III: ORGANIZING FOR THE EVANGELIZATION
OF THE WORLD

ONE of the most important developments in the first summer
conference had to do with the foreign-missionary emphases. Before
describing the more immediate factors in the conference which precipitated that development, however, let us note some of the forces
in the country at the time making for a missionary interest among
students. The results of the Revolutionary War and the consequent
sense of America's having a new national significance had prepared
the way for her people's interest in other countries and a sense of
a world mission.[1] The series of revivals increased the desire to
spread the Gospel among all peoples. Foreign-missionary activity
by societies in England, Scotland, and the Netherlands stimulated
interest in America.[2] This interest, however, "was brought to a
head by a dramatic appeal of a group of students . . . . in 1880,
whose interest and efforts resulted in the organization in the same
year of the American Board of Commissioners for Foreign Missions. . . . The leader of the group had become interested in missions through the efforts of Samuel Hopkins, the minister of the
First Congregational Church at Newport, Rhode Island, to send
two young Negroes as missionaries to Africa." [3] As a student at
Union Theological Seminary, New York, Mr. Wishard had heard
this story. He learned that a group of students, led by Samuel J.
Mills, at Williams College had organized the first American student
missionary society in 1806; that these students, although carrying
through their own desire to be missionaries, had failed in their visits

[1] Sweet, W. W., *op. cit.*, p. 350.
[2] *Ibid.*, pp. 350 ff.
[3] *Ibid.*, p. 361.

to colleges to stir any great interest in foreign missons. He became "possessed" with the idea that students should consummate the "daring purpose of the Williams group." [4] Soon a missionary alliance was formed among students of different theological seminaries. At the International Convention of the Y.M.C.A. in 1879, seven years prior to the conference at Mount Hermon, a missionary department was added to the work of the college associations. Two years later at a similar convention the students decided to open correspondence with missionary colleges in non-Christian lands as a means of extending the organization of the American movement and of securing the reflex missionary influence on the American students. Soon, also, missionary conferences were held among medical students.[5] Also, in founding the Y.M.C.A. in the colleges, Mr. Wishard in a number of instances built the organization upon old missionary societies. "Our work," he said, "exists to promote the spiritual condition of young men, and nothing apart from Bible study conduces to their growth in grace like the development of missionary interest." [6]

Almost from the beginning the willingness to be a missionary was made synonymous with approved Christian living. In a report of one of the medical students' missionary conferences in early 1883, it is said:

"In the meeting . . . . willingness to go anywhere, at any time, to do anything for Christ, was made the test of real, acceptable consecration." [7]

In early March, 1885, one hundred and fifty students in another such conference arranged by the Intercollegiate Y.M.C.A., "spent an hour of solemn waiting before God" to "attain such a degree of consecration that they would be willing to go anywhere for Christ." [8]

[4] Wishard, L. D., op. cit., pp. 94 ff.
[5] Ibid., pp. 98-100.
[6] Ober, C. K., Exploring a Continent, p. 88.
[7] The College Bulletin, Vol. 5, No. 5, Feb., 1883, p. 1.
[8] Ibid., Vol. 7, No. 5, March, 1885, p. 18.

A further factor making for a missionary emphasis in the Intercollegiate Y.M.C.A. was the influence of Mr. Moody, whose revivalism was of a missionary character. Of a visit by Moody to Cambridge, England, in 1882, Tissington Tatlow writes in *The Student Work:*

". . . . He stirred the University, and one outcome was the decision of C. T. Studd, the captain of the cricket eleven, and Stanley Smith, the stroke of the university boat, to go to China as missionaries. This, at the time, was a novel resolution on their part and excited the interest of the student class . . . ." [9]

There was also a reflex from such work by Mr. Moody in England. It was felt by American students through the visit in the colleges during 1885-1886 of J. E. K. Studd, who as a result of Mr. Moody's work had also decided to be a foreign missionary along with his brother, C. T. Studd.[10]

Personalities embodying these forces were conspicuous in the summer conference of 1886 at Mount Hermon. Missionary emphases were expressed through the leaders, and in a peculiarly forceful manner by a student delegate, Robert Wilder of Princeton College. Mr. Wilder's background made him particularly interested in the missionary emphases of the conference. At Andover Seminary his father had been a member of "The Brethren"—a secret society of men pledged to foreign service and founded originally at Williams College. Its constitution declared: "No person shall be admitted who is under any engagement of any kind which shall be incompatible with going on a mission to the heathen. . . . Each member shall hold himself in readiness to go on a mission when and where duty may call." This took Mr. Wilder's parents to India, where the family was for a long time in mission service. Encouraged by his father, Mr. Wilder had helped to organize at Princeton in 1883

[9] Quoted by Ober, C. K., *Luther D. Wishard*, p. 128.
[10] *Ibid.*, p. 116.

a mission band, of which any professing Christian could become a member by subscribing to the following covenant:

"We, the undersigned, declare ourselves willing and desirous, God permitting, to go to the unevangelized portions of the world."

Members of the band held that when this covenant was carried to its logical conclusion, "it was the duty of every Christian to be a foreign missionary if God permitted." [11] It was from this background that Mr. Wilder went to Mount Hermon.

Of the dramatic happenings in this first summer conference Mr. Wishard later wrote:

"Early in the session Wilder . . . . and other kindred spirits . . . . began to hold a daily missionary prayer meeting. . . . Meanwhile, Dr. Ashmore, one of the leading missionaries of China, appeared at the Conference. He and another leader gave addresses on missions. A unique program . . . . was conducted one evening which I led; ten students were there, seven of them natives of foreign lands, three others, sons of missionaries themselves born on foreign fields; each spoke for three minutes, each appealing on behalf of his people. The effect was indescribable. Men went from that meeting alone or in little groups for prolonged prayer on the hillsides overlooking the River. It was a night of decision and destiny. When the last day of the Conference arrived, exactly one hundred students had avowed themselves willing and desirous— God permitting—to become foreign missionaries." [12]

Mr. Wilder and one other man, John Forman, were selected as a deputation to go through the colleges to carry the message of the missionary revival.[13] During the college year, 1886-87, more than 2200 students (of whom 550 were women) in the colleges of the United States and Canada volunteered for foreign mission service.[14] The next college year, however, revealed problems which

[11] *Report of Student Volunteer Movement Convention,* 1891, p. 161.
[12] Wishard, L. D., *op. cit.,* pp. 105-106.
[13] *Ibid.,* pp. 106 f.
[14] Pamphlet: *An Appeal to the Churches from the Student Volunteers for Foreign Missions,* 1887.

demanded serious attention. During that year there was no one traveling in the colleges, and only some 600 new volunteers were listed. In some colleges, also, the groups of volunteers soon became "cold." Varied purposes, with varied sorts of pledges, were soon found in the groups. Some conflicts arose also with the existing student religious agencies.[15] How serious this was may be gleaned from a statement in *The Intercollegian* for March, 1888:

". . . . It was the prevailing sentiment at every conference that the missionary work be continued by the Association [Y.M.C.A.] and that the men who have united with mission bands compose the missionary committee of the Association, and thus avoid becoming a distinct missionary organization. In this way will the Association continue and become more and more permeated with the missionary spirit. The thorough development of the missionary idea *within* the Association is absolutely necessary, if this Association becomes world-wide, as it now promises to become." [16]

By the summer of 1888, however, it was evident that some more effective organization was needed for the missionary emphasis. Accordingly, the Student Volunteer Movement was created, semi-independent, and yet interrelated with the Intercollegiate Y.M.C.A., the Inter-Seminary Student Movement (which later became a part of the Y.M.C.A.), and the student Y.W.C.A., which had developed in the meantime. This newly-formed movement for missions was created by having an executive committee made up of one representative each from the three coöperating organizations.[16a]

It is significant that the Intercollegiate Y.M.C.A. was thus, through the missionary interest, brought into a unique relation with the newly-created intercollegiate Y.W.C.A. so soon after the decision that membership in the Y.M.C.A. should be restricted to men only

[15] Report of the Executive Committee of the Student Volunteer Movement to the First Student Volunteer Convention, 1891, pp. 4-5.

[16] *The Intercollegian*, Vol. 10, No. 4, March, 1888, p. 29.

[16a] The chairman of the Committee from the beginning was Mr. John R. Mott, who joined the Intercollegiate Y.M.C.A. staff in 1888, and soon became the Senior Secretary.

(see pp. 18 f.). Several factors, however, entered to bring that about. Behind the work of Robert Wilder was his sister Grace, who was very influential in the beginnings of the Student Volunteer Movement. "She was praying" says one, "for Robert and with him, and she kept him going forward in getting volunteers." She had prevailed upon him to go to Mount Hermon in 1886. She was instrumental in having him and John Forman, who accompanied him on the first tours in the colleges, visit women's colleges no less than men's. Further, the largest success of the Student Volunteer Movement in the early days was not in the colleges of the East, but in the predominantly co-educational colleges of the West. It would have been difficult for Wilder and Forman to visit a college in the Middle West without including women students in their audiences.[17] Again, the movement assumed the highly-specialized task of finding prospective candidates for foreign mission boards, where women no less than men were needed. The women student volunteers were also members of the student Y.W.C.A.[118] It was such factors as these which made the Volunteer Movement a means for closer relationship between the Y.M.C.A. and the Y.W.C.A.!

The foreign-missionary emphasis was now to be an even bigger factor in the Intercollegiate Y.M.C.A. than ever before. This was manifested in succeeding annual summer conferences at Northfield and in other parts of the country; in special conventions of the Student Volunteer Movement; and in mission-study courses.

BEGINNING QUADRENNIAL CONVENTIONS OF THE STUDENT VOLUNTEER MOVEMENT

The missionary emphases were carried further in quadrennial conventions of the Student Volunteer Movement which were devoted exclusively to foreign missions. The first of these was held at Cleveland, Ohio, Thursday, February 26 to Sunday, March 1,

[17] Interview Document, No. 18; Letter Document, No. 8.
[18] Letter Document, No. 14.

1891. The gathering was intended as a rallying point for representatives of the 6000 men and women who were enrolled by that
time in the lists of the Movement. The convention sought to provide opportunity for contacts between volunteers and missionary
board secretaries, as well as returned missionaries; and for a closer
"union in prayer and purpose" on the part of volunteers, secretaries,
and missionaries, to give a new impetus to the . . . . cause of the
"evangelization of the world in this generation." [19]

The membership of the Convention was made up of 558 students from 151 institutions, 32 board representatives, and 31
returned missionaries.[20] The program included provision for devotional exercises; for addresses dealing with more personal aspects
of religious experience, particularly in relation to missions; for
simultaneous meetings on the requirements of the various missionary
societies and their methods of work, as well as the peculiar features
of the various fields, and also different types of missionary work
on the field. An important issue in the convention concerned the
policy of the Movement. This was given essentially as that of
enrolling volunteers "in sufficient numbers to meet all the demands
made . . . . by the different missionary agencies of the day; and,
more than that, sufficient to make possible the evangelization of the
world in this generation," as well as to develop ways and means
of making that effective.[21]

What was the intended meaning of the phrase, "the evangelization of the world in this generation" and what was to be the basis
of faith in its possibility? Mr. Robert E. Speer explained it to be
"simply this: the presenting of the Gospel in such a manner to
every soul in this world that the responsibility for what is done with
it shall no longer rest upon the Christian Church, or any individual
Christian, but shall rest on each man's head for himself." . . . . In

[19] *Report of the International Convention of the Student Volunteer
Movement,* 1891, p. 3.
   [20] *Ibid.,* p. 3.
   [21] *Ibid.,* pp. 26, 33.

a generation one missionary, "if supplied with the necessary means
and with native helpers," could preach the Gospel to 50,000. Mr.
Speer said the cause "is not a human issue. God is in it. . . . There
is nothing in the world or the Church, except its disobedience, to
render the evangelization of the world in this generation an im-
possibility. . . . Is God dead? If we cannot rely on Him I am
willing to surrender the whole question. But who has arranged the
condition of affairs that I have described? Is not the hand of God
plain in them?" [22]

Another emphasis concerns the sense of responsibility upon every
Christian student. In the statement just cited, Mr. Speer continued:
"From the beginning He has us in mind upon whom the ends are
come. The long years of progress, at times painfully slow, are
culminating now. The walls of exclusion are broken down. . . .
The fortress of the enemy has not long security in the future years.
The field is arranged for the final conflict. . . . The general unrolls
his plan of campaign. Will you take a grasp of his conquering hand
and go forth to the mighty struggle? . . . . It is high time to awake
out of sleep, and banding ourselves with new and deeper devotion,
to swing out on the currents of God's purpose, to accomplish our
mission in the world. Are you ready then, fellow students, to throw
your lives in with this watch-cry: 'Christ to the world before we
die?' " [23]

The same emphasis is found in consideration of the pledge card,
signed by 6000 men and women indicating that they were "willing,
God permitting, to become foreign missionaries." [24] Discussing the
question of renouncing the pledge, Mr. Robert Wilder said this
applied only to those who remain in America without a valid excuse.
As for what is a valid excuse, "that must be settled by each volunteer
with God." After mentioning the possibility of one's exemption by

[22] *Ibid.*, pp. 73 ff.
[23] *Ibid.*, pp. 73 ff.
[24] *Ibid.*, p. 26.

Boards, Mr. Wilder continued, "But such exemption by no means proves that he is exempt before God. Missionary organizations are fallible. . . . One might, like William Carey, feel, 'Go, I must, or guilt will rest on my soul.' " [25]

The sense of urgency was continually present. Mr. W. H. Cossum, a traveling secretary of the Movement, speaking on "Immediate Sailing, Its Advantages, and How Secured," said,

"Six thousand two hundred names are not what we are after. Our object is to evangelize the world in this generation; and it is not until the missionaries pledged are on board ships aiming towards fields that this Movement reaches its true objective point. . . . The honor of the Student Volunteer Movement demands that we reach our fields at the earliest date possible. . . . Don't stay in this country theorizing, when a hundred thousand heathen a day are dying without hope because we are not there teaching the Gospel to them. . . ." [26]

The sense of utter abandon of self to the cause which pervaded the convention was stated succinctly by a delegate:

"If there are young men here who wish to go out, let them believe that God will take care of them." [27]

The force of these emphases is illustrated strikingly in the concluding meeting Sunday evening. Speaking on the perils and privileges of the Volunteer Movement, Mr. Wilder, observing that the volunteer "cools off," said:

"At some meeting the missionary fire was kindled and he signed the pledge. If the fire is not kept up the fault is his own. You say he decided under excitement. That makes no difference. Excitement is often a Godsend. . . . Do not say that God allowed the flame to wane. Have you fed the fire? *Information is the fuel*. . . . You have decided once for all to go unless God blocks the way. Do not reopen that question." [28]

25 *Ibid.*, p. 33.
26 *Ibid.*, p. 42.
27 *Ibid.*, p. 44.
28 *Ibid.*, pp. 161 ff.

There followed a few minutes of silent prayer, and then the "farewell" meeting. In brief addresses the needs of various lands and peoples were presented. Then to Mr. Mott's suggestion that a great many delegates should be heard from, indicating where they were from as well as the dominant impression they received from the convention or the dominant purpose formed under its influence, there were quite a number of responses, including the following:

"Oberlin. Go to India."

"Syracuse University. An indefinite purpose to give my life to foreign missionary work changed to a definite purpose for that work."

"Adrian College. My chief impression has been my own insignificance."

"Yale University. The immense power of prayer."

"Ohio Wesleyan University. Going to China as a self-supporting missionary if possible."

Five brief addresses followed, including one by Mr. F. S. Goodman, who quoted a motto given by Mr. Mott for the college work of the Y.M.C.A. in the state of Ohio:

"Hide the word of God in your heart. Tie yourselves to one man. Fix your eyes on the uttermost parts of the earth."

The concluding address was made by Mr. Speer, who closed his remarks by quoting Tennyson's poem, "Crossing the Bar." [29]

The convention was succeeded by others, which soon began to meet every four years, with essentially the same sort of program.

VOCATIONAL EMPHASES

The emphasis in the programs of the Intercollegiate Y.M.C.A. from its very beginning had a direct bearing on vocation. As we have seen, the foreign-missionary appeal was presented as an

[29] *Ibid.,* pp. 179 ff.

obligation to be faced by every one calling himself Christian. Although missions continued to occupy a large share of attention in summer conferences, other callings came in time to be presented also in a definite "life-work" series. By 1891, the Christian ministry and the secretaryship of the Y.M.C.A. were also included at Northfield.[30] Unlike the development, however, following the presentation of the missionary cause, no separate movement was formed for the presentation of these other callings.[31]

With the inclusion of these (and in time still other professions) some attention was given also to the principles on which one should decide one's vocation. In the first southern summer conference, in 1892, a member of the staff of the Intercollegiate Y.M.C.A., Mr. H. P. Andersen, gave the following as a means for choosing a vocation: Bible reading, prayer, "Godly living," information about the occupation considered, and advice. Another speaker, Mr. I. E. Brown, gave as "the elements of a call": "inclination, fitness, opportunity." A third speaker urged "biblical examples—Moses, Matthew, and Paul." [32]

Accompanying the vocational presentations was usually an appeal to students to have a definite purpose in life. They were generally urged to read, for example, a book by John Foster entitled, *Decision of Character*. In the introductory note to this book is found a statement by Mr. Mott, which is typical of the emphasis in conferences and conventions on decision:

"Whatever may be one's problems and perplexities—whether in the realm of conduct or of faith, the details of everyday life or the larger questions of life work, life attitudes, and the religious, political, and social relationships of life—the acquiring of the habit of conclusive thinking and of prompt, decisive action will be of inestimable value . . . ."

---

[30] *Young Men's Era*, Vol. 17, July 30, 1891, pp. 502-503.
[31] *The Y.M.C.A. Year Book*, 1892, p. 30.
[32] *Young Men's Era*, Vol. 18, No. 26, June 30, 1892, p. 819.

An appeal was also frequently made to a particular type of emotional experience. An example was given by a leader who was speaking on "the Holy Spirit in Missions at the Geneva Conference in the summer of 1891:

". . . . The question is, 'Shall I go?' fellows. I would not dare to set my feet on foreign soil, unless I was sure the Holy Spirit guided me there, and I would not dare stay in America unless I was sure the Holy Spirit kept me there." [33]

Such emphasis on the vocational question naturally magnified for the delegates the significance of those callings which were presented and their sense of obligation toward them, with a corresponding possibility of one's choosing one of these vocations on the basis of highly emotionalized factors.

WORK FOR NEW STUDENTS

Simultaneously with these developments the Association began to give special attention to the new students upon their entry into the institutions as a fruitful field of religious work. As early as the autumn of 1878 the University of Tennessee Association gave a "welcome meeting to new students . . . . at the beginning of the . . . . college year. . . ." Mr. Wishard called the idea "a new one to us. We like it first rate, and believe it would prove to be a most valuable means of leading new students into the Association and persuading them to take a positive open stand for Christ at the very commencement of the college course. . . ." [34] Such an emphasis in work with new students was found in other Associations also. In 1883, a representative of Ohio Wesleyan University reported:

"Students in coming to the university should start right the first day; so we start out as a soliciting committee, and meet them with hearty hand-shakings, and introduce them to our rooms and to one

[33] *Young Men's Era,* Vol. 17, No. 35, Sept. 10, 1891, p. 566.
[34] *The College Bulletin,* Vol. 1, No. 2, Dec., 1878, p. 3.

another. The result of our work this year has been over two hundred conversions among the students in less than three weeks." [35]

At Cornell University in the autumn of 1886, "a Freshman class prayer meeting was started the day the Freshmen registered, and with one exception all present took part Sunday afternoon. . . ." [36]

From this beginning, however, developed in time a practical program of service on the campus, one phase of which consisted in the issuing of "handbooks" by several Associations. This book gave in "detail those facts about the college the Freshmen need to know, but dislike to inquire about too frequently. The book also includes a complete statement of the work of the Association without and within." [37]

PUBLIC EVANGELISM

In addition to the emphasis on personal evangelism and on recruiting for world evangelization, there was also emphasis on public, or mass, evangelism. One means of promoting this was through regular weekly religious meetings, when one of these was systematically devoted to evangelism. Topics and Bible references were suggested by headquarters for the success of such a meeting.[38] The Intercollegiate Association soon began also to foster special meetings led by evangelists. Outstanding in the early beginnings of this means of evangelism was the work of S. M. Sayford, who was endorsed by D. L. Moody as "the best man in my acquaintance for special evangelistic work among students." [39] While doing some work at Amherst, Massachusetts, in the autumn of 1888, Mr. Sayford was invited to speak at Amherst College, and soon afterwards began to tour the country for meetings with other student groups. He was

[35] Report of 1883 International Convention of the Y.M.C.A., p. 115.
[36] The Watchman, Vol. 12, No. 21, Nov. 1, 1886, p. 251.
[37] The Intercollegian, Vol. 12, No. 1, Oct., 1889, p. 2.
[38] The Intercollegian, Vol. 10, No. 2, Nov., 1887, p. 13.
[39] The Intercollegian, Vol. 11, No. 1, Sept., 1888, p. 4.

accompanied in some of his visits to colleges by Professor and Mrs. Towner, whose singing had been a big factor in the Mount Hermon and Northfield summer conferences.[40] In his work Mr. Sayford sought "to promote purity of thought and conversation; to raise the standard of Christian living; to win students for Christ. . . ." His work soon took on the name of the "Higher Ground Movement." And at the end of a five year period, terminating in 1894, twenty thousand had taken his "covenant" for "a higher type of Christian life," resolving "by God's grace to discontinue the habit, or habits," which had hitherto retarded their spiritual growth. Testimonials concerning the work included many references to "the confidential talk of Mr. Sayford," to "wilful habits" of students, and to the effectiveness of his work "when God gave him power" to "lay bare" the "hidden life of students" and their "easily-besetting sins." [41] These emphases were driven in on students by a very forceful personality. As a leader at the southern summer conference in 1892, Mr. Sayford was described in this way:

"It is the sturdy, virile force of voice and figure, the manly, forcible face, and the appalling frankness with which he rifles his hearer of his self-righteousness, along with the brotherly humility in which he leads him not only to lean on Jesus Christ, but to sturdy relentless cutting away from his sin. This is Mr. Sayford's power. . . . . On Thursday morning after his 'confidential talk,' the heart-searching power of that . . . . message, dealing with the errors of young men, almost every man in the conference rose to take with Mr. Sayford the covenant . . . . to give up each the one thing that was befouling his life, or hampering his growth in Christ. . . ." [42]

---

[40] *Ibid.*, p. 4.
[41] Pamphlet: *Mr. Sayford's Work Among the Colleges 1889-94,* and one dated 1898. National Council of Y.M.C.A's.
[42] *Young Men's Era,* Vol. 18, No. 26, July 30, 1892, p. 819.

STUDENT DEPUTATIONS FOR EVANGELISM AND INTERCOLLEGIATE VISITATION

The work of evangelism was also carried on by students with others. This started from an impetus gained from Professor Henry Drummond of Edinburgh University in his visit in 1887, and consisted of "inter-visitation" work by students among students. It was soon extended to include preparatory schools, churches, Sunday-schools, and—especially in vacation periods—city missions.[43]

The intercollegiate deputations were developed as a means of extending the influence of the staff of the Intercollegiate Y.M.C.A. to Associations which they could not themselves visit very often, and of adding the stimulus which the students would carry more widely. Each deputation which went with this purpose to a college included two students, chosen from different institutions; these gave some time each year without pay to the work.[44] Special training conferences were held to prepare the students selected for their work. Emphases at the time are indicated by the themes treated in these special training conferences: "Historic statement of the inter-collegiate movement; the intercollegiate movement of today; importance of organization; personnel and work of the organization; what the college association should do to promote Bible study; how to promote a higher standard of Christian living among so-called Christian students; . . . . the missionary department . . . .," etc.[45]

ROLE OF THE STAFF

One is impressed by the fact that the employed staff rapidly assumed a role of marked influence in the organization. A single report of their activity will suffice to reveal the influence which they were already exerting in the program. The training of the students

[43] *The Intercollegian:* Vol. 10, No. 3, p. 19; Vol. 10, No. 4, p. 27; Vol. 12, No. 6, p. 85.
[44] *The Intercollegian,* Vol. 12, No. 8, p. 118.
[45] *Ibid.*

for the intercollegiate visitation was given by Messrs. Ober and Mott in special gatherings for the purpose. Of the program carried through in that connection it was reported:

"The plan was conceived by . . . . Secretaries Ober and Mott after long study. They arrived at the same plan entirely independent of one another, thus showing the leading of the Holy Spirit. . . . . Secretaries Ober and Mott took full charge of the conference. They had spent much time both in conference and private study in preparation. They gave their instruction in a form somewhat similar to regular university lectures leaving an opportunity at the close of each lecture for informal discussion and questions. . . . Each member took full notes." [46]

About this time also, members of the staff began to give special attention to the training of presidents of the college Associations for their work. This was accomplished through similar training conferences.[47]

EMPLOYMENT OF SECRETARIES FOR LOCAL ASSOCIATIONS

Another early development looking to the direction of local Associations needs to be noted. The erection of buildings for the college work [48] soon led in the larger institutions,[49] as in the city Y.M.C.A., to the employment of secretaries for work with the local Associations. The first man employed for such work in the United States was at Yale, simultaneously with such a development at McGill University in Canada. The rôle of the employed officer in this new post is revealed in the following statement:

". . . . For a number of years it has been the custom in some colleges for baseball clubs, foot ball teams, and boat crews to retain

[46] *Ibid.*
[47] *The Y.M.C.A. Year Book, 1892,* p. 29.
[48] This began with the erection of a building at Hanover College in 1883. Cf. *The Intercollegian,* Vol. 38, No. 9, June, 1921, p. 4.
[49] E.g., Yale University, Cf. *The College Bulletin,* Vol. 8, No. 6, Mar., 1886, p. 22.

for a year or two graduates who have attained preëminence in these different sports, to train men and prepare them for the intercollegiate contests. The Associations in Yale and Toronto Universities have simply applied the same principle to the Christian work of their colleges, and have retained men, who were leaders in the Association, to oversee the work, not to do, but plan it and set committees of students at work in the different departments of the Association. . . ." [50]

These varied developments constituted program emphases, which, with the ascendent role of the staff of the Intercollegiate Y.M.C.A., became crystallized and expanded during the next two decades.

[50] *The Y.M.C.A. Year Book,* 1887, p. xli.

PART THREE: TWO DECADES OF PROGRAM DE-
VELOPMENT AND PROMOTION 1890-1910

Chapter IV. DEVELOPMENT OF "INTELLECTUAL" AND
DAILY BIBLE STUDIES

"INTELLECTUAL" (INDUCTIVE) STUDIES

WE have seen how from the beginning of the Intercollegiate
Y.M.C.A., the Bible assumed primary emphasis. The first special
studies consisted of outlines [1] to train students in "winning souls,"
or "personal work"; these constituted the only kind of Bible study
promoted by the Intercollegiate Y.M.C.A. for several years.
Although this emphasis has never been lost from the organization,
conditions made imperative other approaches as well. The background for one of these is found in the approach to the Bible suggested by the stress upon "higher criticism," a radical emphasis
which precipitated controversy within religious circles during the
latter quarter of the nineteenth century.[2] Within the group of
higher critics was Professor W. R. Harper, who brought a new and
significant emphasis to the Bible study of the Intercollegiate
Y.M.C.A. Professor Harper had been invited to speak to students
in a Y.M.C.A conference on Bible study, but he "demurred, saying
he did not approve of the sort of thing that passed for Bible study
among them at the time." [3] Nevertheless, at a conference of New
England college Y.M.C.A's. held at Yale University in February,
1887, he was a speaker. He recognized the value of Bible study for

[1] See pp. 14 f.
[2] Sweet, W. W., *op. cit.,* pp. 493-494.
[3] Goodspeed, T. W., *William Rainey Harper,* p. 75.

the purpose of "personal work," but he deplored the fact that although such work "aims to be deep spiritually . . . . intellectually, it is confessedly and too often superficial." As a result "questionings and doubt arise." He appealed for an "intellectual . . . . historical . . . . literary work"; for a work of interpretation, "including the application of those great principles common to the interpretation of all great writings. . . . Now so far as this study destroys that Bible-worship of which so many Christians are unconsciously guilty, it is well . . . . ," but it was to be reverent withal. Professor Harper appealed in this way for a method of study consistent with that employed by the student in similar college work.[4] Beginning in May, 1889, and continuing through the next scholastic year, the monthly *Intercollegian* carried a series of "Inductive Bible Studies," specially prepared by Professor Harper and dealing with I Samuel and II Samuel as well as the Psalms of David and of Solomon. In his first study in this series the author urged less attention "to the study of verses, to the neglect of chapters and books. . . . . The habit of reading several chapters, or even an entire book, is one which should be cultivated." [5] The purpose of his plan of study was to enable the student to obtain a comprehensive knowledge of the books of the Bible studied, of the contemporary period of history as a whole, and of "the more important topics which connect themselves with these books and their history," as well as of the practical teachings of the narratives.[6] Directions for individual study were given with a view to applying these objectives to the material, which was divided up by the author into sections of varying length, each around some unifying idea. Such suggestions and questions as the following served as the standard guide for examination of all the material:

[4] (Unpublished paper regarding Fifth Conference of Y.M.C.A's. of New England Colleges, Feb. 18-20, 1887, National Council Y.M.C.A. Library.)
[5] *The Intercollegian,* Vol. XI, No. 5, May, 1889, pp. 11-12.
[6] *Ibid.,* pp. 11-12.

"Jot down in your note-book as you go along the main points of the story. . . . Find a topic which will cover the thought of this section—a topic which will at once suggest to your mind the details, one about which you can group the whole narrative. . . . With now the main topic . . . . and the main points under the topic, ... seize upon the religious lesson which, in the mind of the writer, the narration of these events was intended to teach. . . ." [7]

In the directions for the class work, it was urged that while every member of the class should complete the study, special sections should be assigned to different individuals. The leader was urged to call during the class hour for the special reports on the different sections and to "put the substance on a blackboard." Nevertheless, all were invited to participate in criticism and discussion of these different individual reports. At the same time, it was urged that "commonplace statements, stereotyped expressions, and merely superficial remarks be avoided." It was recommended that emphasis be placed upon "not a single verse, but a complete story; not some particular detail of the history, but the history itself in its entirety. . . . Try to ascertain the connection of events, the philosophy of the history. . . ." [8] Underlying all, however, was the assumption of the preëminent importance of the subject matter. The hearing of "special reports should not be allowed more than half an hour." Then "let the leader endeavor to drill into the class the more important part of the ground covered. . . . The sole purpose is to lodge the material in the mind that it may, in time, be ready for use upon every fitting occasion. . . . Devote the last ten minutes to a consideration of the practical points suggested by the material, i.e., the most significant lesson. . . ." [9]

In the immediately-succeeding Bible studies, the "inductive" method was employed also by several others, including Professor

[7] *Ibid.*, pp. 11-12.
[8] *Ibid.*, pp. 11-12.
[9] *Ibid.*, pp. 11-12.

Beardslee in a course at the first Lake Geneva, Wisconsin, Conference in 1890,[10] and especially by Professor W. W. White. Professor White had found help from Professor Harper at a time when the former was disturbed by studies in "higher criticism." [11] Later, Professor White had assisted Professor Harper in his work at Yale and was impressed by the latter's method of teaching Hebrew—a method which consisted of "actually dealing with the materials instead of theorizing about them—getting the grammar in the Hebrew Bible text." [12] For Professor White this implied that an inductive study of the English Bible meant "taking the Bible as it is, the documents as they are, and coming out to one's own conclusion from the facts, instead of taking preconceptions to the Bible"; it meant also exposing the students to the Bible records, while raising questions for which they must search and think out answers, and allowing them to record the results. More exactly, it meant: (1) analysis of a book of the Bible, asking, "What is here?" and (2) interpretation of the material, "What does it mean?" [13] In connection with a course on Jeremiah given by Professor White at the Lake Geneva summer conference in 1891, the inductive method was defined as: "(1) observation of facts; (2) classification of facts; (3) application of facts." [14] This emphasis upon mastery of the factual material was made central.

"As a drill, each student was assigned a separate chapter, which he was required to analyze by means of this method and submit the result to the class. In this way each student was made authority on some special chapter, and all questions relating to that chapter were referred to him. . . ." [15]

Upon the request of members of this group at Lake Geneva, the

[10] *The Intercollegian,* Vol. 13, No. 1, Oct., 1890, p. 11.
[11] Interview Document, No. 26.
[12] *Ibid.*
[13] *Ibid.*
[14] *Young Men's Era,* Vol. 17, No. 35, Sept. 10, 1891, p. 567.
[15] *Ibid.,* p. 567.

course was repeated by correspondence during the year 1891-92. Twenty-three members of the class became each a leader of a small group in his institution, and Professor White developed the course by mail, passing on weekly a printed outline as well as suggestions on the basis of reports to him. These were combined into a booklet, *Thirty Studies in Jeremiah*. [16]

Within the class of "inductive" studies also fall certain ones by Mr. R. E. Speer. Particularly is that true of Mr. Speer's earliest works, as in the case of a study of the Book of Luke conducted by him at the Northfield summer conference in 1891. [17] The next year, however, in a study of the Book of Acts with a class of some two hundred, Mr. Speer developed more of a lecture approach to the study.

". . . . Mr. Speer does not use the normal-school method; rather

[16] Interview Document No. 26. An excerpt from this set of studies in their final form will indicate their character:
"I. Habakkuk
  1. Read the entire book of Habakkuk and note:
      a. The lament of the prophet over the situation, Chap. I. 2-4, uttered probably during the time of Jehoikim.
      b. God's answer in announcing punishment by the Chaldeans. Chap. I. 5-11.
      c. The impassioned appeal of the prophet to God to punish the Chaldeans. Chap. I. 12 seq.
      d. The twofold woe pronounced upon the Chaldeans. Chap. II.
      e. The prayer of Habakkuk, which, among Hebrew scholars, is regarded as among the noblest efforts of Hebrew genius. Chap. III.
  2. Read the book again without interruption aloud, after noting the following: Habakkuk is the last prophet belonging to the age preceding the destruction of Jerusalem who is master of a beautiful style, of powerful description, and an artistic power that enlivens and orders everything with charming effect.
"II. Uriah
  1. Read the story of Uriah. Chap. XXVI.
  2. Relate the story.
  3. Why is this story introduced in the connection in which it is found?"
W. W. White, *Thirty Studies in Jeremiah*, p. 22.
  [17] *Young Men's Era*, Vol. 17, No. 91, July 30, 1891, p. 503.

the university method, letting those who wish to do so gather impulse from his example to study and teach the book. . . ." [18]

As we shall see, this new method employed by Mr. Speer was a factor in the development of another phase of Bible study starting with Mr. H. B. Sharman. First, however, we must note another emphasis in Bible study which was a forerunner of Mr. Sharman's work.

Along with the "intellectual" study of the Bible and that of the "practical" study intended as preparation for "personal work," the leaders of the Intercollegiate Y.M.C.A. emphasized a "devotional" study of the Bible. ". . . . This line of study should be carried on with special reference to developing the religious life and experience of the Christian. . . ." These three methods were motivated by the same objective:

". . . . If our Associations give themselves up to an intelligent, devout, practical study of the Word of God, we shall have live and telling meetings, active and constant personal work, genuine and contagious missionary enthusiasm, consistent and consecrated living." [19]

Nevertheless, the "devotional" study soon came to receive a special emphasis as a means of making "us better men tomorrow than today," of enabling "us to meet God and to hear His voice and to know that it is His voice. . . . Would we work without friction, strain, anxiety, worry? Then let us apply ourselves to this kind of Bible study. . . . To do the work of God we must have the power of God. To have the power of God, we must have the Spirit of God. The Bible is the channel through which the Spirit comes into life." [20] Along with attention to the "devotional" use of the Bible went an increasing emphasis upon carrying through such an

[18] *Young Men's Era,* Vol. 18, No. 30, July 28, 1892, p. 949.
[19] *The Intercollegian,* Vol. 11, No. 2, Nov., 1888, p. 3.
[20] Pamphlet by J. R. Mott: *Bible Study for Personal Spiritual Growth,* pp. 6 ff.

activity at the very beginning of each day. As early as 1878, students in the Randolph Macon College Association, Ashland, Virginia, were emphasizing an hour's study early every morning instead of the "usual private readings at the end of the day's work, when the mind is dull and the body weary." [21] This emphasis soon became known as the "Morning Watch," which called for the habit of spending "at least the first half-hour of every day alone with God in personal . . . . Bible study and prayer." If "our lives and words and acts throughout the busy day are to possess supernatural value, we must take the earliest opportunity in the day to establish a vital and complete union with God." [22]

DAILY "SYSTEMATIC" BIBLE STUDY

These developments were factors in the new type of study started in this period by Mr. H. B. Sharman. As a visitor to the Northfield Conference, Mr. Sharman had been asked to criticize the Bible study done there. He deemed it useful for the conference, but felt that, since it was presented in lecture form, it would be difficult for the student delegates to reproduce it in their institutions. He was requested soon afterwards to undertake at the Southern Summer Conference at Knoxville, Tennessee, a type of study which he believed could be reproduced. He was then asked to enlarge the study which he developed to meet that request and to make it available for individual and group use. A total of some forty groups were formed in a number of institutions, and Mr. Sharman corresponded with the leader of each group. Each week he received a report on the work and in his reply sent out sheets containing lesson material for the work of that week. The material which was developed in this way was printed in book form in 1896 under the title, *Studies in the Life of Christ.* [23]

21 *The College Bulletin,* Vol. 1, No. 2, Dec., 1878, p. 1.
22 Pamphlet: J. R. Mott, *The Morning Watch,* pp. 3 ff.
23 Interview Document, No. 23.

Compared with previous Bible studies of the organization, this one is neither a study of doctrinal themes running through the Bible, nor of isolated verses, nor of individual books of the Bible. Rather, it is an attempt to explore the life of Jesus. The study is based on *A Harmony of the Gospels,* by Stevens and Burton (published in 1893), which was to accompany it. The text contains work for thirty weeks, as does the study of Jeremiah by Professor White; but it is distinctive in being the first text of the organization to provide for a daily assignment. Each study is divided into seven "days." In twenty-six of the studies devoted to a detailed development of the life of Jesus, the portion for each "day" occupies a page or a bit more than a page. For each day's work a passage from the Gospels is assigned, which is to be looked up and read under directions. There is comparatively little interpretative material, the directions for study being chiefly in the form of questions. Each day is usually closed with a "personal thought," which is sometimes expressed in the form of a question, sometimes in the form of a verse from the Gospels followed by a question, intended to lead to personal application of the central thought in the day's lesson. Very great emphasis is placed on following through each day the assignment for the day.

". . . . The studies are dependent for their highest value upon the principle of daily study by the individual. This is fundamental. . . ." [24]

In this emphasis upon daily study the author was seeking a means of having the material covered with the least inconvenience to the student.[25] He was seeking also to provide opportunity for the habit of daily Bible study and meditation intended as a means of character development:

[24] Sharman, H. B., *Studies in the Life of Christ,* pp. 7-8.
[25] Interview Document, No. 23.

". . . . Give this study the clearest, brightest moments of the day. It is best to begin the day with it; in any case have a regular time and strive to be regular. . . . Strive to overcome any tendency to indefinite meditation; in this, help may be had by centering the meditation about the Personal Thought of the day. Dwell upon it during the study and in the odd moments of the day—not as a means to morbid self-examination but as a joyous help to a fuller appreciation of the privileges of the Christian life. Make each 'Personal Thought' a subject of special prayer and never pass away from one till the life is conformed to its standard. . . ." [26]

Another emphasis is conspicuous in the remaining four studies devoted to review. This procedure recurs at intervals throughout the entire series. Directions accompanying these sections are standardized and repeated in, the same form in all review studies. The directions place much emphasis upon committing to memory the exact titles of the different sections, the summary of the content, and other elements in the historical connection of events. [27] The author's primary interest, as of those immediately before him, was to get the student to "examine the text, to explore the text with his own mind, and to discern the values there, to evaluate independently." [28] Thus, while he sought to develop a life of Jesus in which knowledge about him would find its proper historical setting, the author was at one with his predecessors in attaching significance to the examination of the Biblical records.

One year later there appeared another course, *Studies in the Acts and the Epistles,* by Professor E. I. Bosworth, who had served most acceptably as a leader in the Northfield Summer Conference in 1897. This study is based on the *Records and Epistles of the Apostolic Age,* by E. D. Burton, and is similar in its development to the one by Sharman just discussed.[29] Simultaneously with these developments and in keeping with a general agitation among more progressive

[26] Sharman, H. B., *op. cit.,* pp. 7-8.
[27] *Ibid.,* pp. 52-53.
[28] Interview Document, No. 23.
[29] Miscellaneous Reports, No. 1.

religious leaders for graded courses in the Sunday-schools,[30] the organization put its emphasis more and more upon graded and progressive texts.[31] It was urged that a definite cycle of studies be followed, with the same courses repeated from year to year, and with the privilege of advance conditioned by the completion of the previous year's work.[32] By the autumn of 1898, the Intercollegiate Y.M.C.A. through Mr. Sharman, who had become its first Bible study secretary, was recommending a cycle (No. I) of Bible study texts intended for daily personal study as follows:

Freshman . . . . Sharman, *Studies in the Life of Christ;*
Sophomore . . . . Bosworth, *Studies in the Acts and The Epistles;*

Junior . . . . White, *Old Testament Characters.*[33]

Senior . . . . "To be announced later." [34]

[30] Brown, A. A., *A History of Religious Education in Recent Times,* p. 101.
[31] *Young Men's Era,* Vol. 20, No. 5, Feb. 1, 1894, p. 10.
[32] *Young Men's Era,* Vol. 21, No. 50, Dec. 12, 1895, p. 829.
[33] The course for juniors was issued in parts during the year 1899-1900. The text includes thirty studies, each of seven portions. *The Intercollegian,* Vol. 23, No. 1, Oct., 1900, pp. 16 ff.
[34] *The Intercollegian,* Vol. 21, No. 1, Oct., 1898, p. 10.

By 1901-02 another group of studies, published within the years 1896-99, were being used (as Cycle No. II).

Freshman . . . . Sallmon, W. H., *Studies in the Life of Jesus,*
Sophomore . . . . Sallmon, W. H., *Studies in the Miracles of Jesus, Studies in the Parables of Jesus,*
Junior . . . . Sallmon, W. H., *Studies in the Life of Paul.*
The Intercollegian, Vol. 25, No. 9, June, 1903, p. 212; Miscellaneous Reports, No. 4.

The studies in the first cycle were arranged for daily study; those in the other cycle were in the form which had developed before the appearance of Mr. Sharman's book. Developed by Mr. Sallmon in his work with groups at Yale, the material was printed in the form chiefly of topics and questions, with pertinent references from books of the New Testament. At the same time, other texts were developed specifically to follow earlier emphases (see pp. 12 ff.) on preparation for "personal" work, including, for example, H. A. Johnston's *God's Method of Training Workers—The Intercollegian,* Vol. 23, No. 1, Oct., 1900, pp. 16 ff.

This series of texts was completed by the publication in 1901 of Bosworth's *Studies in the Teachings of Jesus and His Apostles* for seniors.[35] The same general plan was carried through in this text as in the previous ones of this series, except that much more explanatory material is found here than had been included in the previous studies.

Although there was a change of Bible study secretaries in this period, the policy inaugurated previously of helping Bible study leaders by correspondence was continued. During the year 1902-03, the Bible study secretary coöperated in this way with the leaders of 1808 circles.[36]

With further changes, however, in the personnel of the Bible study staff, there were soon brought in slightly different emphases in policy from those introduced in Mr. Sharman's study. Beginning about 1902-03 and continuing for nearly a decade, various types of courses were developed as a part of a program for popularizing Bible study.[37] The main emphasis came to be placed more on expansion, or increased enrollment, than upon any definite organizing principle for the courses of study. Beyond revision by the organization of its own courses to meet popular demands as well as the preparation of some studies to meet certain special requests, the Bible study texts published in this period were largely outgrowths of programs in operation in different colleges or universities which were discovered to be popular. An example is a text, *The Political and Social Significance of the Teachings of Jesus,* by Professor J. W. Jenks, then at Cornell University. Published in 1906, the book grew out of a series of Sunday morning talks, which the author

[35] *The Intercollegian,* Vol. 24, No. 9, June, 1902, pp. 221 ff.
[36] Miscellaneous Reports, No. 52.
[37] For example, an alternative course on the life of Christ was prepared in 1904 for freshmen by Professor Bosworth. This latter course takes up the four Gospels one by one, rather than in the form of a harmony. In 1908 appeared by the same author *New Studies in the Acts,* prepared as a simpler and less exacting study to replace his *Studies in the Acts and Epistles.*

had given five or six years before for the Cornell Y.M.C.A.[38]   The text contains twelve "studies," each divided into seven "days," in keeping with the arrangement initiated by Mr. Sharman for daily study.   In a similar fashion was published in 1909, *The Will of God and a Man's Life Work,* by Henry B. Wright.   This text had a widespread popularity, due no doubt to the more immediate interest in the practical problem with which it deals, viz., one's vocation. Developed from studies prepared for seniors in the Association Bible classes at Yale University,[39] the text carries through a definite idea; it argues that God has a plan for every life, a plan which may be discovered by one's dedicating one's self completely to God. "The act of surrender . . . . is a definite, conscious act . . . . between the man and God personally, made without reservation, in the path, not of inclination but of duty. . . . " [40]   After one has successfully met this "crisis" of surrender, one is ready to discover the will of God for one's vocation and other particulars.[41]   Four conditions must be met before the will of God can be learned or expressed in one's work: these are "purity"; "honesty"; "unselfishness"; and "love."   They are to be developed in one's life and also to be applied as tests to any vocation contemplated.[42]   The rapid development of Bible-study texts and their wide variety may be indicated by the following list of standard studies published by the Intercollegiate Y.M.C.A. in this period:

I. OUTLINE STUDIES (giving authorship, teachings of the books considered, etc.) :

1892, R. E. Speer, *Studies in the Gospel of Luke*
1892, R. E. Speer, *Studies in the Book of Acts*
1896, W. W. White, *Thirty Studies in Jeremiah*

[38] Jenks, J. W., *Political and Social Significance of the Teaching of Jesus,* Preface, p. vii.
[39] Wright, H. B., *The Will of God and a Man's Life Work,* Preface, p. v.
[40] *Ibid.,* pp. 69 ff.
[41] *Ibid.,* pp. 70 ff.
[42] *Ibid.,* pp. 167 ff.

1896, W. H. Sallmon, *Studies in the Life of Paul*
1897, W. H. Sallmon, *Studies in the Parables of Jesus*
1897, W. H. Sallmon, *Studies in the Life of Jesus*
1899, W. H. Sallmon, *Studies in the Miracles of Jesus*
1901, W. W. White, *Studies in the Gospel of John*

II. TEXTS IN ESSAY, OR LECTURE, FORM:

1896, R. E. Speer, *Studies of the Man Christ Jesus*
1900, R. E. Speer, *Studies of the Man Paul*

III. TEXTS ARRANGED FOR DAILY USE:

1896, H. B. Sharman, *Studies in the Life of Christ* (Based on *A Harmony of the Gospels*, by Stevens-Burton)
1898, E. I. Bosworth, *Studies in the Acts and Epistles* (Based on *Records and Epistles of the Apostolic Age*, by E. D. Burton)
1900, W. W. White, *Old Testament Records, Poems, and Addresses*
1900, W. W. White, *Studies in the Old Testament Characters*
1901, E. I. Bosworth, *Studies in the Teaching of Jesus and His Apostles*
1904, E. I. Bosworth, *Studies in the Life of Jesus Christ*
1904, R. A. Falconer, *The Truth of the Apostolic Gospel*
1906, J. W. Jenks, *The Political and Social Significance of the Teachings of Jesus*
1906, G. L. Robinson, *Leaders of Israel*
1907, C. F. Kent-R. S. Smith, *The Work and Teachings of the Early Prophets*
1907, J. E. McFadyen, *Ten Studies in the Psalms*
1907, H. T. Fowler, *Studies in the Wisdom Literature of the Old Testament*
1908, E. I. Bosworth, *New Studies in Acts*
1909, H. B. Wright, *The Will of God and a Man's Life Work*
1910, G. L. Robinson, *The Book of Isaiah*

IV. TEXTS ON "PERSONAL WORK" (arranged for daily study):

1900, H. A. Johnston, *Studies in God's Methods of Training Workers*
1901, H. C. Trumbull, *Individual Work for Individuals*

SMALL, STUDENT-LED GROUPS

In connection with the study programs in this period marked emphasis came to be placed upon small groups led by students. With the first Bible study promoted by the intercollegiate organization, emphasis was placed on the choice of a leader from the group or of some one else who would help to make possible participation by the members.[43] The stress upon an intimate group was now carried further. A student reflecting an attitude which had more and more weight said that student leaders were used because "professors tend to degenerate into lecturers." [44] In contrast to the formal class organized primarily to impart knowledge, emphasis was placed upon student leaders in order also to stimulate discussion of practical problems of common concern to the members of the group.

The same factors entered into the determination of the size of the group. One of the leaders in the Intercollegiate Y.M.C.A., J. Campbell White, discouraged the tendency of classes to organize with as many as sixteen members. He urged that two classes of eight members each be organized instead: he believed that such smaller classes could be more easily led, that they would stimulate greater interest and participation, and that they would make possible the development of more leaders.[45] A bit later a somewhat larger number was recommended for a group by the first Bible study secretary, Mr. Sharman; he felt that the number enrolled would inevitably shrink after the beginning, and that consequently, a very small group would remain. Such a small group, he felt, would produce only a small intellectual stimulus from different points of view and thus force the leader to talk too much; accordingly, he recommended that the group start with about twenty.[46] With the change

---

[43] See p. 16.
[44] Young Men's Era, Vol. 21, No. 50, p. 829, Dec. 12, 1895.
[45] The Intercollegian, Vol. 13, No. 4, Jan., 1891, p. 59.
[46] Interview Document, No. 23.

of Bible study secretaries, there in turn followed another emphasis on the size of the groups. Much larger classes were recommended, but only for a while.[47] Several factors operated to bring about a return to the smaller group. Among these was the fact that the large classes, which generally employed the lecture method, tended to "decrease in attendance and interest as the college year advanced, and the teachers would rarely be able to secure personal study outside of the class hour. Every year, however, a band of ten or twelve men . . . . would finish the year together, and would, moreover, become thoroughly attached to the study and to one another." Accordingly, small groups of ten or twelve men each were developed, led for the most part by students.[48]

To help train these student leaders, "normal" classes, led by professors, clergymen, laymen, or the employed officers of the Association were promoted. Their program was intended to give the student leader an intelligent grasp of the subject matter which he was to present in turn to his group; and to help him in applying it practically.[49]

Bible-study institutes running from one to four days were developed also to help in training the leaders of the classes, the teachers of the normal classes, and the committees promoting the Bible study in the colleges. This consisted in instruction on principles and methods of promoting the work. Beginning as early as 1896, when such an institute, led by Professor W. W. White, was held at the Indiana State Normal School,[50] these multiplied rapidly, and in the year 1903-04 one hundred such institutes were held over the country.[51]

Other means for promoting the Bible-study program included

[47] Interview Document, No. 24.
[48] Pamphlet, Cooper, C. S.: *Brief Historical Sketch of the Voluntary Bible Study Movement among North American Students*, p. 7.
[49] Pamphlet, Cooper, C. S.: *The Training of Bible Teachers*, pp. 8 f. and 21.
[50] *Young Men's Era*, Vol. 22, Feb. 20, 1896, p. 118.
[51] Miscellaneous Reports, No. 53.

lectures in the colleges on the Bible intended also to popularize the movement, Bible study reference libraries, special classes for special groups, e.g., fraternity groups or groups for athletes, and receptions and socials for members of the Bible-study classes. All such activities were usually initiated by a Bible-study "rally" and a campus-wide canvass for members.[52] Such a pronounced emphasis on Bible study was felt that a secretary was added to the staff of the University of Illinois Association in the year 1902-03 to promote this phase of the program alone and another institution took similar steps for the next year.[53] Other Associations followed suit, including the one at Columbia University, which in 1909-10 added a secretary on part-time for this purpose.[54] The Bible-study staff for the national movement also increased from one to two in 1904-05 and to three in 1906; in 1911, however, the number again dropped to one.[55] The Bible-study program received further emphasis in a national student Y.M.C.A. Bible-study conference, the first and only one of its kind, at Columbus, Ohio, October 22-25, 1908. A total of 1022 delegates were present, made up of 694 students, 124 professors and administrative officers, 90 college pastors and editors, and 114 employed secretaries of the Y.M.C.A.[56] At the same time there was a marked emphasis upon numbers, expressing itself in a pronounced effort to "double the enrollment." [57] The Bible-study secretary reported that, as a result of a campaign in the colleges during the year 1902-03, 390 institutions had pledged allegiance to the policy of doubling the enrollments.[58] Not a little of the printed matter intended to promote the studies from year to year among the students in this period showed such an emphasis as the following, taken from the cover page of one leaflet:

[52] *The Intercollegian*, Vol. 26, No. 6, March, 1904, p. 136.
[53] Miscellaneous Reports, No. 5.
[54] *The Intercollegian*, Vol. 32, No. 6, March, 1910, p. 164.
[55] Miscellaneous Reports, Nos. 6, 11.
[56] Miscellaneous Reports, No. 8.
[57] *The Intercollegian*, Vol. 26, No. 4, Jan., 1904, p. 98.
[58] Miscellaneous Reports, No. 5.

CAMPAIGN FOR FIFTY THOUSAND COLLEGE MEN IN BIBLE STUDY
College Year 1907–08

Threefold aim of campaign:

I. Enrollment: 50,000 students in Bible classes
II. Attendance: For two months or more.
III. Training: 500 normal classes in charge of college professors and Bible scholars.

Bible study was popularized in a way never achieved before. A special letter-head for the Bible study department was developed, carrying a special Advisory Council.[59]   Outstanding educational leaders were listed as sponsors of the Bible-study program, and statistics on the study groups included thousands of fraternity men, a well as many athletes, scholarship men, and other outstanding leaders. The results, however, of these emphases were not altogether satisfactory. A report of how the Bible-study program worked out in one Association (the University of Illinois), suggests something of its strength and weakness. Following a convention of the Y.M.C.A. in which students had been urged to employ the system used by Tammany in New York City, a leader in the University of Illinois Association made a preliminary directory of men students, so that, within the first week of school, the association leaders knew where 90 per cent of the men were located. There followed in the second week a big Bible-study "rally," when a prominent man spoke on the Bible; this was then followed up by a carefully-organized canvass, the territory having been divided among the various workers. Even in the beginning years of this effort as many as 1000 men were enrolled. Unfortunately, however, only about 80 per cent of these ever appeared at any of the classes and only about 50 per cent would continue for two months or more.[60]

[59] This was discontinued in time, however, because of apparent danger of developing a tangential movement away from the Intercollegiate Y.M.C.A. —Miscellaneous Reports, No. 49.

[60] Interview Document, No. 19.

The large enrollments secured by such means, with the falling off in interest afterwards, became an increasing problem for the inter-collegiate organization. This was undoubtedly a large factor in difficulties leading to criticisms, which began to appear in connection with the Bible-study program as this period was coming to a close. We shall take up these factors in the next section.

Chapter V. FOREIGN MISSION STUDIES

It is now necessary to review briefly the mission-study program in this same period. It will be recalled that the Student Volunteer Movement was started in 1886 and definitely organized in 1888, with a small executive committee, whose chairman, Mr. Mott, was a secretary of the Intercollegiate Y.M.C.A. Mr. Mott soon became the senior secretary of the Intercollegiate Y.M.C.A. and remained in that capacity until 1915. He also remained chairman of the Student Volunteer Movement Committee until 1920. Thus a unified program between the two organizations was assured and it was possible for the Intercollegiate Y.M.C.A. in sending in its first annual report to the World Student Christian Federation to call the Student Volunteer Movement its "Missionary Department." [1]

Similar to the topical outlines prepared in 1885 as the first "studies" of the Intercollegiate Y.M.C.A. on the Bible was a series of "studies" on foreign missions started in the early nineties by the Student Volunteer Movement. This first series appeared in eleven sections in the weekly *Young Men's Era* within the period, October, 1891 to June, 1892. These outlines were devoted to the "historical background of modern missions," including such topics as "Moravian Missions," the "Danish-Hall Missions," and the "Jesuit Missions of Southern India," as well as "The Beginning of American Foreign Missions." Reference books were listed, and topics, questions, and readings from these references were suggested. The last study is a review.

Underlying these studies was the belief that a mastery of the facts of the missionary enterprise would, more than anything else,

[1] Miscellaneous Reports, No. 5, 1897-98.

"deepen the convictions and strengthen the purpose of the individual volunteer" for foreign missionary service.[2]

Following this course there was an effort to develop studies by the method of correspondence with the "Volunteer Bands,"—the groups of student volunteers on the campuses.[3] This approach was in turn supplanted by topical outlines in a small monthly magazine, *The Student Volunteer,* started by the Student Volunteer Movement in February, 1893. Beginning with the very first number, studies were prepared, in outline form, together with suggestions about desirable texts. In eighteen months the following courses were developed: two on records in the New Testament concerning the Apostolic Church and the lessons to be drawn therefrom on missions;[4] one on different religions;[5] one each on China and India, with material on history, government, education, and religions;[6] and one on "Practical Studies" related to becoming a missionary.[7]

Beginning with the autumn of 1894, however, the Movement was forced to undertake its educational program far more seriously. From the first there were religious leaders who did not favor the procedure of the Movement in pledging students for foreign mission service. Among these was Mr. Moody, who, although deeply interested in the missionary cause, did not at first give his endorsement to the Student Volunteer Movement because he objected to pledging in principle.[8] Developments in the Movement led several years afterwards to sharp criticism by others equally interested in the foreign-missionary enterprise. One of these, Dr. John Nevius, an influential Presbyterian missionary in Chefoo, China, said in

[2] *Young Men's Era,* Vol. 17, No. 38, Oct. 1, 1891, p. 612.
[3] Interview Document, No. 18.
[4] *The Student Volunteer,* Vol. 1, No. 5, June, 1893, pp. 86 ff.; No. 7, Oct., 1893, pp. 126 ff.
[5] *Ibid.,* Vol. 1, No. 8, Dec., 1893, pp. 147 ff.
[6] *Ibid.,* Vol. 1, No. 1, Feb., 1893, pp. 8 f.; Vol. 1, No. 6, Oct., 1893, pp. 105 f.
[7] *Ibid.,* Vol. 2, No. 1, Feb., 1894, pp. 4 ff.
[8] Moody, W. R., *Dwight L. Moody,* p. 358.

1893, "the Student Volunteer Movement has not increased the number of missionaries actually going to the field to the extent that the reported number of volunteers led us to expect." Of the volunteers, "one-tenth of the whole number have applied to mission boards and been either sent or rejected, while one-tenth have 'renounced'; two-tenths have been 'hindered.' . . . . There has certainly been great lightness in assuming or renouncing the pledge. . . . Another cause of disappointment . . . . is an evident estrangement, amounting in some cases almost to antagonism, between those who expect to go abroad and those who do not." This condition, Dr. Nevius believed, was due to an "unwarranted assumption and too much pressure on the part of volunteers." He criticized the volunteers for claiming that the greatest need is in the mission field, and for "appealing too strongly" to students "and too exclusively to their sympathies and imaginations." He felt that the presentation of missionary work frequently gave "only the bright side of it," so that many who reached the field on such a superficial basis found cause for deep regret afterwards. He believed also that it was ill-advised to pledge young men and young women "three, four or five years before they are expected to enter upon their work. . . ." Moreover, "volunteers who are rejected for reasons which existed when they signed the volunteer pledge, and should have prevented their doing so, are subjected to needless disappointment and chagrin. . . ." [9]

This statement by Dr. Nevius made a deep impression on missionary leaders, and for at least a while caused a dropping off of support of the Student Volunteer Movement by the missionary boards.[10] Appreciation by the Volunteer Movement of the significance of the statement is reflected in part in the report of the executive committee in its convention at Detroit, Michigan, in 1894. The leaders of the Movement called attention to the fact that they had already changed the wording of the pledge card which volunteers

[9] The Missionary Review, Vol. 16, May, 1893, pp. 336 ff.
[10] Interview Document, No. 18.

were signing. The early form read, "I am willing and desirous, God willing, to become a foreign missionary." This was changed in 1892 to read, "It is my purpose, God willing, to become a foreign missionary." The new form was also called a "declaration" instead of a pledge.[11] This change was made with the thought of eliminating those who signed simply as evidence of their consecration.[12] The executive committee also discussed other "perils," chiefly those mentioned by Dr. Nevius, which were facing the Movement at the time.[13]

The statement of Dr. Nevius had an immediate bearing on the mission-study program. The article made quite an impression on Mr. D. W. Lyon, who had grown up in a missionary family in China, where he had known Dr. Nevius, and who was the traveling secretary for the Student Volunteer Movement at the time. Mr. Lyon's contact as a young man with China caused him to be concerned also about the materials used to interest students in the missionary cause and the manner of presenting it. He frequently found in tears students who were hindered from going out because of the attitude of their parents or of their sweethearts. He felt that the missionary cause was presented too much as a romance, so that many of those who did reach the field had a difficult time in adjustment. Again, some of those who were working for the Movement held pre-millennial views, believing that Christ would return the next year or when the Gospel was preached to the whole world. The idea of having a part in bringing this about was something which entered also as a factor into the decisions of students for foreign service.[14] Mr. Lyon urged the executive committee of the Movement

[11] *Report of 1894 Student Volunteer Convention,* pp. 62 f.

[12] This new form has remained essentially the same since then, undergoing more recently only slight modification. As now used, the statement reads, "It is my purpose, if God permit, to become a Christian missionary abroad."—Interview Documents, Nos. 18 and 27.

[13] *Report of 1894 Student Volunteer Convention,* pp. 66 ff.

[14] In 1892 it was reported that among 7000 enrolled as volunteers there were those whose purposes varied from that of an old man of seventy who

sciousness" in the rank and file of students.[25]   Again, as with Bible study, emphasis was placed more and more in this period on student leadership of the mission-study groups.   As early as 1902 it was reported that students were "the most usual leaders."   As with the Bible-study programs, also, stress came to be placed more and more on multiplying small groups, led by students, with normal classes led by older people for training the leaders week by week.[26]

Again, at this time students began to make visits to churches to create interest in the missionary cause, conducting large numbers of mission-study circles among young people of the churches.[27]   In connection with this projection of the missionary interest beyond the campus, leaders of the Intercollegiate Y.M.C.A. helped to stimulate the organization of an independent "Young People's Missionary Movement" in the churches.[28]

In keeping with the type developed by Mr. Lyon, the early courses by Mr. Beach continued to be prepared in topical outline form and published in *The Student Volunteer*.   Soon, however, these began to be replaced by texts in essay form, prepared by Mr. Beach himself and supplemented by others prepared at his request or that of his successor.   Many of these were adopted by other missionary agencies.[29]   The large number and wide variety of standard texts published by the Movement during the period under consideration will be revealed by the following list:

I. COUNTRIES

> 1895, Beach, H. P., *The Cross in the Land of the Trident* (Studies on India)
> 1898, Beach, H. P., *Dawn on the Hills of T'Ang-* (Study of missions in China)
> 1899, Thornton, D. M., *Africa Waiting*
> 1899, Cary, Otis, *Japan and Its Regeneration*

[25] Letter Document, No. 9.
[26] *The Intercollegian,* Vol. 27, No. 4, Jan., 1905, p. 89.
[27] Miscellaneous Reports, No. 69.
[28] Miscellaneous Reports, No. 53.
[29] Letter Document, No. 9.

1903, Brown, A. J., *The New Era in the Philippines*
1904, Beach, H. P., *India and Christian Opportunity*
1911, Zwemer, S. M., *The Unoccupied Mission Fields of Africa and Asia*
1912, Speer, Robert E., *South American Problems*
1912, Brown, A. J., *The Chinese Revolution*
1915, Eddy, Sherwood, *The Students of Asia*

II. BIOGRAPHY

1896, Beach, H. P., *Knights of the Labarum*
1899, Thompson, A. C., *Modern Apostles in Missionary By-ways*
1901, McDowell, W. F., *Effective Workers in Needy Fields*
1903, Walsh, W. Parkham, *Heroes of the Mission Fields*

III. HISTORY AND PRINCIPLES

1897. Bliss, E. M., *Development of the Mission Field*
1897, Bliss, E. M., *Organization and Methods of Mission Work*
1900, Beach, H. P., *Protestant Missions in South America*
1901, Lawrence, E. D., *Introduction to the Study of Foreign Missions*
1903, Thompson, A. C., *Protestant Missions: Their Rise and Early Progress*

IV. TYPES OF MISSION WORK

1899, Rutter, W. J., *The Healing of the Nations*
1909, Edwards, Martin R., *The Work of the Medical Missionary*
1913, Barton, James L., *Educational Missions*

V. BIBLICAL STUDIES

1899, Beach, H. P., *New Testament Studies in Missions*
1907, Fiske, Martha T., *The Word and the World*

VI. GENERAL

1900, Mott, John R., *The Evangelization of the World in This Generation*

1904, Mott, John R., *The Pastor and Modern Missions.* A Plea for Leadership in World Evangelization
1907, Brown, Arthur J., *The Foreign Missionary*
1908, Barton, James L., *The Unfinished Task*
1908, Mott, John R., *The Future Leadership of the Church*
1909, Murray, J. Lovell, *The Apologetic of Modern Missions*
1910, Mott, John R., *The Decisive Hour of Christian Missions*
1914, Mott, John R., *The Present World Situation*

VII. RELIGIONS

1901, Kellogg, S. H., *A Handbook of Comparative Religion*
1905, Richards, E. H., *Religions of Mission Fields*
1907, Zwemer, S. M., *Islam: A Challenge to Faith*

VIII. SURVEY OF MISSION FIELDS

1901, Beach, H. P., *A Geography and Atlas of the Protestant Missions:* Vol. I, Geography
1903, Beach, H. P., *A Geography and Atlas of the Protestant Missions:* Vol. II, Statistics and Atlas
1910, Dennis, James S., *World Atlas of Christian Missions*

Chapter VI. OTHER DEVELOPMENTS

EXPANSION

WE must note briefly other developments in the direction of an expansion and an institutional character of the program, as well as some problems arising in connection therewith, particularly toward the end of the period. There was an expansion of the staff for the Intercollegiate Y.M.C.A. from two in 1890 [1] to twelve two decades later.[2] In this period also the Intercollegiate Y.M.C.A. began to stimulate the development of similar work among students in other countries. This was promoted chiefly by Mr. Mott, who took a leading part in organizing to that end in 1895 the World's Student Christian Federation.[3] Summer conferences similar to those at Northfield (Massachusetts), Lake Geneva (Wisconsin), and Knoxville (Tennessee) were added at Cazadero (California) in 1896,[4] at Gearhart (Oregon), and Lake Erie (Ohio) in 1903,[5] at Ruston (Louisiana) in December, 1903,[6] at Cascade (Colorado) in the summer of 1908,[7] and Pocono Pines (Pennsylvania) in the summer of 1910.[8] With one exception all of these conferences have continued to date, each being held, if not in the same place, then in the same general area of the country. The conference at

---

[1] The Y.M.C.A. Year Book, 1890, pp 24, 32, 36.
[2] The Y.M.C.A. Year Book, 1909-10, p. 37.
[3] Men, Vol. 22, No. 22, Oct. 10, 1896, p. 356.
[4] Young Men's Era, Vol. 22, No. 15, April 9, 1896, p. 232.
[5] The Intercollegian, Vol. 25, No. 6, March, 1903, p. 140.
[6] Ibid., Vol. 26, No. 3, Dec. 1903, p. 68.
[7] Ibid., Vol. 31, No. 2, Nov., 1908, p. 40.
[8] Ibid., Vol. 32, No. 8, May, 1910, p. 205.

Lake Erie (Ohio) was discontinued after 1911 in favor of one at Eagles Mere (which succeeded the one at Pocono Pines).[9]

CONTINUED SEGREGATION OF MEN AND WOMEN

The principle established in the previous period of developing a work made up exclusively of men (cf. pp. 18 ff.) was rigidly adhered to in this period, this being carried through even in the face of some criticism of such a policy. For example in 1893, Mr. A. A. Stagg, president of the Association at the University of Chicago, said that the organization for men and the one for women in the same institution had similar constitutions, that both were alike except in name, and that they had joint meetings to silence the critics of separate work for men and women "when boys and girls are so closely connected in other ways." [10] Another example of this emphasis upon segregation of the sexes is found in the organization two years afterwards of a new Y.M.C.A. at the University of Michigan. This group was formed within the "Student Christian Association," which had been organized in 1858, and which had related itself to the Y.M.C.A. At that time it included only men; after 1870, however, when women were admitted to the University, the membership included both sexes.[11] Although there was also some criticism at the University of Michigan of the segregation caused by the organization of the Y.M.C.A., the plan was adhered to. It was urged that men would express themselves more freely in religious meetings when alone, and that their moral and spiritual needs could be dealt with more effectively under such conditions.[12] Moreover, there was a desire to develop a group with an intensive missionary and evangelistic emphasis.[13] This principle of segregation was manifested as well

[9] *Ibid.*, Vol. 34, No. 6, March, 1912, p. 142.
[10] *Young Men's Era*, Vol. 19, No. 5, Feb. 2, 1893, pp. 145 ff.
[11] Letter Document, No. 7.
[12] Interview Document, No. 9-A.
[13] Interview Document, No. 15.

in the summer conferences, where the leadership sought also to eliminate visiting by women around the conference grounds during the period of the gatherings.

The problem of getting the undivided attention of the men students was undoubtedly a very real one. The emphasis, however, put upon segregation of the sexes was sometimes pushed to an extreme. Programs for new students came to include a reception at the beginning of the college year. In discussing this phase of the program in 1891, it was said that students were "divided in their opinion as to whether or not women should be invited"; in 1895, there was "no sentiment against it. There is, however, a growing sentiment in co-educational colleges in favor of the young men and young women holding separate receptions the first week, and later in the year holding a joint reception." In 1901, however, it was definitely suggested that "whenever practicable let the reception be for men only," with, perhaps, a joint reception later.[15]

PUBLIC EVANGELISM

In this period also, programs of evangelism were developed more extensively than previously. Methods of preparation and follow-up, no less than the actual carrying through of the "campaign" itself became standardized and put into pamphlet form.[16] In addition to Mr. Sayford's evangelistic work begun in the previous period, was that of members of the staff, particularly Mr. Mott, who had become the leader of the staff. His own commitment to the Christian faith had been very much of a crisis experience. "His student days," writes Miss Ruth Rouse, "were crucial in his development. . . . At Cornell University . . . . John Mott passed from agnosticism to faith and went through the experience of conversion. . . . It was

[14] *Ibid.*
[15] Pamphlets issued in 1891, 1895, and 1901 on work for new students.
[16] Pamphlet: Elliott, A. J., *Meetings for Christian Decision.*

Moody's death that called . . . . Mott to do the work of an evangelist. . . ." in the colleges.[17]

The staff of the Intercollegiate Y.M.C.A defined the objects of evangelism in 1906 as that of making "men not simply followers of Christ as the greatest religious teacher, but as Lord and Saviour. This issue of evangelism is righteousness, a recognition of the supernatural claims of Christ. Evangelization other than this is superficial." [18] The results in one instance of such an emphasis in 1900 by Mr. Mott are suggested in a letter by a secretary of a local Association:

"That group of four agnostics and sceptical students . . . . are meeting twice a week and studying the resurrection and Christ's life." [19]

Moral problems, however, of young men continued to be emphasized, particularly, "sins of the body," and "sins of the mind," as well as gambling, dishonesty, and profanity.[20] A delegate at the Lake Geneva Conference in 1897 reports that Mr. Sayford was present and gave addresses in his "usual dramatic way" on sex. "He told blood-curdling stories of men, who because of masturbation, had become insane and had to be tied hand and foot. . . . He terrified the youngsters. . . ." [21] Another evangelist was used for "clean-up" nights at summer conferences, with results the value of which may be questioned:

". . . . Everybody knew when the night was coming, and not a few were afraid. Everybody was selfconscious. . . . With the lights turned low, all gathered around the fire place for the discussion of 'secret sins.' " [22]

[17] Rouse, Ruth, *The Student World,* Vol. 22, sheet 17, April, 1930, pp. 102 ff.
[18] Miscellaneous Reports, No. 42.
[19] Letter Document, No. 15.
[20] Interview Document, No. 15.
[21] Interview Document, No. 16.
[22] Interview Document, No. 10.

Other special speakers were secured for this work in the colleges. One type of experience which was emphasized is suggested by the title of a booklet, *Down and Out and Up Again*. This booklet describes the work of one of the special speakers, who in one college year (1909-10) visited 55 institutions, giving 148 public addresses and conducting "369 group meetings in Greek letter fraternity houses, in athletic training quarters, in club houses, and dormitories. These group meetings averaged from 15 to 75 men." In all of these meetings much attention was given to the question of "purity." [23]

Sometimes the emphases in evangelism dealt not only with overt acts, but tended to give an unwholesome connotation to the normal sex impulses of developing adolescence as well. A leader in the Intercollegiate Y.M.C.A. urged that all members of the staff should, in connection with their visits to local Associations, "have at least one meeting where you can strike a blow for spiritual results," and "sink in the knife with reference to possible and probable secret sins. . . ." [24]

The special evangelistic efforts naturally stirred great numbers of students. One writes of a campaign:

"We are trying to have each man fight his particular sin biblically; making Bible study for each . . . . an individual matter. . . . . Each man is reading through parts of the New Testament and writing out those verses that apply to his particular weakness. . . . [X] has taken down all the smutty pictures in his room. . . .Another man . . . . smashed up a picture" following the meeting Sunday, "began systematic study, and feels the power of Christ." [25]

The definite things suggested for students desiring help on personal problems included observance of the habit of daily Bible study and prayer, confession of faith and joining the Church, entering a Bible class, and engaging in some sort of service for others.[26] A

[23] Miscellaneous Reports, No. 9.
[24] Miscellaneous Reports, No. 43.
[25] Letter Document, No. 15.
[26] Interview Document, No. 15.

positive step forward is registered here, particularly in the emphases which enabled a student to forget his problem through contact with groups and through activity in service programs. Nevertheless, the most fundamental aspect of at least one problem is hardly cared for. The treatment of the sex question in such "campaigns," as Professor George Albert Coe has observed, sometimes amounted to the offering of a religious emotional escape from bad habits instead of providing a basis of new habits.[27] Sometimes, indeed, the problem of the student was magnified, as when through certain emphases he was led to infer that his impulse toward the other sex was evil. Under such conditions attention was directed to the sex problem, with a consequent tension and worry, particularly so in the case of the student who was conscientious about his religious life.[28]

A more positive approach to the problem was implied in an address [29] delivered at the Northfield Conference in 1901, by President H. C. King, of Oberlin University. He urged that one seek character through "the conditions . . . . involved in our very natures"; for through careful heeding of the laws of nature "are we to be saved." The author insisted on the unity of mind and body, and urged that one keep one's self "persistently at your best." Fatigue and vagueness of thought are to be avoided. Further, control of the emotions is always indirect. "Emotion spontaneously arises in the presence of its object." In trouble, one can direct one's attention to something else. "Not your environment makes you, but that part of your environment to which you attend. . . . Surrendering, persistent personal association with those who have such characters as we seek" was emphasized; for "character is caught, not taught." An emphasis was also placed on action: body and mind are made for action; any idea, "if it is really to be yours, you must express . . . . in some way. . . . That which is not expressed

[27] Interview Document, No. 4.
[28] Interview Document, No. 10.
[29] King, H. C., "How to Make a Rational Fight for Character."

dies." [30]   Although this address was printed in pamphlet form and listed in the publications from 1902 to 1918, and although the point of view was found in some of the evangelistic work, it remained for a later period to develop its full implications.

TRAINING OF COLLEGE ASSOCIATION SECRETARIES

The institutional development of the Y.M.C.A. work in the colleges and universities is found also in the attitude toward the secretaryship as a vocation.   It will be recalled that at first men were employed for work with the local Association for a period of only a year or two.   (Cf. pp. 39 f.)   In 1892, a conference of the ten secretaries who were then serving in local college Associations, drew out the observation that up to that time employed officers had been serving just one year each.[31]   The development in this phase of the work, however, was quite rapid.   In 1899 a member of the Intercollegiate Y.M.C.A staff reported that "it is not a matter now of having" to urge universities and colleges to employ secretaries, but rather of keeping some institutions from doing so.[32]   About the same time it became evident that there was a growing sentiment "in the larger universities for more experienced secretaries, as well as longer terms of service, and consequently higher salaries. . . ." [33] In 1907, Mr. W. D. Weatherford, a member of the Intercollegiate Y.M.C.A. staff, ventured to prepare an article declaring the college association secretaryship to be a life work.[34]   This was the first printed statement to that effect.[35]   Other printed statements concerning the work and training of college secretaries soon followed.[36]

[30] *Ibid.*, pp. 4 ff.

[31] *Young Men's Era*, Vol. 18, No. 4, Jan. 28, 1892, pp. 115 ff.

[32] Miscellaneous Reports, No. 2.

[33] Miscellaneous Reports, No. 3.

[34] Weatherford, W. D., "The Secretaryship of the Student Y.M.C.A.," *College Problems*, 1907.

[35] Letter Document, No. 13.

[36] Pamphlets: Hurrey, C. D., *The Student General Secretary;* Weatherford, W. D., *Student Secretaries in Training.*

And in 1910, Mr. Mott said to a group of church leaders, "There has come a new conception about the leadership of the Young Men's and Young Women's Christian Associations . . . . that the secretaryship of the Associations may be made a life work." [37]

Simultaneously with the developing conviction that the college secretaryship could be a vocation there was also a growing interest in the training of the men engaged in this work. In so far as this had been achieved already, it had been accomplished largely through conferences of the intercollegiate staff, and through their contacts with other college secretaries, as well as through informal conferences among the latter. Believing that more specialized training was necessary than the regular A.B. degree made possible, leaders in the work in the South held a summer school for college secretaries in that section in 1907, for a period of two weeks.[38] The specific aim of the school was twofold: to give courses to prepare the men for meeting the intellectual problems of students concerning religion, as well as to help on the best methods for developing the work.[39] The school was repeated the next year, at which time also similar efforts were started in the Central West,[40] and soon afterwards in other parts of the country. College secretaries were also encouraged to take two or three years of graduate study as another means of training.[41]

There soon developed, however, the idea of having from time to time one national training school for the whole country. The first of these was held for three weeks during August, 1910, at Lake Forest, Illinois. This was repeated again in 1911, when it was decided to hold the gathering biennially.[42] It has been generally recog-

---

[37] Galpin, C. J., Ed., *Church Work in State Universities,* p. 59.
[38] *The Intercollegian,* Vol. 30, No. 1, Oct., 1907, p. 12.
[39] Weatherford, W. D., *College Problems,* 1907, Foreword, p. 6.
[40] Elliott, A. J., *College Leadership,* 1909.
[41] Miscellaneous Reports, No. 10.
[42] *College Leadership,* Vols. I and II, 1910, 1911; and reports of subsequent assemblies of college secretaries, Library National Council of Y.M.C.A's., New York.

nized that among other things these biennial gatherings have created an interest in the national character of the organization and have engendered a spirit of solidarity.[43]

SOCIAL SERVICE

The program of practical service by the Association also revealed expansion in this period. By 1892, a great many of the college Associations had established employment bureaus as a part of their campus service activities.[44] The work for new students was continued, with many features of practical service added.[45] Interest in community service found a new outlet through the social settlement, through summer camps, through deputations for religious meetings, through city mission work, through industrial service programs, through work with foreigners, and through other means.[46]

DEVELOPMENT OF SPECIAL MEMBERSHIP BASIS

The basis of membership in the Intercollegiate Y.M.C.A. also received attention at this time, bringing the organization into greater selfconsciousness within the general Y.M.C.A. Already, the Intercollegiate Y.M.C.A had been the occasion of questions arising regarding the supervision of certain phases of the work with students. This was related to a larger problem, that of dual supervision by the state committees and the International Committee, the latter being the committee under which the intercollegiate work was promoted. The problem was so acute by 1899 that in the International Convention of Y.M.C.A's. that year a resolution was adopted providing for a committee of seven to study the whole problem.[47] This

[43] Miscellaneous Reports, No. 58.
[44] Young Men's Era, Vol. 18, No. 18, May 5, 1892, p. 559.
[45] Cf. pamphlets issued in 1891, 1895, and 1901 on work for new students, Library National Council of Y.M.C.A's., New York.
[46] The Intercollegian: Vol. 30, No. 9, June, 1908, pp. 214 ff.; Vol. 26, No. 9, June, 1904, pp. 205 ff.; Vol. 30, No. 9, June, 1908, p. 219.
[47] Report of International Convention of Y.M.C.A's., 1899, p. 71.

committee was continued in the next convention.[48]   In the following convention (1904) a majority report was adopted which was not generally satisfactory to those representing the emphasis of states' rights.   This left the problem an unsettled one.[49]

One aspect of the intercollegiate work which had become involved was that relating to control of summer conferences.   This question had become acute in the Middle West, where strong state committees had developed for the promotion of the Y.M.C.A. work in its various phases.   The management of the summer conference at Lake Geneva, Wisconsin, was claimed by both the International Committee and the state committees in the area which that conference was serving.   After prolonged discussion, however, it was generally conceded that the International Committee should continue to manage the summer conferences.   Nevertheless, the manifestation of strength on the part of the state committees in the West stimulated some other state committees also to assert their own strength.   In at least one instance this led to the development of a state summer conference in competition with the one for the area in which that state is located.[50]

A special problem now arose with reference to the basis of membership.   The prevailing "evangelical" basis [51] had been a stumbling block to some students and professors from the beginning.   Revision was finally proposed at a general convention of the Y.M.C.A. in Washington, D. C., in 1907.   A rephrasing of the "evangelical" basis was adopted to authorize as active members in college Associations—

". . . . students and members of faculties who are either members of evangelical churches or accept Jesus Christ as He is offered in the Holy Scriptures as their God and Saviour, and approve the objects of the Association, which are as follows:

[48] *Report of International Convention of the Y.M.C.A's.,* 1901, p. 284.
[49] Interview Document, No. 13.
[50] *Ibid.*
[51] *See* Footnote 33, p. 8.

'To lead students to become disciples of Jesus Christ as their Divine Lord and Saviour. To lead them to join the Church. To promote growth in Christian faith and character, and to enlist them in Christian service. Only active members shall have the right to vote, and only active members who are members of evangelical churches shall be eligible for office.' " [52]

This represented a special concession for the college work. It is significant, however, that although the attitude of students, along with that of professors, stimulated criticism of the prevailing basis of membership, the actual appeal for the change on the floor of the convention was presented by others than students. Mr. Mott, the senior secretary for the intercollegiate work, was the outstanding champion of the change, successfully meeting in debate the objections of so prominent a figure as William Jennings Bryan. Naturally, the result heightened the self-consciousness and the sense of distinctiveness of the intercollegiate organization, particularly so in the minds of those directing its work. [53]

ALL-CAMPUS MOVEMENT

These various developments were expressions of a movement which was seeking increasingly to influence the total student life. Through the more intimate and informal Bible-study groups, with the opportunity for the members to deal with their more practical problems; through the changes in the basis of membership developed in view of the attitude of students and professors; through an increasing number of practical activities developed on behalf of students—through such means the organization, which at first had represented a small group banded together for mutual helpfulness in

---

[52] Report of International Convention of Y.M.C.A's., 1907, pp. 109, 111, 122.

[53] Interview Document, No. 22. The significant rôle which had come to be occupied by the staff of the intercollegiate work, compared with that of the student members, was a factor in later developments looking to the democratization of the work with students.

Christian living, came to express a much more inclusive constituency and program. A report of a meeting at Columbus, Ohio, in 1904, of secretaries working with students on behalf of the intercollegiate and state committees of Y.M.C.A's., indicated the following as the type of Association on the campus for which they stood:

One that "embraces all the students—all faculties. The whole range of the moral and religious life of students and the whole range of the moral and religious life of the institution so far as this can best be done by a voluntary organization. . . ." [54]

So effectively was the organization deemed to be functioning in that rôle that in 1909, a prominent church leader in the South urged that the Y.M.C.A. "should be in the middle of college life where it can influence the ideals of every department of college activity. . . ." To that end he urged recognition of "the right of the Association to the controlling position in college life." [55]

RELATIONSHIPS WITH DENOMINATIONAL AGENCIES

Note must be taken also, however, of developments in the relationship of the organization with denominational agencies. The attitude of the general Y.M.C.A. toward the Church at the time the intercollegiate work was started was expressed by the first "agent" of the general committee, Mr. Robert Weidensall, in giving his report for the year 1878-79:

"No pains have been spared to show the intimate and subordinate relation of the Association to the Church, and to make manifest the distinctive work of the Associations,—viz., the salvation of young men, through the agency chiefly of young men. . . ." [56]

This attitude naturally became the policy also for the college work. An argument frequently advanced by leaders of the work for the

[54] Miscellaneous Reports, No. 41.
[55] Miscellaneous Reports, No. 72.
[56] *The Y.M.C.A. Year Book*, 1878-79, p. 11.

"evangelical" basis of membership was that it gave evidence of the
Association's being a co-worker with the (Protestant) Church. The
special concession on membership granted for the college work in
1907 [57] was in no sense a change of policy. Moreover, when the
problem of a more satisfactory basis of membership was again up
for discussion in a meeting of the intercollegiate staff in 1910,
Mr. Morse, the General Secretary of the International Committee,
said:

"The great thing is not that we shall have a test, but the fact
that the basis declares . . . . the Association is allied to the Church
and that the two will stand together. . . . The word 'evangelical'
was defined at the Portland Convention because no other agency
had made such a definition. If there had been anything to com-
pare with the Federation of Churches, no such definition would have
been prepared. In 1905 the Federation of Churches excluded the
Unitarian denomination, declaring their essential belief in Jesus
Christ as Lord and Saviour. Since the adoption of our North
American test" (evangelical), the Associations "have gotten on a
much better footing with the churches." [58]

By that time, however, another aspect of the organization's relation to the Church had begun to present itself. In the early days
the Y.M.C.A. and Y.W.C.A were the only religious agencies working on the campuses of many institutions. Later, however, with the
rapid growth of state universities some church leaders began to feel
that the work of the Y.M.C.A. (as well as that of the Y.W.C.A.) was
either not adequately meeting the needs of their students or not
properly conserving the denominational loyalties. [59] At first establishing guild houses at three or four institutions, certain denominations then employed assistant pastors, "in many cases a graduate
or senior student, on a part-time basis, to give special attention to

[57] Cf. p. 77 f.
[58] Miscellaneous Reports, No. 47.
[59] Cf. Article by Dr. Frank Strong, *Religious Education Magazine,* Vol.
II, No. 6, Feb. 1908, p. 211.

student work," [60] and by 1904 some denominations were employing full-time clergymen for work with students.[61] The relationships between the denominational workers and those representing the Y.M.C.A in state institutions were considered so important a question that in 1906 the Presbyterian General Assembly appointed a committee to confer with the one directing the Intercollegiate Y.M.C.A. work.[62] At the same time the Intercollegiate Y.M.C.A. reported that one of its problems was that of "how to relate our movement to denominational work for students so as to avoid friction and duplication." [63]

In addition, there were problems arising with reference to volunteer and professional leadership for the Church. Participation in Y.M.C.A. work did not guarantee interest, it was said, in church work afterwards:

". . . . Men may be live, vigorous, consecrated workers in the University Association, and after their course is finished go out into their communities to take no part in the work of organized religion there. They were trained in a different school . . . . ; it was a strange thing to them when they went out." [64]

Further, it was charged that the Association was failing to present to students the call to the ministry in the home church in as forceful and challenging a way as it was presenting foreign work.[65]

There was also a feeling that the policies of the local Association were determined too much from the outside, i.e., from national headquarters.[66]

[60] Urbach, W. F., *A History of the University Pastor Movement in State Colleges and Universities of the United States*, pp. 24 ff.
[61] *Ibid.*, p. 27.
[62] *Ibid.*, p. 36.
[63] Miscellaneous Reports, No. 55.
[64] Baker, Rev. J. C., *Church Work in State Universities*, Galpin, C. J., Ed., p. 51.
[65] Interview Document, No. 15.
[66] Miscellaneous Reports, No. 45.

The association leaders sought to deal with the situation in several ways:

1. They endeavored to meet their obligations to the Church by getting more of the lay alumni to identify themselves with, and to help in, the programs of churches upon graduation. They reported in 1907 that they were making progress on that score.[67] This was carried further in the next period by a member of the staff, employed specifically to stimulate continued activity and service on the part of alumni.[68]

2. They began to put greater emphasis upon recruiting more able young men for the ministry. In 1908, Mr. Mott published a book, *Future Leadership of the Church,* which was prepared as a "diagnosis of the problem and program." [69]   Addresses on "the claims of the ministry" were presented during the same year in two hundred institutions.   In addition, special "institutes" were held for the same purpose, and local ministerial "clubs," or "bands," were formed for those intending to become ministers; also, students planning to become ministers were encouraged to make visits to neighboring colleges and universities and present the call to others.[70] Early in 1909 the Association published a series of pamphlets, dealing with the claims and opportunities of the ministry; in this effort in particular, as well as in the recruiting of students for foreign service, the coöperation of the church leaders was actively sought.   For, said Mr. Mott, "the problem of enlisting men for Christian work as a life work will not be solved save by . . . . the coöperation of . . . . the men who know the work facing the Church. . . ." [71]

3. The Associations also felt that the problem would be solved best by placing emphasis upon the local church in the college town instead of developing separate church work for students.   The in-

[67] Miscellaneous Reports, No. 56.
[68] Cf. p. 90.
[69] Miscellaneous Reports, No. 57.
[70] *Ibid.*
[71] Galpin, C. J., *op. cit.,* p. 62.

vestments by the denominations, Mr. Mott felt, should be "related largely to the parish church and its various plans and establishments. . . . . The ablest ministers . . . . should be stationed in the state university towns. . . . I would put [the money] more largely into men than into buildings. . . . Assistant pastors, chosen with reference to helping the church to minister more largely to students, should be officially related to the local parishes." [72]

4. The association leaders took the position that the religious life of students should be approached as a unit and that the Associations should be recognized as the organizations to make this possible. ". . . . The distinctive function," said Mr. Mott, of the Young Men's and Young Women's Christian Associations, "is that of leadership in the interdenominational efforts, and . . . . all work so far as it is interdenominational, should function through them; . . . . in distinctively denominational matters, the . . . . Associations should serve and help the regular parish churches." [73] Further, ". . . . the . . . . Associations are to be the one great comprehensive voluntary principle of student initiative. . . . ." Mr. Mott urged also the value in *esprit de corps* which comes to the Association from the consciousness of its members that, through the World's Student Christian Federation, they are united with similar societies in other nations.[74] Action in line with this point of view is found particularly in the religious-work directorship, which was developed for a while in this period in some of the state universities of the Middle West. The plan was started at the University of Minnesota, where, upon the suggestion of certain local church leaders, the Y.M.C.A. and Y.W.C.A. employed a clergyman to represent the various religious interests, with particular reference to the churches. Rev. W. S. Richardson began work in that capacity in 1909, developing in various ways a program of religious work in

[72] *Ibid.*, pp. 60 f.
[73] *Ibid.*, p. 64.
[74] *Ibid.*, p. 58.

coöperation with the churches and the Associations. In spite of a change in personnel, the plan was continued at the University of Minnesota for some six years, but was then discontinued.[75]

5. The Associations sought also to provide stronger employed leadership for the direction of its work, particularly in the state universities of the Middle West. This was due in part to the reasons given above, in part to the criticism that the policies of the local Association were determined too much from headquarters,[76] and in part to desire of the Associations to strengthen their program of religious work.[77]

Representing a somewhat different point of view was another approach to the problem which was started at the University of Pennsylvania. This was intended primarily as a means of extending the work of the denominational leaders to the students without any denominational affiliation.[78] Beginning in 1908, this took the form of a coöperative endeavor between the denominational agencies and the local Association,[79] and soon developed into an actual unity of forces. By this means each of the pastors of the participating denominations began to serve not only in a pastoral relationship to his denominational constituency, but also as a part-time secretary of the Association, with a responsibility for certain of its functions.[80] Although this plan was extended later to Cornell University,[81] one of its immediate effects was to stimulate certain denominational leaders to organize their approaches independently of the Y.M.C.A.[82] This problem is dealt with further in the next period.

[75] Interview Document, No. 12.
[76] Cf. p. 81.
[77] Letter Document, No. 6.
[78] Interview Document, No. 15.
[79] Urbach, W. F., *op. cit.*, p. 2.
[80] *Summary of the Cleveland Conference*, 1915, p. 4.
[81] *The Intercollegian*, Vol. 37, No. 8, Nov., 1919, p. 8.
[82] Interview Document, No. 15.

PART FOUR: SOCIAL EMPHASES
1910–1917

Chapter VII. NEW SOCIAL EMPHASES

RISE OF THE SOCIAL GOSPEL

ABOUT 1910 the Intercollegiate Y.M.C.A. began to reveal decidedly new program emphases, in keeping with the growing social consciousness of the time. The latter half of the nineteenth century gave rise to unusual social and industrial problems. Although the Civil War did much to quicken a sense of idealism, the post-war period revealed other attitudes as well. Wealth increased rapidly, and in the midst of the social and political confusion the direction of business and politics frequently fell into the hands of unscrupulous men.[1] The liquor evil took on renewed vigor.[2] Immigration grew rapidly,[3] creating problems of congestion and intensifying others.[4] The expansion of capitalism in industry led to the rapid rise of organized labor.[5] Conflicts between the two groups soon developed, and in this controversy the churches were charged with having passed over into the control of big business.[6]

Reference to several of the developments in response to these conditions will be suggestive of forces of another character. To deal

---

[1] Sweet, W. W., *op. cit.,* p. 477.
[2] *Ibid.,* p. 478.
[3] The number of immigrants entering the country increased from 72,183 in 1862 to 788,992 in 1882, and to 1,285,349 in 1907—*World Almanac,* 1932, p. 331.
[4] *See* the writings of Josiah Strong: for example, *The Challenge of the City.*
[5] Sweet, W. W., *op. cit.,* p. 503.
[6] *Ibid.,* pp. 503 ff.

with the liquor problem, the Women's Christian Temperance Union was organized in 1874.[7]   Attention was directed also to the problem of making democracy efficient, an issue, says Professor James T. Shotwell, which slowly came to the fore in the 80's and 90's, although it did not reach maturity until the first decade of the twentieth century. "At that time a new moral tone became evident in American social and political ideals, a tone which showed itself in the new conception of wealth as a trusteeship for social service instead of as the symbol of individual success. . . ."[8]

These various factors, together with a rapidly increasing study of sociology in the universities, challenged church leaders.[9]   They began to voice a new "Social Gospel." "The new civilization," wrote Professor Strong, "with its new social problems, has led us to search for the social teachings of Jesus, which had been long neglected; and we find that these teachings fit modern conditions as a key fits a lock."[10]   A bit later Professor Walter Rauschenbusch wrote:

"There are texts and allusions in the New Testament which have been passed by as of slight significance; now they are like windows through which we see miles of landscape. . . . Christians had always bowed in worship before their Master, but they had never undertaken to understand his life in its own historical environment and his teachings in the sense in which Jesus meant them to be understood. . . . He has stood like one of his pictures in Byzantine art, splendid against its background of gold, but unreal and unhuman. . . . Slowly . . . . his figure is coming out of the past to meet us . . . . and the better we know Jesus, the more social do his thoughts and aims become."[11]

[7] *Ibid.*, p. 478.
[8] *The New York Times*, Vol. 80, No. 26,860, Section 3, Aug. 9, 1931, p. 7.
[9] Sweet, W. W., *op. cit.*, p. 504.
[10] Strong, J., *The Challenge of the City*, p. 169.
[11] Rauschenbusch, W., *Christianity and the Social Crisis*, pp. 45 f.   Mr. t'Hooft has called attention to the fact that "higher criticism and the general historical interest in the biographical study of the personality of Jesus went hand in hand."—W. A. V. t'Hooft, *The Background of the Social Gospel in America*, p. 154.

The force of the rising social interest is found in the fact that by the end of the century courses in Christian sociology or social service were being offered in many theological seminaries; while college settlements had been established in most of the larger American cities, where students of sociology might receive practical training in dealing with the problems of society.[12]

Church bodies began also to take action. At first this was on behalf of labor, but by 1908, it was recognized "that the labor problem was but one phase of a larger complex social problem," a conviction evidenced by a social creed which was adopted that year by the Federal Council of Churches.[13]

Leaders of the Intercollegiate Y.M.C.A. were influenced not only by these developments, but also by the attitude of the British Student Christian Movement, particularly through its publications on social and economic questions.[14] Moreover, although some of the leaders in the American organization at first expressed concern lest the "social-democracy movement" develop into a tangential agency,[15] there were others whose attitude constituted a strong stimulus to a new social emphasis. The executive secretary, Mr. E. C. Carter, had caught from his father a deep interest in social questions. The latter, after serving as a Congregational minister, was for twenty years the secretary of the Charity Organizations Society of Lawrence, Massachusetts, where he was instrumental in developing such new social movements as hospital visiting service, baby clinics, milk stations for infants, and other phases of child welfare. Later as a student at Harvard, Mr. Carter was impressed with the emphasis placed on the practical, ameliorative character of religion. Following his graduation there, and while serving as secretary of the Harvard Christian Association, he was instrumental in leading students to become active as volunteer workers in social

12 Sweet, W. W., *op. cit.,* p. 506.
13 Rowe, H. K., *History of Religion in the United States,* pp. 150 f.
14 Interview Document, No. 7; Miscellaneous Reports, No. 58.
15 Miscellaneous Reports, No. 44.

institutions of Boston, Cambridge, and New York. This was done in addition to work with boys' clubs and social settlements in order to expose the students to modern social problems.[16]   Mr. Carter's interest in getting Americans to face their own social problems was accentuated by service afterwards in India, where he felt criticism from time to time of certain aspects of American life.[17]   From that background he returned to America to direct the work of the Intercollegiate Y.M.C.A.   The social interest already felt in the organization was soon manifested actively in a number of different ways.[17a]

INTEREST IN NEGRO LIFE

One specific expression of the general social interest is found in relation to the Negro, a development stimulated particularly by another member of the staff, Mr. W. D. Weatherford.   Before the birth of the intercollegiate movement, general Y.M.C.A. work had been started among Negroes.

". . . . At the Toronto Convention in 1876, the delegates from the South urged the importance of work among colored young men in that section.   Rev. Stuart Robinson, of Louisville . . . . led the discussion and made the first contribution to place an agent in the field for that purpose.   General George D. Johnston, late of the Confederate army, acted as the representative of the committee in this department until the Louisville Convention in 1877." [18]

This beginning in the general Y.M.C.A. led to a special department, directed largely by Negroes.

Early in the intercollegiate branch also some attention was given to the status of the Negro, an interest which was expressed in terms

[16] Interview Document, No. 3.
[17] Ibid.
[17a] Although the social service program was accentuated and expanded by Mr. Carter, several phases in the developments which are discussed here were effected under his successor, Mr. Charles D. Hurrey.
[18] The Y.M.C.A. Year Book, 1884, p. 54.

of the prevailing emphasis upon evangelism. Of the Northfield summer conference in 1894, it was reported:

". . . . Rev. C. L. Phillips, secretary of the Home Missionary Association, ... Presbyterian Church, South, ... spoke on the 'Moral Aspect of the Negro Question.' The Negro is in America to stay. . . . Our responsibility for them is eternal, until it is fully discharged. After a season of prayer for the preaching of the Gospel to the Negroes in the Black Belt, Mr. Sankey sang the 'Ninety and Nine' . . . ." [19]

Another approach was now undertaken. Mr. Weatherford was stimulated by the rising social consciousness no less than by the intimate contacts which, as a Southerner, he had with individual Negroes. He felt that something should be done to interest white students in the Negro and to make them intelligent regarding such factors in his life as the new social consciousness was emphasizing, as well as to establish interracial good-will and understanding. In 1909 he called together three Negro men and two white men in addition to himself. After a day's discussion of the question, it was felt that he should prepare a text for study by white students in order to secure their interest.[20] His *Negro Life in the South* appeared the next year, giving facts concerning Negro education, Negro religious life, economic conditions, and conditions of health and housing. This text was followed soon afterwards by another, *Present Forces in Negro Progress,* by the same author. Such interest was created by the special attention given to the status of the Negro and to the responsibility of whites in the South,[21] that the Intercollegiate Y.M.C.A. secured special funds to further its program along this line. A special worker, Mr. A. M. Trawick, with training in sociology, was added to the staff to stimulate and direct the

[19] *Young Men's Era,* Vol. 17, No. 29, July 16, 1891, p. 471.
[20] Letter Document, No. 13.
[21] For expressions of this newly-created interest, see an article by C. D. Daniel on "Southern Students' Interest in Negro Education,"—*The Intercollegian,* Vol. 31, p. 168.

interest in the question.[22]   At the same time Mr. C. H. Tobias was added as an additional Negro staff member in the colored department of the general Y.M.C.A. for work among Negro students. Very soon afterwards, a special summer conference was started at King's Mountain, North Carolina, for Negro students.[23]   This work was furthered also by the organization of an advisory committee consisting of representative educational and religious leaders in the South.   At the same time there was developed a "library of race relations," consisting of several books by both Negroes and whites and seeking to give neither an "ultra-northern" nor an "ultra-southern" view.[24]

INTERESTING STUDENTS IN POST-COLLEGE SERVICE

Already there had been put under way another special project, an attempt to have students continue as alumni their social-service interest.   This was stimulated to a degree by the feeling that something should be done to have professional men match the sacrifices of those going out as missionaries.[25]   The effort was a response on the whole, however, to the social interest of the time.   Appalled by "the realization . . . . that the great majority of students who were interested in religious and social service in college failed to ally themselves with altruistic enterprises in the communities to which they go after graduation," the leaders of the intercollegiate organization appointed a special "secretary[26] . . . . to investigate the problem and try out in a few typical cities and country communities what an organization of college graduates can do in personally relating college men who come into the community to church, civic, and social service."[27]

22 Letter Document, No. 13.
23 Ibid.
24 Miscellaneous Reports, No. 49.
25 Interview Document, No. 3.
26 Mr. Oliver Cutts.
27 Miscellaneous Reports, No. 58-A.

DIRECTOR OF SOCIAL SERVICE

The interest in social service was deemed so significant that another secretary [28] was added to the staff in 1912 to facilitate the promotion of the service programs throughout the country as a whole and to undergird them with an adequate philosophy. The service activities already under way [29] were extended to other areas. By 1914, some twenty-five different forms of volunteer service were being developed, including:

Campus Service: work with new students, employment bureaus, sick visitation, tutoring, hospitality to students from abroad, social recreation, and maintenance of moral standards.

Community Service: Bible classes and other forms of religious education, religious deputations, clubs and other work with boys, service visits to families and institutions, public speaking for social and moral reform, recreational service, educational classes and other service for working men, assistance in surveys, investigations, and exhibits, summer vacation work, alumni work.[30]

The philosophy of the work also came to be clarified and reinterpreted. It was held that social service was a benefit to the student on the ground that it enabled him to unify his life; it was also believed to be an effective means both of interesting some students in Christianity and of deepening the religious experience of others.[31] More and more, however, attention was directed to the purpose of advancing "the kingdom of God, ... the Christian social order. . . . . Human need must lay hold of the man who would serve. . . . . Service must be for the sake of those to whom one goes." [32]

[28] Mr. R. H. Edwards.
[29] Cf., p. 76.
[30] Pamphlet: Edwards, R. H., *Volunteer Social Service by College Men,* pp. 14 ff.
[31] *Ibid.,* p. 9.
[32] *Ibid.,* pp. 10 f.

This work was furthered by the publication of such pamphlets as the following:

1912, Trawick, A. M., *College Men and Community Service*
1912, Trawick, A. M., *Social Investigation, with Special Reference to the Race Question in the South*
1914, Trawick, A. M., *Service Visits to Families*
1914, Porter, D. R., *Clubs and Other Work with Boys*
1914, Edwards, R. H., *Volunteer Social Service by College Men*
1914, Edwards, R. H., (Ed.) *The Challenge of American Social Problems to College Men and Women*
1914, Edwards, R. H., *How to Work Out a Service Program*
1915, Rindge, Fred, *Educational Classes and Other Service with Workmen*

In addition, special texts [33] were prepared which, with those already referred to, included:

1910, Weatherford, W. D., *Negro Life in the South*
1910, Weatherford, W. D., *Race Relationships Library*
1912, Weatherford, W. D., *Present Forces in Negro Progress*
1912, Wood, H. G., *Personal Economy and Social Reform*
1912, Devine, E. T., *The Family and Social Work*
1913, Fiske, G. W., *The Challenge of the Country*
1913, Trawick, A. M., *The City Church and Its Social Mission*
1915, Edwards, R. H., *Christianity and Amusements*
1915, Edwards, R. H., *Popular Amusements*

SUMMER SERVICE GROUPS

Supplementing these efforts was another intended to enable a small group of students to have first-hand contact with problems of social congestion in the cities. It was hoped that bringing the students into contact with some of the social problems in city life would not only give them a valuable experience, but, upon their return to college would also make such problems more vivid to their fellow-students. It was also hoped that through this first-hand

[33] For other studies incorporating the social point of view, *See* pp. 113 f.

contact with conditions, the students would find help on their own vocational questions.[34]

The plan was started in New York in the summer of 1916, with twenty-two college students participating. They were placed for residence in selected institutional churches, settlements, Christian Associations, and other agencies—one or two in each. Their duties varied, including responsibility for a shop meeting each day for several weeks; for play-grounds, outings, and picnics; for week-end camps for boys; for work as assistant ministers in institutional churches. The entire group spent a part of one day each week together in round-table discussion of leading social questions, and in visits to social institutions.[35]

New Vocational Emphases

In this period also an advance was made by the Intercollegiate Y.M.C.A. in its approach to the vocational problems of students. It will be recalled that the Bible-study text, *The Will of God and a Man's Life Work,* published by the Y.M.C.A. in 1909, had emphasized the significance of the layman and insisted that he, also, ought to seek the will of God in his vocation. The principles, however, which were enunciated in connection therewith carried little of the rising social consciousness.[36] The social movement challenged the idea that consecration in its highest state was restricted to missionary service, and at the same time brought a new possibility for, and significance of, service in the homeland. "The work at home requires the same spiritual fitness, the same intelligence and devotion, the same unselfish sacrifice for the good of others that foreign missions demand." [37] Again, "the call to war came to our fathers—

---

[34] Interview Document, No. 7.
[35] *The North American Student,* Vol. 5, No. 1, Oct., 1916, p. 26.
[36] Cf., p. 52.
[37] Pamphlet, Trawick, A. M., *College Men and Community Service,* p. 3.

the social crisis calls us!—The task of the real patriot today is to do his share in righting social wrongs. . . ." [38]

This attitude was at first identified with the new vocational opportunity through the agencies for social amelioration. There was a feeling that the Intercollegiate Y.M.C.A. should do for this new "profession of social and civic workers" the same thing that it had done through the Student Volunteer Movement for the mission boards. It was hoped in this way to get better men into such work and at the same time to keep the movement close to the Church.[39]

Implications for other professions as well, however, were quickly developed. The program of the first national summer school for college secretaries [40] in 1910 included discussions on the service program of the Association. These were closed with an address by Professor Graham Taylor, who urged among other things that the secretaries "impress upon students the need of men in all professions, not only the ministry, who will go into these callings for the sake of the reforming power they may exert in them." [41] Four years later leaders of the Intercollegiate Y.M.C.A., along with those of kindred movements, were in conference with such men as Professors Walter Rauschenbusch, Graham Taylor, and Harry Ward. Conscious of "a new vision of men today," they felt that "there must be raised up thinkers, scholars, and men of affairs . . . ." with the new vision. "Apostles and leaders must come forth. Whole generations of students are needed who will accept their full responsibility as doctors, business men, lawyers, as well as those who will carry on the social service of the Church." [42] The opportunities in ordinary call-

[38] Pamphlet, *The Challenge of American Social Problems to College Men and Women,* 1914, p. 7.

[39] Miscellaneous Reports, No. 48. This led the Intercollegiate Y.M.C.A. to coöperate with the Department of Social Workers of the Intercollegiate Bureau of Occupations, e.g., in producing a bulletin on, "Salaried Positions in Social Work."—Miscellaneous Reports, No. 13.

[40] Cf., pp. 75 f.

[41] Cf., *College Leadership,* Library, National Council of Y.M.C.A's.

[42] Pamphlet, Council of North American Student Movements, *Social Needs and the Colleges,* 1914, pp. 3, 7.

ings were emphasized. "The doctor . . . . as a Christian socialized man will labor for preventive medicine, ignoring the lowering of his own business and the opposition of unworthy members of his profession; the lawyer [will frame laws so that] there will be less litigation; the engineer . . . . will use his humanizing influence in construction camps, showing that he places men above efficiency." [43]

A means was sought by the Intercollegiate Y.M.C.A. for carrying over these emphases into a "consecration of men to social service for Christ." To that end, a declaration similar to the form used for volunteers for foreign missions was considered but rejected, "for, is not the world needing today to learn of the God-given service inherent in every calling . . . . ?" [44] The following form, therefore, was developed and used with all students who were willing to apply it in deciding their vocation: [45]

A Christian's Fundamental Life Work Decision

I will live my life under God for others rather than for myself, for the advancement of the Kingdom of God rather than my personal success.

I will not drift into my life work, but I will do my utmost by prayer, investigation, meditation, and service to discover that form and place of life work in which I can become of the largest use to the Kingdom of God.

As I find it I will follow it under the leadership of Jesus Christ, wheresoever it take me, cost what it may.

Signed. . . . .

The reverse side of the card carries the following:

Think over prayerfully what is implied for you in signing this card. Sign it. Memorize it. Keep it in your Bible. Test your purposes by it daily.[46]

[43] *Ibid.*, pp. 25 f.
[44] *Ibid.*, p. 26.
[45] This was written by Mr. R. H. Edwards, one of the secretaries of the Intercollegiate Y.M.C.A. *See* p. 91, Note 28.
[46] Pamphlet, Council of North American Student Movements, *Social Needs and the Colleges,* p. 26.

Thus was afforded a concrete means of enabling the student to associate in his mind the concept of vocation with the concept of religious loyalties and values, dignifying all vocations and enriching and broadening the content of religion.   Another forward step was that of beginning summer service groups, which through actual experience offered a concrete means in enabling one to find help on vocational problems.[47]

Although the full implications of these developments could not be immediately and fully incorporated in the vocational emphasis of the organization, advance was registered in its procedure of recruiting for such professions as foreign missions, the ministry, and the Y.M.C.A. secretaryship, with the new calling of the social worker now added.   In keeping with the special emphasis made through conventions and conferences (chiefly of the Student Volunteer Movement) to present foreign service, the Intercollegiate Y.M.C.A. had developed in some sections of the country special conferences on behalf of one of these callings, and other conferences on behalf of another.   These various gatherings increasingly became combined at this time into one, when all four types of callings were presented.   This was prompted by an effort to open before students larger areas "of need and opportunity, rather than specifically to urge them to decision for a single form or a single place of service."[48]

SOCIAL EVANGELISM

Another expression of the social gospel in this period was a new emphasis in public evangelism, brought chiefly through Mr. Raymond Robins.   Mr. Robins was invited to some of the summer conferences as a lecturer, and was soon pressed into service as a speaker for the Intercollegiate Y.M.C.A. to college and university communities.   Difficulties had to be surmounted, however, for the

[47] Cf., pp. 92 f.
[48] Letter Documents, Nos. 4 and 5.

immediate demands which were placed on all such work were essentially the satisfaction of the more traditional evangelistic emphases. This is evidenced in the fact that social service raised questions in the minds of some, who feared that certain values were being lost.[49] It is evidenced again in the force of the more traditional emphases in public evangelism still being employed by some in the Intercollegiate Y.M.C.A. Of a "campaign" in a college in 1913, for example, it was reported that for months a group of students and professors had been earnestly praying and working in preparation. During the campaign itself they were busy in "personal work" and in relating students to the speaker for interviews. The series of addresses given during a period of several days included near the end a "decision meeting." This was followed by an "after-meeting." Forty-five minutes later public decisions were called for, and some sixty men who before had not regarded themselves as Christians, "publicly declared their purpose to live a Christian life. . . . All of these . . . . remained to a second after-meeting, where further" instructions were given and arrangements made for their uniting with the churches of the city. In response to the request of the speaker, ninety-eight turned in cards with their names and addresses, indicating decisions in the way of a "forward step" in the Christian life. These included such statements as the following:

"Resolved to cut out soft pedal Christianity."
"To attend church more regularly; to stop desecrating the Sabbath."
"I will join the church and write more often to my mother."
"Decided to have a more constant communion with my Savior in prayer."
"I will stand for what is right."
"I have decided with the help of God to cut out swearing."

[49] For the force of these criticisms and the answers, See *The North American Studant*, Vol. 4, No. 4, Jan., 1916, p. 179; and Vol. 4, No. 6, March, 1916, p. 272.

"To keep the morning watch as well as the evening watch; and
as far as possible to cut out Sunday studying."
"Cut out self-abuse."
"Cut cigarette smoking."
"More personal work."

The last gathering ran for two hours and consisted of a "testimony meeting. . . . One minute the audience was in a perfect up-
roar over some very unique expression of an experience; the next,
every man would be in tears over the recital of some harrowing
struggle through which some man had come to victory. . . ." [50]

In this period the machinery, also, of such an effort to challenge
the life of a campus had become highly organized.   Of such a campaign in a state university in 1913, the following statistics were
given:

Student workers (80 women, 341 men)	421
Speakers (35 from outside, 4 local)	39
Personal interviews with speakers	468
Decisions for Christian life	827
Number of meetings	256
Total attendance	18,486

The public meetings for this campaign were held within a period
of six days; two days before the meetings were employed in more
intensive preparation with the help of some of the leaders, and
seven days following the public meetings were used for "follow-up"
purposes.[51]   Essentially the same kind and extent of preparation
was demanded for the work of Mr. Robins.[52]   Moreover, the ultimate objective was the same as that which characterized the evangelistic programs of the organization.   Indeed, Mr. Robins was pressed
into service because it was believed that his approach offered the
advantage of "gathering up the general social interest which is so

[50] Miscellaneous Reports, No. 17.
[51] Ibid.
[52] Miscellaneous Reports, No. 19.

prevalent in the life of our colleges today and turning it into definite evangelistic channels." [53] Moreover, Mr. Robins had a deep conviction concerning the value of the more personal aspects of religion emphasized by the organization—the significance of Christ in the experience of the individual and of Bible reading, prayer, and service as means of spiritual growth.[54]

As a labor leader and, therefore, acquainted with the problems of industry; as one who, with Graham Taylor, had worked on civic problems in Chicago; and as one active in national political affairs, Mr. Robins brought a rare background of experience. This, with an appeal directed to the heroic and the vicarious in men, plus a rare gift for simple and effective presentation, drew everywhere a ready audience for him.[55] He laid great emphasis on righteousness and service as the expression of religion. After presenting, however, various aspects of social, economic, and political problems of the day, Mr. Robins emphasized individual duties in relation to them. He sought to interpret the difficulties of the tasks facing the students and dealt with such "personal problems" involved in preparation for them as impurity, gambling, and drinking.[56]

Students who were challenged by Mr. Robins' message were asked to sign and turn in a "decision" card as follows:

Grateful for the deeper revelation I have received of the power and meaning of the Gospel of Jesus Christ, and believing that Christian living is the only way for the complete redemption of the individual and social life, and desiring to do God's will and to have His power in my personal experience and life work. . . .

I hereby make decision to seek a daily life of victory and fellowship in service with Jesus Christ as Savior and Lord.

Name ....
College Address ....
Church Preference ....

[53] Miscellaneous Reports, No. 18.
[54] Miscellaneous Reports, No. 19.
[55] *Ibid.*
[56] Miscellaneous Reports, No. 20.

Students were given opportunity to state on the back of the card any decision in case the one above did not suit their needs.[57]

The wide sweep of interests appealed to in the addresses by Mr. Robins is suggested by the following typical program for a "campaign" of four days on the Pacific Coast:

First Day: 1. All-college assembly: "The Challenge of the Changing Social Order."
2. Address to faculty: "The Redemptive Principle in Education."
3. Men's mass meeting: "College Men and Community Leadership."

Second Day 1. Address to law department: "The Lawyer of Tomorrow."
2. Address to mass meeting of women students.
3. Men's mass meeting: "Fundamentals in the Industrial Conflict."

Third Day   1. Engineering Department: "The Engineer of Tomorrow."
2. Address to the Association and other leaders supporting the "campaign."
3. Men's mass meeting: "Mastery and Power."

Fourth Day 1. Chamber of Commerce: "Challenge of the Changing Social Order."
2. College and community mass meeting: "Faith." [58]

In one year alone—1915-16—Mr. Robins, assisted by Mr. John L. Childs, a member of the staff of the Intercollegiate Y.M.C.A., delivered addresses on such topics in forty-two colleges and universities throughout the country.[59] The character and force of the new social emphasis in these addresses will be suggested by a report of one of the meetings which was held with law students in a state university:

[57] Miscellaneous Reports, No. 19.
[58] Miscellaneous Reports, No. 21.
[59] Miscellaneous Reports, No. 19.

". . . . No one . . . . present will soon forget the profound impression made at the close of the law school meeting. There were . . . . 400 present, and in trenchant and challenging words Mr. Robins put before them the opportunity of the lawyer of tomorrow. At the conclusion of the address, Judge . . . , Dean of the school, spoke simply but with great feeling to his students. In closing he asked all who would purpose to go into their profession in the spirit of unselfishness and service, who would courageously stand for the working out of social justice through law, and who would pledge themselves to a fair and honest administration of the law for rich and poor alike, to stand with him. . . . There were few who did not stand on this call." [60]

Such was the new social emphasis brought through evangelism at this time.

SEX EDUCATION

Still another significant development at this time in the program of the Intercollegiate Y.M.C.A. was its approach to sex education. We have seen that the organization had been dealing with the question in meetings with students in the colleges and in the summer conferences. Although much of this work undoubtedly had a wholesome effect, some of it was of such a nature as to intensify the problem for students.[61] Nor was the program during the period under consideration entirely void of such a consequence. Some of the addresses on sex problems were characterized by strong feeling, thus creating tension on the part of the students in connection with the question. Not infrequently a speaker measured his success by the number of young men stirred to come for personal interviews, instead of by such evidence of liberation from tension and fear as the absence of interviews would suggest.[62]

Simultaneously, however, with this approach, the Association sought to make its work more constructive by increasing use of

[60] Miscellaneous Reports, No. 20.
[61] Cf. pp. 71 ff.
[62] Interview Document, No. 10.

medical doctors, notably Drs. L. B. Sperry, F. N. Seerley, and W. S. Hall. A forward step was registered in adding to the staff a man who was to give all of his time to work on the question in a more scientific spirit. With the rise of the social gospel, the Intercollegiate Y.M.C.A. began to be interested in the problem of the white slave traffic.[63] Mr. John D. Rockefeller Jr. had been a member of a commission to deal with the vice situation in New York City, and as a result had become interested in sex education. Believing that a program to that end ought to be developed in the colleges, he suggested that this be undertaken by the Intercollegiate Y.M.C.A., and Dr. M. J. Exner was employed to develop the undertaking.[64] Under Dr. Exner's direction the Intercollegiate Y.M.C.A. in 1912 established a bureau for the study and promotion of sex education in the universities and colleges; the bureau undertook to gather the best available thought and experience and to coöperate with educators toward the objective of making sex education an indigenous feature of the college curriculum.[65] With this approach, especially at a time when newer points of view on sex were being developed by certain educational leaders, the Intercollegiate Y.M.C.A. soon began to introduce new emphases into its own programs. Dr. Exner sought to treat the subject not only with reference to health, but also with relation to "efficiency, character, and fullness of life." [66] A study of answers by 948 college men to a questionnaire led to further development of that point of view:

". . . . We find a large proportion of students in whom the subject of sex occupies altogether unduly the field of consciousness and creates severe struggle for self-control," with "their energy and attention taken up so largely with personal struggle as to seriously handicap their efficiency and to cause much mental misery. . . .

[63] Miscellaneous Reports, Nos. 48 and 49.
[64] Interview Document, No. 10.
[65] Exner, M. J., "Progress in Sex Education," *Journal of Social Hygiene*, Vol. 15, No. 7, Oct., 1929.
[66] Exner, M. J., *The Rational Sex Life of Men*, Preface.

Most of the sex teaching thus far has been on too purely a physical basis. The psychological and idealistic aspects of the question need most to be stressed. . . . The sex instinct must be treated as natural, necessary, and therefore wholly honorable, not as a necessary evil. . . . Sex education should seek to normalize, not to repress, social relationships between the sexes." [67]

This work was interrupted, however, by the World War, and in 1920, the work of the bureau, as well as the personnel in connection therewith, was transferred to the American Social Hygiene Association.[68] Other developments on sex education will be taken up in the next section.

SOCIAL SERVICE AND FOREIGN MISSIONS

Although there was no change in the process of recruiting for foreign service, nor in the fundamental policies of the Student Volunteer Movement, some attention was given to social service as a factor in preparation for foreign-missionary activity. At the quadrennial convention of the Student Volunteer Movement in 1914, Mr. A. M. Trawick spoke on, "Social Service as a Necessary Preparation of Missionaries." He urged training and experience in methods of social work—social observation, social surveys, social service, social welfare work, and social legislation:

[Missionaries often bring back valuable facts, but too few] "bring back a convicting body of . . . evidence touching the facts and forces that make human life what it is." [69]

The need of socialized religion was also urged by Mr. Trawick:

". . . . A religion that appeals only to an individual and seeks only the salvation of his soul is a self-limiting and self-destroying force. . . . Prevention is better than cure, and a society Christianized from its foundations is better than palliatives applied to evil

[67] Exner, M. J., *Problems and Principles of Sex Education*, pp. 29, 31, 37.

[68] Interview Document, No. 10.

[69] *Report of Student Volunteer Convention*, 1914, pp. 430 ff.

conditions. . . . Men, high in Church councils and powerful in giving type to Christianity, control industrial plants, own houses for rent, manage banks, manipulate politics, and live such lives of unenergetic complacency that they rob their neighbors of hope and render a full, satisfying, abundant life absolutely unattainable." [It is such sorts of exploitation that are imposed on the East. We must regenerate and purify society here as an apologetic in the East. Otherwise, our efforts there will be futile.][70]

The address also implied a challenge of the prevailing basis on which the missionary program was being propagated:

". . . . To . . . . Christianize the East, missionaries must know how to value the importance of social heritage, and must guide the development of the new consciousness according to the genius of racial spirits. The new order in the East, commercial, industrial, political, and religious, must be Oriental as well as Christian. . . ." [71]

The significance of these observations, however, did not become apparent in the Volunteer Movement until the next convention, after the war.[72]

GROUP APPROACH TO ENTIRE CAMPUS

At the same time the effort to influence the standards and ideals of the entire campus [73] was now carried much further in a new method of attack. Along with the mass approach, which had come to be used extensively by the organization, particularly in its program of evangelism, there was also developed in many cases a group approach. This was found especially in the larger institutions of the Central West. It came with the new social emphases, even though it was started in some instances as a practical procedure for furthering more effectively traditional aspects of the program. Thus, at the University of Wisconsin in preparation for an evangelistic

[70] Ibid., pp. 433 f.
[71] Ibid.
[72] Cf. Chapter XI.
[73] See pp. 78 f.

campaign a special promotion committee was organized. The members of the committee were encouraged to solicit by personal invitation the participation of students in the campaign meetings. The committee functioned throughout the campaign and was continued as an organization to conserve its results.[74]

Later the chairman of this committee, Mr. Conrad Hoffmann, developed the same general plan at the University of Kansas, where he became general secretary of the Y.M.C.A. The committee at the University of Kansas was composed of ten captains, each leading a group of ten members, each of whom in turn was responsible for ten students on the campus. Through this committee of one hundred, an effort was made to reach every male student. In the same way the Association organized its Bible-study groups, raised its funds, and promoted other aspects of its University-wide program. An example of the significance of the organization for this procedure, particularly in its relation to the groupings of students, may be seen in that for the Bible-study work. A large map was used to represent every house in and around the campus, as well as every student residing in it. Pins with heads of one color were used to represent the students enrolled in Bible groups; another color was used for those not enrolled. In this way one could tell at a glance where the organization in at least one phase of its program had failed to penetrate.[75]

Under the direction of Mr. R. L. Ewing, general secretary, the Association at the University of Nebraska developed a program with reference to the institution as a whole and around regularly-organized units. An effort was made to locate key men in the fraternities and other groups and to project program activities through them in their respective centers. An intricate organization was developed and blueprinted; men who constituted the promotion force were brought weekly into a meeting called the "Round Up,"

[74] Letter Documents Nos. 7-A and 6-C.
[75] Ibid.

when campus standards were discussed, activities and efforts reviewed, and new activities undertaken.[76]

Under the leadership of the secretary, Mr. M. H. Bickham, the Association at Iowa State College adopted a similar program. This was centered in Bible classes but with the definite purpose of influencing the moral tone of the various residence units and so affecting the whole atmosphere of the campus. During the winter of 1910-11, the number of Bible-study discussion units on this basis reached fifty, with some fifteen hundred students enrolled. The students and professors who were leading these groups met weekly in a normal class directed by the secretary.[77] Later this effort was developed further and expanded under the general direction of Mr. Fred M. Hansen. Following the War the number enrolled included some three thousand, with some 50 per cent of the men enrolled in the college generally present in the seventy-five groups. These met once a week for eighteen weeks. Each week there were also four sessions of group leaders, so as to allow each leader to attend one of these meetings. This group program claimed practically the full time of one member of the staff.[78]

The leaders developed by the Association in each instance constituted, generally, its "Promotion Force" or "Friendship Council." Thus, the Intercollegiate Y.M.C.A., in seeking to become an effective, all-campus influence, developed a distinctive and significant type of organizational procedure: it did so by projecting its intimate-group idea into the various groups of the campus. This went beyond Bible study as such and became the organizing method of the Associations.[79]

[76] Letter Documents, Nos. 6-B and 6-C.
[77] Letter Documents, Nos. 1 and 6-C.
[78] Letter Documents, Nos. 7-B and 6-C.
[79] The type of organization was extended to other parts of the country. For a full statement concerning the method of work in one institution, together with a chart illustrating the organization, see an article by Ray Sweetman, "The Promotion Plan of Committee Service,"—*The North American Student*, November, 1915.

The University of Chicago Association, to which Mr. Bickham transferred, developed a modified form of the same method. The approach to campus ideals and moral standards was made through groups in the schools at the University rather than through fraternity and other house groups. In each instance the unit consisted of interested students and professors, who met and discussed the ideals and standards prevalent among the men of the particular school, especially those related to class honor and to the practice of the profession. In addition to members of the faculty, prominent lay and religious leaders were brought in from the outside to meet with these groups.[80]

In some instances the idea was also carried over into the summer conferences of the Intercollegiate Y.M.C.A. Particularly was this true at the conference held each summer at Lake Geneva, Wisconsin, under the general direction of Mr. A. J. Elliott. The six- to eight hundred delegates were organized into some fifty groups, with a tent captain in each tent and a leader for each two tents. It was possible thus to combine with the mass impact the intimacy and personal contacts of small groups. Moreover, it made possible more of a carry-over of the planning and program to the campuses.[81]

[80] Letter Documents, Nos. 1 and 6-C.
[81] Letter Documents, Nos. 6 and 6-C.

Chapter VIII. DEVELOPMENT OF CORRELATED VOLUN-
TARY STUDIES

SIMULTANEOUSLY with these developments, which were brought
in with the rise of the social emphasis, there were significant happenings in the realm of voluntary studies. Many new factors had
arisen which vitally affected the Bible- and mission-study programs.
These factors were made evident by growing criticism within the
organization itself of its Bible-study work, making evident the
need of some kind of change. Conferences on the part of Mr.
Harrison S. Elliott, who had become the new Bible-study secretary,
with the secretary for developing similar work of the student
Y.W.C.A., Miss Ethel Cutler—a fact which in itself represented a
new approach to the work—revealed a number of problems common to both the Y.M.C.A. and Y.W.C.A. These included dis-
satisfaction with available Bible-study texts; feeling that enrollment
outran competent leaders; confusion in regard to the relation of
voluntary study to curriculum study; misunderstandings and duplication of effort between the Association and the Sunday-school on
account of the Bible-study program; and growing difficulty in the
attempt to promote both Bible study and mission study simultaneously among the same students, especially among those only nominally interested.[1] Moreover, with the rising social interest there
was at the same time an increasing demand that special studies of
a social nature be prepared and recommended to students.[2]

[1] Elliott, Harrison S., Unpublished manuscript on the development of
the correlated voluntary studies. At first it had been comparatively easy to
promote both Bible study and mission study at the same time, but as early
as 1906 a group of college Y.M.C.A. secretaries devoted a large part of a
conference together to the question of how to correlate the Bible and mission studies.—Miscellaneous Reports, No. 41-A.
[2] Interview Document, No. 9.

At the request of the Bible-study secretary of the Intercollegiate Y.M.C.A., a commission was appointed by the organization in 1912 to conduct an investigation of its Bible study and to make recommendations. The commission sent a questionnaire to professors, secretaries, and other friends of the organization—a development which represented the first effort to get the attitude of the constituency of the organization on such an important problem. Two hundred and nine replies were received from various parts of the country.[3] The commission, in reporting, made recommendations which called for significant changes in the program of the voluntary studies:

1. Bible study should not be considered an end in itself, but should find its rôle in relation to the function of the Association which the Commission conceived to be, "to cleanse men's lives, to develop a distinct conviction upon the vital relation between religion and life, ... individually and socially, and to inspire service. . . ."

2. The texts should attempt to cover less material; they should be reduced to twelve weeks; the principal material for each week should not be divided into seven parts, but should be presented as a unity, with provision for the "Morning Watch" (daily Bible reading, meditation, and prayer) and topics for group discussion.

3. A curriculum should be developed on a graded basis and in the light of the experiences to which the student is subjected from his Freshman year through his Senior year, together with the readjustments and problems of faith which most usually arise. Those parts of the Bible should be used, along with extra biblical material, which would best help in meeting these problems.

4. The objectives of Bible study, mission study, and social study should be considered essentially the same. Voluntary religious education, therefore, should "be considered a study as a unit and" ought to correlate these three phases of the program.

5. Account should be taken of all the religious education forces related to the student.

[3] Miscellaneous Reports, No. 12.

6. ". . . . A committee or a conference, sufficiently representative of both curriculum and voluntary . . . . study" should prepare "a correlated outline covering both curriculum and voluntary work in Bible, mission, and social study." [4]

To meet the problem of duplication of association Bible-study and Sunday-school work, some of the Associations in the Middle West were actually trying to unite their work with that of the Sunday-schools. The leaders of the Intercollegiate Y.M.C.A. deemed this a valuable means of giving students a conception of the significance of Sunday-school work; they also regarded this as an opportunity to emphasize the value of leadership of Bible-study classes after graduation.[5]   Any thought of general adoption of such a plan, however, drew out three phases of opposition: leaders in the organization were opposed to the classes and work as carried on at the time in the Sunday-schools, insisting on special student groups, special texts, and special leadership; pastors were on the whole anxious to have large classes and were reluctant to relinquish any part of the responsibility for Sunday-school work; and it was generally felt that very few churches had proper facilities.[6]

Following conferences by representatives of a Committee of the Religious Education Association on teachers' training in colleges and universities, of the Association of Biblical Instructors, of the Intercollegiate Y.M.C.A. and Y.W.C.A., of the Student Volunteer Movement, of the Sunday School Council of Evangelical Denominations, and others, the rôle of voluntary study came to be more definitely delimited.[7]   ". . . . All education, and particularly religious education, whether curriculum or voluntary, should be planned primarily for the development of character and the training of efficient leaders. . . ."   The curriculum courses for credit, it was felt, of-

[4] Wright, H. B. *et.al., Report of Commission on Student Voluntary Bible Study Texts*, pp. 5 ff.
[5] Miscellaneous Reports, No. 48.
[6] Elliott, H. S., *op. cit.*
[7] *Ibid.*

fered broad and thorough training in the Bible and kindred subjects in the field of religious education; voluntary study, on the other hand, was concerned with the more "immediate and pressing religious problems, either personal or social, on which students are coming to some basis of personal belief and action. . . ." It was deemed possible in the "more intimate circle of a voluntary group, where the conference or discussional method is used, to face these immediate problems of students in a more intimate way than the academic class usually makes possible." Although the method distinctive of each was believed to be found in both types of work, voluntary study was defined as having a narrower and more restricted field: It was declared to be "functional. . . . It seeks to lead students to answer two questions: What does it mean to me? What am I going to do about it?" [8]

There soon followed an effort to develop a program of studies worked out coöperatively by all the interested bodies. This was facilitated by the "Council of North American Student Movements," which had developed in the meantime.[9] The organization of this council—to represent the Intercollegiate Y.M.C.A. of North America, the Intercollegiate Y.W.C.A., and the Student Volunteer Movement—was a significant evidence of need for coördination of endeavor. "Its chief function" was "to provide regular and established channels through which the . . . . ideas, plans, and purposes of one group . . . . may pass to the others." [10] The Council sponsored the new approach to the total problem of voluntary studies, and authorized (1913) for the preparation of such studies a committee representing these various constituent bodies. The Sun-

[8] Pamphlet: Council of North American Student Movements, *A Suggested Curriculum for Voluntary Study Groups in Colleges and Universities*, pp. 4 ff.

[9] Cf. *The North American Student*, Vol. I, No. 1, March, 1913, p. 1 f.

[10] *Ibid.* One immediate development by this council was a magazine, *The North American Student*, which was started in March, 1913, and continued until June, 1918. During this time *The Intercollegian*, the organ of the Intercollegiate Y.M.C.A., was supplanted by the new magazine.

day School Council of Evangelical Denominations also authorized a sub-committee of its committee on courses to coöperate fully with the committee appointed by the North American Student Council.[11]

These two committees, conscious of the demands for Bible, mission, and social studies, sought to deal with the difficulties involved in promoting these simultaneously by correlating them into one series of studies. They adopted a definite principle for developing the series, viz., that of building the curriculum in the light of four periods, believed to represent the dominant problems and interests of undergraduates:

Freshman Year: Period of Adjustment to New College Environment.

Sophomore Year: Period of Aspiration for Leadership and of Life Work Decision.

Junior Year: Period of Discussion of Fundamental Religious Problems.

Senior Year: Period of Decision as to Community Relationships.[12]

Themes were then adopted for each of these periods, and courses were mapped out accordingly. A number of texts, prepared by different authors, soon appeared in the series, and were made available through not only the organizations represented in the Council of North American Student Movements, but also the publishing houses of the church bodies participating. The significance of the coöperative phase of this development is made evident by a statement essentially the same as the following, found on the inside title page of all the studies:

[11] Miscellaneous Reports, No. 14. *See* Pamphlet: *The Denominations' Part in the College Voluntary Study Courses.*
[12] Pamphlet: Council of North American Student Movements, *A Suggested Curriculum for Voluntary Study Groups in Colleges and Universities,* p. 11.

"Written from an Outline Prepared by Sub-Committee on College Courses, Sunday School Council of Evangelical Denominations, and Committee on Voluntary Study Council of North American Student Movements."

Each text contains twelve chapters, each of which (with minor exceptions) is divided in turn into three parts: "Daily Readings"—one for each day of the week, as a basis for the observance of the "Morning Watch"; "Study of the Week"—dealing more thoroughly with the theme of the chapter; and "Suggestions for Thought and Discussion"—presenting suggestive questions for group discussion based on the week's theme. Readings were selected from the Bible and other sources which, it was believed, would help meet the needs being considered.

The following courses appeared in the series:

For Freshmen:
First Part:
Elliott-Cutler, *Student Standards of Action,* 1914, with chapters on "The College Purpose," "Readjustments," "An Expense Account," "Real Efficiency," "A Budget of Time," "College Friendships," "The Student and the Church," "Student Honor," "The Laws of Achievement," "Christian Chivalry," "Christian Loyalty," "Student Initiative and the College Ideal."

Second Part:
Murray-Harris, *Christian Standards in Life,* 1915, biographical sketches illustrating from the lives of men and women in different kinds of service at home and abroad the application of the theme of the book.

For Sophomores:
First Part:
Edwards-Cutler, *A Life at Its Best,* 1915, giving principles of living illustrated from the life of Paul.

Second Part:
Harris-Robbins, *A Challenge to Life Service,* 1916, a consideration of one's approach to one's vocation along lines already partially indicated. (Cf. pp. 93 ff.)

For Juniors:
　First Part:
　Never prepared. A text on *The Meaning of the Christian Religion,* a book really in fact on fundamentals of religion, had been contemplated.[13]

　Second Part:
　E. D. Soper, *The Faiths of Mankind,* 1918.

For Seniors:
　First Part:
　Rauschenbusch, *The Social Principles of Jesus,* 1916.

　Second Part:
　Ward-Edwards, *Christianizing Community Life,* 1917.

Thus was initiated an entirely new approach to the program of religious education, an approach starting from, and based on, the fundamental problems and situations being faced by the students, and using the Bible and other resource material as an aid to the solution of these problems.

SPECIAL BIBLE STUDIES

The foregoing correlated voluntary studies represented a minimum program to be promoted on behalf of Bible, mission, and social problems. Following an effort to secure as many students as possible for this minimum program, a supplementary effort was urged in order to enroll as many as possible in special studies of the Bible, of missions, and of North American problems.[14] The production of special studies dealing with these interests was continued by the Intercollegiate Y.M.C.A. and the Student Volunteer Movement. We shall indicate here the special Bible-study texts.[15]

[13] *Ibid.,* p. 22.
[14] Pamphlet: Council of North American Student Movements, *Voluntary Study Groups,* p. 29.
[15] For the special texts prepared in this period on foreign missions, cf. pp. 66 f.; and on North American social problems, cf. p. 92.

While the "College Voluntary Study Courses" were being developed, Rev. Harry Emerson Fosdick was asked to prepare a study on the life of Christ, based on a series of Wednesday evening lectures which he had delivered in the First Baptist Church, Montclair, New Jersey.[16] This new text, *The Manhood of the Master,* was published in 1913. Instead of following in detail the life of Jesus according to a harmony of the Gospels or of making a more theological approach to his teachings, the author developed another emphasis. Attention is directed to the character of the man Jesus. The arrangement of the material took on largely the form determined for the curriculum of voluntary studies. There are twelve "studies," each divided into three sections: daily Bible readings, comment for the week, and questions for group discussion. The daily Scripture lessons are printed in full.[17]

There followed in the same general form three other books by Mr. Fosdick: *The Meaning of Prayer* (1915); *The Meaning of Faith* (1917); and *The Meaning of Service* (1920). This arrangement of Daily Readings, Comment for the Week, and Suggestions for Thought and Discussion, became a standard form for a series of studies edited by the executive secretary of Association Press, Frederick M. Harris, and known as the "Everyday Life Series." Later, because of the demand for a continuation of the more systematic Bible study, Mr. H. B. Sharman was asked to prepare a new book on the life of Christ. Twenty-five years previous, as Bible Study Secretary of the Student Y.M.C.A., he had developed a new type of textbook which set the standard for that period.[18] Mr. Sharman had continued his contact with the Student Movement through leading Bible-study groups in connection with the

[16] Interview Document, No. 19.

[17] Inasmuch as this text was published while the curriculum for the correlated series was being developed, this new arrangement of materials was tried as an experiment. The results confirmed the committee's plans, which were carried through in subsequent studies.—Miscellaneous Reports, No. 15.

[18] Cf. pp. 4/ ff.

Canadian universities. He embodied the results of this experience and study in a new textbook, *Jesus in the Records,* published in 1918. This represented a distinct form of Bible study, since it took a situation and problem approach to the life of Jesus but confined attention to a careful exploration of the records and an attempt to understand the situations Jesus faced, but made no effort to make a present-day application. Special studies bearing on "personal work" included *Introducing Men to Christ,* by Mr. W. D. Weatherford (1911), and *Personal Evangelism among Students,* by Stewart-Wright (1913).

LEADERSHIP TRAINING

Simultaneously with the developments looking to a correlated program of voluntary studies, the Intercollegiate Y.M.C.A. was giving attention to the training of leaders for its groups. The failure of student leadership in certain places led to a demand on the part of some for expert leadership of all Bible-study classes, implying that students should be replaced by professors. Investigation, however, revealed that failure in leadership of these groups was not restricted to students alone.[19] It was quickly discovered that although not enough care had been exercised generally in choosing student leaders for the classes, the trouble lay principally with the leaders' training group.[20] To meet this practical problem, the Bible-study secretary sought the aid of several experts in pedagogy, notably Professor H. H. Horne, who prepared a syllabus on *The Leadership of Bible Study Groups.* This was made available to the Associations through *The Intercollegian* [21] and developed immediately afterwards into a text with the same title.[22] Professor Horne and others helped also in training leaders in summer conferences.

It soon became evident that the training classes had been too

[19] Miscellaneous Reports, No. 12.
[20] Miscellaneous Reports, No. 50.
[21] *The Intercollegian,* Vol. 34, No. 8, May, 1912, pp. 215 ff.
[22] Association Press, 1912.

much of a model Bible-study class, in which the professor taught the lesson and the students later attempted to reproduce it with the members of their groups. Moreover, the leaders often had no training in the principles involved, and apparently secured little skill in the leaders' training class for using the material.[23] It became a conviction in the Intercollegiate Y.M.C.A. that the director of the leaders' training class should not lecture, but instead be the chairman of a discussion in which group leaders would themselves work out questions, topics, and lesson plans; at the same time the leaders' training conference should make possible the development of principles of group leadership and skill in applying them.[24] This new approach to the problem of group leadership made much greater demands on both the group leaders and the teacher of the training class. To help meet the problem, the work at summer conferences was supplemented by special leaders' training conferences, to which professors also were invited, and the effort was also carried on by various other means throughout a period of years.[25]

These various developments in the program of the Association were interrupted by new emphases brought on by the World War and America's participation therein. The new program of activities and the new emphases which grew up in that connection will be discussed in later chapters. Before leaving this period, however, it is necessary to note developments of another character.

[23] Miscellaneous Reports, No. 50.
[24] For full statement, cf. Pamphlet: Elliott, H. S., *Training an Adequate Leadership for Voluntary Study Groups*, 1918.
[25] Miscellaneous Reports, No. 59.

Chapter IX. OTHER DEVELOPMENTS

THIS period gave rise also to efforts looking to the development of a more democratic organization for promoting the intercollegiate work of the Y.M.C.A. In the beginning of the era the chief problem, as envisaged by the leaders of the intercollegiate organization in its relationship with the general Y.M.C.A., was still that of securing a large degree of freedom for the promotion of the college work within the general movement. One phase of this problem, as we have seen, related to the basis of membership. The special membership basis, however, granted in 1907 by the general Y.M.C.A. for the college work,[1] quickly proved unsatisfactory. Indeed, an investigation three years later revealed the fact that 35 per cent of the college Associations were irregular in practice and were using various statements of membership.[2] Official action, however, authorizing a new membership basis had to be delayed until 1922.[3]

Another aspect of the problem continued to be that of supervision—the relation of the state and international committees respectively to this function, in which the question of supervision of the college work became acute. There was general feeling on the part of the leaders of the Intercollegiate Y.M.C.A. that the existing dual arrangement was wasteful and that it made impossible the working out of the best arrangements for meeting the needs; that secretaries employed by state committees were changing too frequently (in some instances every year or two); that the college

[1] Cf. pp. 77 f.
[2] Miscellaneous Reports, Nos. 46, 47.
[3] Cf. p. 141.

work was regarded by the state forces as an adjunct of the city Y.M.C.A. work "and not in the light of the college problem as it actually exists"; and that students were drawn into state functions not related to student problems. Moreover, the leaders of the intercollegiate organization desired to work out a policy and a unified program for the country as a whole, in view especially of developments on the part of denominational agencies.[4]

Although there was general agreement among the leaders of the Intercollegiate Y.M.C.A. that single control for the entire country was a desirable ideal, some felt that it could not be achieved because the supervision had been started on a dual basis.[5] To meet this general problem, the Intercollegiate Y.M.C.A. sought to build up its staff so far as possible, in order to supervise the work more effectively. This was attempted particularly in the South in 1911, where some of the states were without secretaries for college work.

That policy, however, was discontinued in 1916, for developments in the general Y.M.C.A. in the meantime had resulted in the decision that only one man should be assigned by the Intercollegiate Y.M.C.A. committee to a single area.[6] Moreover, measures had also been taken, through the appointment by the committee for the general Y.M.C.A. of field "executive secretaries," to provide more efficient relationships with the state committees and to strengthen the work of the latter.[7]

A quite different aspect of the question relating to the development of the college work was that voiced in a call for "democratization." This had been heard in connection with the rising activity on the part of denominational agencies among students in state institutions. When leaders of the Intercollegiate Y.M.C.A. urged upon denominational representatives that the work on a campus should be developed as a unit and in the light of the campus

[4] Miscellaneous Reports, No. 16.
[5] Miscellaneous Reports, No. 49.
[6] Letter Document, No. 13.
[7] *Report of International Convention, Y.M.C.A.,* 1913, p. 58.

needs, some of the latter contended that that was impossible because the programs and policies of the local Associations were controlled too much from without.[8]

There developed a general feeling on the part of a number of
men related to the college Y.M.C.A. work that its policies were
controlled too much from the general headquarters of the organization; and secretaries related to state committees for college work and
those working with local college associations, began to give expression to this feeling.[9]   That their attitude was a matter of no small
consequence may be realized from the rapid increase in their numbers.   By 1913, the staff of the Intercollegiate Y.M.C.A. had increased to sixteen, while the number of full- or part-time employed
workers related to state committees for college work had grown
to fifteen, and the number of those related to particular institutions
as "local" secretaries had grown to ninety-six.[10]   Indeed, the very
strength and influence of the employed workers gave rise to another
question—that of the rôle of the student member.   Pleas for freedom to develop the college work had been made by secretaries
and other men who were not students.   The prominent part played
by the executive leader of the Intercollegiate Y.M.C.A. in obtaining
a special membership basis in 1907 has been noted.[11]   It also became apparent that no student voice had been heard in any signifi-

---

[8] *See* p. 81. Nor did such criticism pass immediately.   In the preliminary discussions of the "Cleveland Conference" in 1915, the question
of unification in Christian forces in state universities was under consideration. This implied democratic counseling together by all the religious workers
on the campus, and the development of the program in a similarly democratic fashion, with student initiative as an important factor to be con-
served.   One of the university pastors asked if national supervision of the
college work was not "superimposed from the top." Mr. Mott replied:
"This matter of student initiative was more than an incident. . . . The
Movement is not now as democratic as originally, but a Commission is at
present at work looking to the greater democratizing of the student
work."—(*See Summary of the Cleveland Conference,* 1915, pp. 4 f.)

[9] Interview Document, No. 22.

[10] *The Y.M.C.A. Year Book,* 1912-13, pp. 13, 16 ff., 224 ff.

[11] Cf. p. 78.

cant gathering on the problem of supervision, or on that of emphasis upon the rights of the "field" as over against "headquarters." Foreign delegates to the World's Student Christian Federation, meeting at Lake Mohonk in 1913, remarked to Americans present that the organization of the latter seemed to them to be an employed secretaries' movement! [12] The former also stimulated thought on this issue through visits to local Associations and summer conferences. [13]

These impressions, together with the problem of securing a larger participation by the "field" in shaping the organization's policies, were discussed by the college secretaries in their summer school at Estes Park, Colorado, in 1913. A general feeling was expressed that the movement should be "democratized," and that the students should be encouraged to assume a bigger rôle in determining the policies of the work. Following a request by the school, the International Committee appointed a commission on "Increase of Efficiency" and tentative reports were made from time to time. Further consideration of the problem by the college secretaries in 1915 stimulated similar discussion in other sections of the general Y.M.C.A.; these finally resulted in authorization for the general convention of the Y.M.C.A. "to sit as a convention in sections in the afternoon sessions. . . . This authorization for the first time in the history of the . . . . conventions gave the delegates from student associations . . . . the opportunity to meet . . . . and discuss their own vital problems."

At the general convention of the Y.M.C.A. in 1916, the section on college work secured the adoption of a resolution permitting election from the summer conferences of a "Committee of Counsel" authorized to "give counsel to the Student Department of the In-

[12] Interview Document, No. 22.
[13] For immediately succeeding developments, the author has drawn on an article by M. H. Bickham, in *The North American Student*, Vol. 5, No. 7, April, 1917, pp. 288 f.

ternational Committee. . . ."[14] From the conferences held in 1916
a total of twenty-three members were elected for the Committee of
Counsel, which was convened at Chicago in 1917 by Mr. D. R.
Porter,[14a] who in the meantime had become senior secretary for the
intercollegiate organization. The work of this committee was interrupted, however, by the entry of the United States into the World
War, leaving the matter to be taken up again following the war.[15]

RELATIONS WITH DENOMINATIONAL AGENCIES

The question of relations between the Intercollegiate Y.M.C.A.
and the denominational agencies also received attention in this period. The problem became so acute that in November, 1912, a commission was appointed by the International Committee of the
Y.M.C.A. to give it special attention.[16] Church leaders claimed
that, instead of the organization developing interdenominational
work, it fostered work which was really undenominational. At the
same time it was said that the students "must function religiously
all the rest of their life through the Church and its institutions and
from them must be sought the leadership of the Church at home
and abroad, yet their relations with the Church are unsettled. The
four to six years' gap between leaving the home church and graduation is a denominationally dangerous period."[17] In 1913, a convention of the general Y.M.C.A. recognized the problem of relationships with denominational agencies. It passed a resolution declaring allegiance to the Church, and approving and welcoming
the entrance of denominational agencies into the state university.

[14] *Report of International Convention, Y.M.C.A.,* 1916, p. 176, Resolution xxxiii, Sec. 1.
[14a] Mr. Porter led the movement for democratization, emphasing particularly student participation.
[15] Cf. p. 140.
[16] Urbach, W. F., *op. cit.,* p. 78.
[17] Miscellaneous Reports, No. 73.

Conviction was expressed, however, that the Y.M.C.A. should continue to be recognized as the chief interdenominational agency.[18]

To help meet the criticism that the student members of the Y.M.C.A. were not supporting the Church or its sacraments, the intercollegiate organization sought the help of leaders in the Anglican Church.   In 1912 Father Kelly of the Society of the Sacred Mission, and the Reverend Neville Talbot, Chaplain of Balliol College, Oxford, both of whom had an intimate relation to the British Student Christian Movement, made a visit to a number of universities and colleges in the East, seeking to interpret the significance of worship and to give help on the general problem.   Shortly afterwards an ordained minister of the Episcopal Church [19] was added to the staff of the Intercollegiate Y.M.C.A. to help on this issue along with other specific responsibilities.[20]

In a further effort to deal with this problem, representatives of the various groups concerned began to confer together on the relation of the church and the association forces in state universities.   To that end, the "Cleveland Conference" was held at Cleveland, Ohio, in 1915, with participating representatives from the Council of Church Boards of Education and the Conference of Church Workers in State Universities, as well as the Intercollegiate Y.M.C.A. and Y.W.C.A.   The problem had become defined by this time largely as that of the respective functions of the Church and the Associations, as revealed by the findings agreed upon at this conference.   These include emphasis upon a close unification of the Christian forces in state universities; recognition of the right of all agencies to direct access to the state university field; and of the place of the Y.M.C.A. and Y.W.C.A. as voluntary interdenominational agencies, as well as the need of maintaining their individuality and autonomy.   But it was agreed that they should be so con-

[18] Report of International Convention of Y.M.C.A's., 1913, pp. 139, 149.
[19] Reverend Paul Micou.
[20] Interview Document, No. 15.

stituted that all the denominations coöperate in forming their policies; specifically that "on the supervisory or advisory bodies of the Association, both local and national, should be . . . . representatives of the various Christian communities, which representatives shall be nominated by the Association's supervisory . . . . board, ... approved by the proper ecclesiastical authority" and elected by those representing the Association, or Associations. Emphasis was placed also on identification of interests of all forces, on the need of regular consultation by the leaders of the various organizations, and of mutual consent on any policies and measures of common concern which were adopted. The desirability of undergraduate initiative and control in all the agencies was recognized. It was recommended further that all denominational activities should be related as closely as practicable to the churches in the university communities.[21]

The succeeding year a second "Cleveland" conference adopted principles in which these same emphases largely figured. In addition, there was recognition of the unified community life of the university and of the consequent obligation of all to develop together a unified program, planned with reference to the entire university, in order to work for a university community consciousness favorable to the Christian life. In the work of the churches, their plans should be measured in their effectiveness not only in relation to the individual churches, but in relation to the coöperative projects. It was recognized that students should be kept loyal to the church of their preference, and it was agreed that every student should be urged to identify himself with a local church.[22] As a result of developments in this second "Cleveland" conference, representatives of these agencies began to make visits together to state universities and to seek to work out with the local forces united plans for the university

[21] Elliott, H. S. et al., "Christian Work in State Universities," Report of Cleveland and Chicago Conferences, p. 3.
[22] Ibid., pp. 7-8.

community. These processes, however, were discontinued with the war.[23]

About this time also the Intercollegiate Y.M.C.A. asked that each of the various denominations send two official representatives to the summer conferences, one to represent the denomination's home mission work and the other its foreign mission work.[24] We shall see in the post-war period the results of this proposal.

[23] Interview Document, No. 24.
[24] Minutes of the Committee of Reference, "Cleveland Conference," New York, March 14, 1916.

PART FIVE: WAR PERIOD
1917–1918

Chapter X. WAR TIME EMPHASES AND PROGRAMS

THE war-time programs of the Intercollegiate Y.M.C.A. are significant chiefly in reflecting factors which helped to bring decidedly different emphases in the period since the war.

The programs maintained in the preceding period were largely continued until the conversion of colleges and universities into the Student Army Training Corps made that no longer possible. With that development, the Intercollegiate Y.M.C.A. in the early autumn of 1918 correlated its work with the National War Work Council of the Y.M.C.A.,[1] and its program shifted largely to that for soldiers in training camps, in which recreational activities carried on in huts and directed by uniformed secretaries figured extensively. The war was the occasion, however, of new and significant emphases.

RAISING FUNDS FOR WAR SUFFERERS

Through the instrumentality of the Intercollegiate Y.M.C.A. and Y.W.C.A., students were the first in the United States to give money, as a class, to war relief. Within a few months after the outbreak of hostilities in 1914, students began spontaneously to raise funds for Belgian relief, for the Red Cross, and for other causes.[2] Very soon, work in prison camps in Europe and Russia was undertaken by the general Y.M.C.A. Some of the workers with the college associations in the United States began to help in this new activity, and funds were solicited by the Intercollegiate Y.M.C.A. to

[1] *The Intercollegian,* Vol. 36, No. 1, October, 1918, p. 9.
[2] *The North American Student,* Vol. III, No. 4, January, 1915, pp. 181 f.

carry it on. Support was also requested for the Student Christian Movements of the different countries in Europe which were extending their own work, as well as for the World's Student Christian Federation. To all such appeals there was a generous response by students and faculty.[3] They were appeals to sacrifice. Students were asked to "give until it hurts," and they responded in that spirit, finding under the stress of the war innumerable ways of sharing unstintedly.[4] An appeal in the autumn of 1916 for a "Friendship War Fund," primarily for prisoners of war, brought in during the college year over $200,000.[5] During the following year, after America's entry into the war, an amount of some million and a half dollars was secured through the same agencies for war prisoners' aid and work with the men in the armies.[6] Nor did such appeals cease immediately with the close of the war. In the college year 1918-19 gifts were collected through the same processes for continuance of the war prisoners' work and for relief work carried on by other American agencies.[7] Before the following year had closed appeals were being made for the relief of students and professors in Central Europe.[8]

DISCUSSION OF SOCIAL AND INTERNATIONAL ISSUES

Another significant emphasis by the Intercollegiate Y.M.C.A. is found in the attitude of some of its leaders toward the institution of war itself. Through the magazine of the organization and through other ways, the question of whether a Christian should

[3] The North American Student, Vol. IV, No. 1, Oct., 1915, p. 17; Vol. IV, No. 3, Dec., 1915, p. 125; Vol. IV, No. 6, Mar., 1916, p. 257.
[4] Ibid., Vol. VI, No. 3, Dec., 1917, p. 96.
[5] Ibid.: Vol. V, No. 6, Mar., 1917, pp. 253 f.; Vol. VI, No. 2, Nov., 1917, p. 47.
[6] Ibid.: Vol. VI, No. 4, Jan., 1918, p. 139; Vol. VI, No. 8, May, 1918, p. 404.
[7] The Intercollegian, Vol. 36, No. 2, Nov., 1918, p. 2.
[8] For further developments cf. pp. 146 f.

fight was frequently raised and discussed, particularly so in the early part of the war.[9]

During the war and immediately afterwards, the organization gave much consideration as well, through its summer conferences, to other social and international issues suggested by the war.[10] Forums on these issues were also developed in the colleges and universities. The program of voluntary studies offering a variety of courses was often superseded by the development for the entire campus of single courses for different periods of time which dealt more and more with national and international issues.[11]

EMPHASES ON PERSONAL RELIGION

Although the war precipitated new and significant social and international emphases, its immediate effect was to accentuate the more traditional aspects of personal religion. In 1917, a leader of the organization reported:

"In many Associations there has been a marked tendency to simplify and intensify the work. . . . The Association leaders have seen the necessity of abandoning secondary activities and with great urgency stressing the essentials of the Christian life. . . ." [12]

This point of view was expressed in such ways as the development of a "league of prayer for workers," as well as increased emphasis on evangelism and Bible study.[13]

[9] See *The North American Student,* Vol. IV, No. 2, Nov., 1915, pp. 47-50; Vol. V, No. 7, April, 1917, p. 302.
[10] Miscellaneous Reports, No. 61.
[11] Miscellaneous Reports, No. 60. *A New World Democracy,* by H. S. Elliott, an outline to facilitate discussion of a new world order in the light of Jesus' ideals, was used a great deal during the latter part of the war and immediately afterwards.
[12] Miscellaneous Reports, No. 59.
[13] *The North American Student,* Vol. VI, No. 3, Dec., 1917, p. 125.

RECRUITING FOR FOREIGN MISSIONS

The same emphasis was found especially in accentuation of the missionary cause and recruiting therefor. A conference of the Student Volunteer Movement held, with the coöperation of the Intercollegiate Y.M.C.A., in January, 1918, to anticipate its post-war program, drew out an editorial in *The North American Student,* from which we quote as follows:

". . . . Men and women must be summoned in great numbers to confess Jesus Christ as their Lord and Savior and to dedicate themselves to His program for the individual and the world. This we must do on a hitherto unimagined scale. . . . Our present situation demands . . . . a call for a very large number of those in the colleges to offer and prepare themselves as foreign missionary candidates. . . . We all long for a real righteous peace that shall abide. The foreign missionary enterprise . . . . is the only sure promise of peace. . . ." [14]

As a result of the conference, the delegates agreed "to enlist two hundred thousand students in study and discussion of Christian principles . . . . ; to call students to live those principles at whatever cost on the campus, in the nation, and in the world; to enlist a sufficient number of qualified men and women for the foreign-missionary program of the Church; to secure at least one-half million dollars during the academic year 1918-19 for the foreign-missionary program of the Church. . . ." [15] Although such traditional missionary activities were not to be challenged by students until the next convention of the Student Volunteer Movement, one of the conditions operating to bring about a different emphasis was already present. From the Negro race only one of their number, an employed officer of the Y.M.C.A., attended the gathering, and that for only a part of the time. When it was later asked why the colored stu-

[14] *Ibid.,* Vol. VI, No. 4, Jan., 1918, pp. 140 f.
[15] *Ibid.,* Vol. VI, No. 5, Feb., 1918, pp. 191 ff.

dents were absent, one of the Negro leaders indicated that the church boards were employing very few Negro missionaries. He pointed out at the same time a very grave problem meriting attention:

". . . . As Negro students, we are tremendously interested in having Christ's principles become the guiding principles of life for all; for we realize that if these principles are made vital in the relationships between men, savage orgies like those of East St. Louis and most recently of Tennessee, will no longer be tolerated. . . ." [16]

This condition, however, received little, if any, attention at the conference. When the gathering was closing, its chairman, Mr. Mott, said that in view of the world situations, "we are summoned to prepare ourselves for vast reconstruction tasks." [17] But these were presented largely in terms of the foreign-missionary program and recruiting therefor.

This emphasis was extended by the Intercollegiate Y.M.C.A., especially in the immediate post-war period, to include other Christian callings also. Around such slogans as, "Christ the Way Out," and "Let's Finish the Job," emphasis was placed on recruiting "for the great gigantic task ahead." [18] This meant a call for "large numbers of the ablest American college and university men." [19] "Unquestionably," said a member of the staff, "the imperative need . . . . is the discovery and training of a much greater number of full-time Christian workers. Evidently they are going to be needed by the tens of thousands. . . ." [20] Indeed, the "supreme test" of a successful Association was envisaged by some in terms of its number of students committed to the Christian callings. [21] In coöpera-

[16] *Ibid.,* Vol. VI, No. 7, April, 1918, pp. 343 f.
[17] *Ibid.,* Vol. VI, No. 5, Feb., 1918, p. 198.
[18] See leaflets announcing the Seabeck and Geneva summer conferences in 1919, as well as *The Intercollegian,* Vol. 36, No. 1, Jan., 1919, pp. 3 f.
[19] *The Intercollegian,* Vol. 36, No. 9, June, 1919, p. 8.
[20] Miscellaneous Reports, No. 22.
[21] *The Intercollegian,* Vol. 37, No. 8, May, 1919, p. 11.

tion with the Interchurch World Movement—and, after its collapse, in various other ways—the Intercollegiate Y.M.C.A. sought vigorously to push its program of recruiting.[22] Something of the difficulties involved in furthering such an emphasis, however, soon became apparent in the post-war period.

[22] Miscellaneous Reports, No. 23.

PART SIX: POST-WAR PERIOD
1919–1930

Chapter XI. INTRODUCTION TO POST-WAR DISILLU-SIONMENT

INTRODUCTORY STATEMENT

THE period following the war called out new forces which were destined to be quickly reflected in the program of the Intercollegiate Y.M.C.A.[1] With the nation thrust out into a world conflict there had been released influences which tended to widen and deepen international-mindedness. At the same time, the spirit of provincialism on the part of some and of greed and selfishness on the part of others became more manifest.

Moreover, as the real facts of the war filtered through, these made increasingly evident how far the people had been misled through the use of propaganda. This impression was accentuated by the results of the war, as interpreted by the peace treaties and the refusal of the Senate to assume commitments to the League of Nations.

The people, however, continued to think and act with the mind which the war had engendered. Patriotism came to be expressed by many in a perverted spirit of nationalism, manifested in the standardization of ideas, and an intolerance toward minority races and sects. At the same time, a few became equally pronounced against such an attitude, as well as against war as such and the instruments of war.

---

[1] The author is indebted in this introductory statement to Frederick Lewis Allen's *Only Yesterday,* on which he has drawn for data to supplement his own observations.

Again, the emphasis during the war upon making the "world safe for democracy" stirred minority groups to assert themselves on behalf of democracy at home against the dominant ones, and youth in pursuit of self-determination against the older generation. In particular, morals and manners underwent a rapid change, stimulated by the exigencies of war and its annihilation of restraints. This was accentuated by the growing independence of women: their movement was furthered by the important rôle which they played during the war and by the suffrage, which they won in 1920. Emphasis was placed on professions for women as a factor in securing self-expression and economic independence. With this movement also went an emphasis, stimulated by the "New Psychology," upon the fact that sex is a force to be recognized in the life of women no less than in that of men.

Moreover, the prestige of science, the consequences of prosperity, and the natural let-down from the tension and idealism of the war period, as well as criticism of Christianity because of its countenancing the war—these led to a discounting of the traditional expressions of religion.

Again, the prosperity gained by so many in connection with the war led to rapid increase in the enrollment of students in the colleges and universities.

It was within such forces and factors that the Intercollegiate Y.M.C.A. developed its post-war program.

THE DES MOINES CONVENTION

The reflection of the post-war disillusionment and questionings is seen strikingly in developments at the quadrennial convention of the Student Volunteer Movement held at Des Moines, Iowa, just after the Christmas holidays in 1919.[2] In October of that year the staff of the Student Volunteer Movement had met with secretaries of the Intercollegiate Y.M.C.A. and Y.W.C.A. and decided

[2] See Report of Student Volunteer Convention, 1920.

that the central emphasis in the convention should be that, essentially, of a moral equivalent of war.[3] The program was set up largely on the basis of previous conventions, but with this new sense of urgency engendered by the war. In the course of the opening address the chairman, Mr. Mott, indicated some of the more imminent problems needing attention: in industry, commerce and finance; in attitudes toward other races; in international politics; and in the impact of Western civilization on the East.[4] These emphases were carried further in addresses by others, notably by Bishop Francis McConnell, who spoke on "Practical Christian Principles in National and International Life." [5]

The question of racial discrimination, particularly toward the Negro, was a peculiarly pertinent issue at the time.[6] Mr. George E. Haynes, speaking at this convention on "The Negro Students," asked that barriers—"economic, educational, social, civic, and religious, be removed." Nevertheless, these barriers were to be removed in order that the Negro students might "go forth to their black brothers throughout the world" with the missionary message.[7]

Although various social and international issues were recognized, the convention program was not prepared to deal with them. Stress was placed on the more traditional appeal to the individual in such a way as to lead him to volunteer for foreign missions. A typical expression of this emphasis is found in an address on the "Significance of Present-day Conditions to the Students of North America," by Mr. Sherwood Eddy, who closed with this appeal for workers:

"And I heard a voice saying, 'Whom shall I send and who will go for us?' Who will answer, 'Here am I; send me!' " [8]

[3] Interview Document, No. 22.
[4] *Report of Student Volunteer Convention*, 1920, pp. 17 ff.
[5] *Ibid.*, pp. 124 ff.
[6] *See* pp. 129 f. for a development on this point in connection with the Northfield Conference of the Student Volunteer Movement during the war.
[7] *Report of Student Volunteer Convention*, 1920, pp. 94 ff.
[8] *Ibid.*, pp. 49 ff.

Not a few delegates, however, particularly students, soon became disappointed with the program. Among those present were some students who had been chosen as delegates, not because of their interest in religious activities, but because they were leaders on their respective campuses. These declared the traditional evangelical message to be meaningless to them.[9]

Among the critics were also students who had served in the army and who had developed in consequence an individualism with reference to one's vocation and the prevailing interpretations of Christianity more marked than that of previous student groups. Some felt that President Wilson's "Fourteen Points" and other aspects of international diplomacy and politics and commerce, as well as problems in America, needed to be considered thoroughly along with the missionary program.[10] Some students wished to take immediate action in view of peoples in need of relief; others wished to petition the government to accept a mandate for Armenia.[11]

It is significant that among the critics were several young men whose fathers had been pioneers in developing the Volunteer Movement and were still prominent leaders in the convention. These young men sought to interpret to the elders the convictions of the youthful critics, and urged that an opportunity be made for democratic expression of student sentiment on questions about which they were concerned, as well as concessions on the subjects already being considered.[12] Moreover, they felt deep concern themselves about the validity of the missionary program to which previously they had felt committed. "Why," said one, "should I go out as a missionary to. . . . ? Have I any message?" [13]

Leaders of the convention admitted from the platform that there was criticism of the program but sought again to direct the conven-

[9] Coe, G. A., *Report to the Faculty of Union Theological Seminary.*
[10] Interview Document, No. 28.
[11] Coe, G. A., *op. cit.*
[12] *Ibid.*
[13] Interview Document, No. 15.

tion to the original focal point. They said the gathering was designed as a missionary convention and they challenged the Christian loyalty of the critics.[14] Mr. Sherwood Eddy in a second address recognized the need of a world brotherhood, of a lasting league of peace, and of attention to social and industrial problems in America. He turned then on the students and asked if they were meeting their personal problems of sin:

". . . . Are you pure? Are you a clean man? . . . . Are you honest? . . . . Are you surrendered or leading the selfish life? . . . . Get off the side-lines of criticism and get in the game. . . . Some of you said to me yesterday, 'Why do you bring us this piffle, these old shibboleths, these old worn-out phrases?' . . . . But, my friends, the trouble isn't with . . . . these men who have spoken to us. . . . Perhaps the trouble is, that you haven't yet found . . . . that living God. . . ." [15]

Disappointed, the dissenters created at the convention small conferences on their own initiative to deal with issues which they felt most pertinent.[16] They felt that there was a great diversity between their point of view and that of the leaders and that the latter were unyielding.[17] This attitude was carried over in a measure toward some of the leaders of the Intercollegiate Y.M.C.A. as well;[18] and it was undoubtedly a factor, along with other developments, which led to the insistence by students at times later on that older

[14] Coe, G. A., *op. cit. See also report of address by Mr. Robert E. Speer, Report of Student Volunteer Convention*, 1920, pp. 175 ff.
[15] *Ibid.*, pp. 191 f. That the fundamental assumptions of the Movement had undergone little change over the years is evidenced by the fact that so many of its statements were printed in pamphlet form and continued as standard literature from their beginnings up to the time of this convention. *See* Chart No. I, pp. 138-9. This chart is based on the Movement's lists of its literature available from year to year.
[16] Coe, G. A., *op. cit.*
[17] Interview Document, No. 24.
[18] *Ibid.*

people should absent themselves from the meetings when important policies of the Intercollegiate Y.M.C.A. were being discussed.

The next convention of the Volunteer Movement, four years later, showed by its program the significance attached to developments at Des Moines, but it will be necessary first to turn to other developments.

NO.	AUTHOR	TITLE
1	MOTT	HISTORY OF THE STUDENT VOLUNTEER MOVEMENT
2	SPEER	PRAYER AND MISSIONS
3	SPEER	THE VOLUNTEER BAND
4	WHITE	THE SELF-PERPETUATION OF THE VOLUNTEER BAND
5	WHITE	TEN LESSONS ON THE BIBLE AND MISSIONS
6	WILDER	THE BIBLE AND FOREIGN MISSIONS
7	GATES	CHRISTIAN MISSIONS AND THE HIGHEST USE OF WEALTH
8	GATES	THE MISSIONARY FACT RECORD BOOK
9	LYON	THE VOLUNTEER BAND
10	LYON	THE VOLUNTEER DECLARATION
11	SCHAUFFLER	MONEY: ITS NATURE AND POWER
12	EDDY, S.	THE SUPREME DECISION OF THE CHRISTIAN STUDENT
13	EDDY, S.	THE OPPORTUNITY OF THE HOUR
14	EDDY, S	CYCLE OF PRAYER OF THE S.V.M. FOR FOREIGN MISSIONS
15	MOTT	THE MISSIONARY DEPARTMENT
16	MOTT	BIBLE STUDY FOR PERSONAL GROWTH
17	SPEER	WONDERFUL CHALLENGE TO THIS GENERATION
18	MOTT	THE STUDENTS OF NORTH AMERICA UNITED
19	SPEER	WHAT CONSTITUTES A MISSIONARY CALL
20	BROCKMAN	IF GOD PERMIT [STUDY OF MISSIONS
21	TURNER	SOME REASONS WHY A STUDENT SHOULD PROMOTE THE A
22	FOX	SCRIPTURE PRINCIPLES OF GIVING
23	JOHN	MOTIVES IN FOREIGN MISSIONS
24	HASS	DOCTOR'S REASONS FOR GOING TO CHINA
25	MOTT	THE WATCHWORD AS A SPIRITUAL FORCE
26	MOTT	COMPARATIVE STUDIES IN MISSIONARY BIOGRAPHY
27	STREET	INTERCESSORY FOREIGN MISSIONARIES [MEN
28	SPEER	NON-CHRISTIAN RELIGIONS INADEQUATE TO MEET THE NEEDS OF A
29	FRASER	SPIRITUAL PREREQUISITES FOR THE PERSUASIVE PRESENTATION OF y
30	FOSTER	PRESENT CONDITIONS IN CHINA [CHRIST
31	SAILER	GENERAL SUGGESTIONS TO MISSIONARY LEADERS
32	BARTON	WHAT IS INVOLVED IN MISSION STUDY ?
33	ROBSON	SUPREME BUSINESS OF THE CHURCH
34	MOTT	URGENCY OF THE CRISIS IN THE FAR EAST
35	MOTT	THE WORLD'S EVANGELIZATION
36	MURRAY	BENEFITS DERIVED FROM MISSION STUDY AMONG STUDENTS
37	ZWEMER	THE MESSAGE AND THE MAN
38	MOTT	CONSECRATION
39	MOTT	MODERN WORLD MOVEMENTS: GOD'S CHALLENGE TO THE CHURCH
40	WRIGHT	SECRET PRAYER A GREAT REALITY
41	MURRAY	BENEFITS DERIVED FROM MISSION STUDY
42	MURRAY	IS MISSION STUDY WORTH WHILE ?
43	TURNER	WHY PROMOTE THE STUDY OF MISSIONS ?
44	DAY. D.	HINTS ON MISSION STUDY CLASS METHODS
45	ZWEMER	THE IMPENDING STRUGGLE IN WESTERN ASIA
46	ZWEMER	HOME TIES AND THE FOREIGN MISSION FIELD
47	ZWEMER	HOW SHALL THEY HEAR ?
48	TURNER	MISSIONARY UPRISING AMONG STUDENTS
49	SPEER	PLACE OF MISSIONS IN THE THOUGHT OF GOD
50	WARNECK	PRAYER FOR MISSIONS
51	BRETHERTON	VALUE OF A PURPOSE [ASSOCIATION
52	MURRAY	MISSIONARY MEETINGS OF THE STUDENT CHRISTIAN A
53	ZWEMER	ARE MORE MISSIONARIES NEEDED ?
54	MOTT	CALL OF THE NON-CHRISTIAN WORLD
55	EDDY, S	MESSAGE TO STUDENT VOLUNTEERS FOR FOREIGN MISSIONS
56	EDDY, B	STUDENT MISSIONARY DEPUTATIONS AMONG CHURCHES & YOUNG V
57	MOTT	A VISION REALIZED [PEOPLES SOCIETIES
58	MOTT	STUDENT VOLUNTEER MOVEMENT AFTER TWENTY-FIVE YEARS
59	MURRAY	BIBLIOGRAPHY OF MISSIONARY LITERATURE
60	ROSS	PHILOSOPHY OF MISSIONS [MOVEMENT
61	MOTT	INFLUENCE AND RESULTS OF THE STUDENT VOLUNTEER A
62	MACKENZIE	FUNDAMENTAL QUALIFICATIONS OF THE MISSIONARY
63	MOTT	INTERCESSORS THE PRIMARY NEED
64	TURNER	WHAT IS INVOLVED IN SIGNING THE DECLARATION OF THE S.V.M.
65	TURNER	WHO IS QUALIFIED TO PREPARE FOR FOREIGN MISSIONARY SERVICE ?
66	BURTON	WORLD FELLOWSHIP
67	MURRAY	WHY I STUDY MISSIONS
68	MURRAY	TWELVE STUDENTS EXCUSED FROM MISSION STUDY
69	BEAVER	WORLD BROTHERHOOD, FIRST ESSENTIALS OF

CHART No. I

PAMPHLETS OF THE STUDENT
PUBLISHED TO 1920 WITH

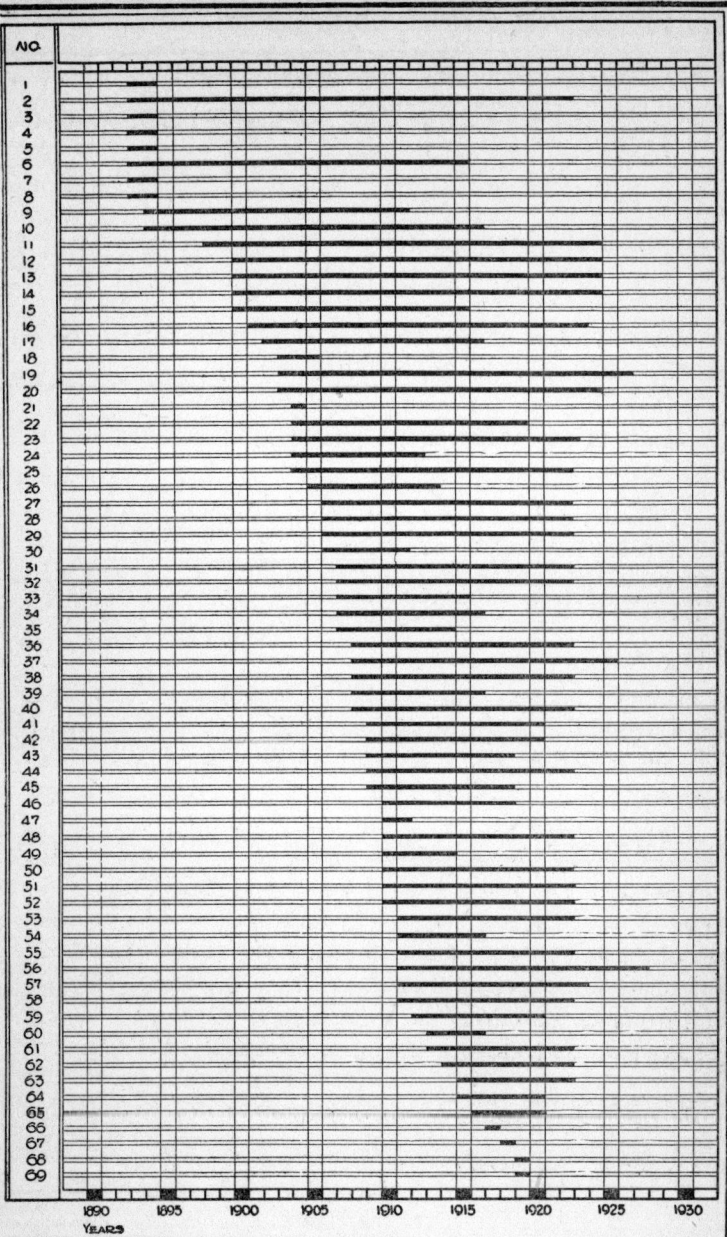

VOLUNTEER MOVEMENT
LENGTH OF TIME USED

Chapter XII. DEVELOPMENTS IN ORGANIZATIONAL
SELF-DETERMINATION

VARIOUS influences now converged to accentuate emphasis upon self-determination in the Intercollegiate Y.M.C.A. The stress in connection with the war upon political autonomy had stimulated the desires of the leaders of the organization along this line. A former member of its staff writes:

"I wonder if there is any place in American society where the emphasis upon democracy . . . . took firmer rootage than in the student movement. [At the conclusion of the war] we found ourselves hedged about and inhibited by our absorption in the general Y.M.C.A. movement. Then began the struggle for a larger freedom. . . ." [1]

A significant influence was felt also in developments in Canada which eventuated in the withdrawal of the student organizations from the Y.M.C.A. and Y.W.C.A. and forming an independent movement.[2]

The Committee of Counsel of the Intercollegiate Y.M.C.A. which had held its first meeting during the war,[3] was continued by a convention of the Y.M.C.A. held in 1919 at Detroit.[4] At this gathering, however, other happenings accentuated the self-consciousness of the leaders in the Intercollegiate Y.M.C.A. and their desire for autonomy. A group had submitted to the Resolutions Committee a resolution embodying the social creed of the Federal Council of Churches. Such changes, however, were made in the statement,

[1] Letter Document, No. 1-A.
[2] *Report of International Convention of Y.M.C.A's.*, 1922, p. 56.
[3] Cf. pp. 121 f.
[4] *Report of International Convention of Y.M.C.A's.*, 1919, pp. 10, 249.

as finally prepared by the Resolutions Committee, that a member of the Intercollegiate Y.M.C.A. staff took the floor of the Convention and secured the adoption of the original resolution.[5]

Following these events came the convention at Des Moines, with results which had a significant bearing on the problem of self-determination for the Intercollegiate Y.M.C.A.:

> "Des Moines marks the turning point. . . . The leadership of the student movement—local and traveling secretaries, and interested laymen—were soon mobilized. More and more the one issue of freedom became dominant. . . . Matters of program necessarily were subordinated. . . ." [6]

Developments at Des Moines revealed also the potential contribution of students to the struggle for autonomy, and by the time of another convention of the general Y.M.C.A. at Atlantic City in November, 1922, the leaders of the Intercollegiate Y.M.C.A. had made progress in drawing them into prominence. At this convention one of their number presided over the section relating to the student work. Significance attaches chiefly to the participation of students, because their primary interest at the time was in the question of the membership basis. They asked the convention to grant a new alternative basis of membership, known as the "purpose basis." [7] Students were active also on the floor of the convention,

---

[5] Letter Document, No. 1-A.

[6] *Ibid.*

[7] This basis of membership includes the following objectives:

"1. To lead students to faith in God through Jesus Christ.

"2. To lead them into membership and service in the Christian Church.

"3. To promote their growth in Christian faith and character, especially through the study of the Bible and prayer.

"4. To influence them to devote themselves in united effort with all Christians to making the Will of Christ effective in human society, and to extending the Kingdom of God throughout the world. . . ."

(*Report of International Convention of the Y.M.C.A.,* 1922, p. 184.) A similar statement of purpose had been adopted six years before by the second "Cleveland" conference, made up of representatives of the

arguing for this new statement of purpose. An eyewitness, impressed with the eagerness of the convention to coöperate to the limit, said the situation was a "spiritual experience. . . . There was no debate. The new basis was just voted. . . ." [8]

The convention showed its attitude to the college work further by approving action looking to the creation of regional and national councils, made up of students and others, to give more adequate direction to the college work.[9] This made possible a meeting, a few months later, of the first national assembly of the Associations in the colleges and universities, thus instituting a more effective means of dealing with various problems related to the status of the intercollegiate work within the general Y.M.C.A.

One of these was the question of dual control and supervision which was continued from the period prior to the war.[10] It had become so acute after the war that not a few of the leaders related to the state committees, as well as of those connected with the national movement, felt a grave concern about the future of the college work. A state secretary related to college work wrote in 1922:

". . . . At the present time there is no nation-wide program accepted, understood, and carried on with our whole might. Often our best energies are consumed in long hours in diplomatic maneuvring of relationships instead of the larger creative work which our leadership should undertake. . . ." [11]

Such conditions spurred the feeling of many that there should be inaugurated a national program of advance. The regional council

Y.M.C.A., Y.W.C.A., Student Volunteer Movement and denominational agencies. See pp. 123 f., and cf. Elliott, H. S., "Christian Work in State Universities," Report of Cleveland and Chicago Conferences, p. 6.

[8] Interview Document, No. 22.
[9] Report of the International Convention of Y.M.C.A's., 1922, pp. 54-55.
[10] Cf. pp. 118 ff.
[11] Letter Document, No. 10.

for the central area in its meeting in October, 1922, had expressed the need of infusing "new vitality into the Student Christian Movement" and urged a great forward program, on the basis of a five-year period, terminating in 1927, which marked the fiftieth anniversary of the Intercollegiate Y.M.C.A.[12] The situation was discussed at the 1922 convention. Figures were offered showing great increases in student bodies following the war, as a basis of appeal for authorization of an advance program. A resolution was passed by the convention authorizing the committee on intercollegiate work to appoint a commission on an advance program.[13]

The problem of supervision, however, continued to receive a great deal of attention by the secretaries related to the college work, and increasingly by the newly-formed councils.[14] The question was debated at the assembly of secretaries related to college work held at Estes Park, Colorado, in the summer of 1923, and at other meetings prior to a constitutional convention of the general Movement at Cleveland the same year.[15] A majority report went from these conferences favoring supervision through a single agency, which was to have the privilege of setting up and approving its own budget,[16] but the constitutional convention provided for neither a single-agency control nor a separate budget for the intercollegiate work. Following further discussion of the problem, a commission was appointed in 1924, charged to study various possibilities, including experiments in supervision of the college work in the Southwest and in New England;[17] and to recommend to the newly-created general board

[12] Letter Document, No. 10-A.
[13] *Report of International Convention of Y.M.C.A's.*, 1922, p. 340. For emphases in the "advance program," *see The College Situation and Student Responsibility*—Student Young Men's Christian Associations, 1924.
[14] Cf. p. 142.
[15] It was also discussed in subsequent assemblies of the student secretaries, as well as in the meetings of the councils.—*See* reports of these gatherings.
[16] Interview Document, No. 22.
[17] In 1918, with the development of the Student Army Training Corps,

of the Y.M.C.A., as well as to the state and interstate organizations, a practical plan for more adequate secretarial supervision of the college work.[18]

Various proposals were made, but it was not possible to develop a plan which would be satisfactory for the entire country. The situation became acute in the Middle Atlantic area. There the Field Council set up in early 1927 [19] an independent agency of supervision, employed secretaries, raised a budget, and projected its programs.[20] In the South, certain Associations threatened to form an independent federation.[21] Conditions reached such a state that the Ad-Interim Committee of the Council directing the intercollegiate work and its executive secretary, Mr. D. R. Porter, resigned in June, 1927. They did so largely as a protest against the interpretation being placed upon the constitution of the National Y.M.C.A., an interpretation which tended to magnify state control. At the same time they demanded that responsibility for policies, staffs, and budgets, reside solely in the National Council of Student Associations. They were later urged to withdraw their resignations, and did so. The commission had been superseded in the meantime by a "Committee of Eleven," whose proposals resulted in the elevation of the Intercollegiate Y.M.C.A. to the rank of a "Division," providing in this way a means to meet essentially the desires of the organization relative to budgets and staffs. This also assured freedom of approach to the local associations, but with responsibility at the same time to

---

the association work in the New England colleges was supervised by two secretaries. This was continued afterwards by a joint committee representing five states, with the coöperation of the national forces, and later was extended to the Southwest. This plan of unified supervision made possible supervision also according to types of institutions.—*The Intercollegian*, Vol. 42, No. 2, Nov., 1924, p. 27.

[18] *Report of Meeting of National Council, Y.M.C.A.*, 1924, p. 38.
[19] Miscellaneous Reports, No. 31.
[20] Letter Document, No. 2.
[21] Miscellaneous Reports, No. 30.

coöperate fully in the coördination of all the forces.[22] In the college year immediately succeeding, the staff of the Intercollegiate Y.M.C.A. was more than doubled and the total budget for college work also greatly increased.[23]

The victory was not won, however, without some cost to the complete and harmonious unity of all the Y.M.C.A. forces. At the same time the results accentuated activity by some of the state committees on behalf of work with students.[24] Accordingly, the problem of determining the final form of the organization in its relationship with the general Y.M.C.A. still remains. For, although the greater degree of self-determination secured by the intercollegiate organization looks to the building of a movement directed nationally, the relationship of the state committees of the Y.M.C.A. to the college work has not been severed. Moreover, although the struggle greatly strengthened the "national consciousness" of the intercollegiate organization—a feeling which its leaders had been seeking to develop—some felt that this took on the form of a "fighting complex." [25] The significance of the attitude of struggle is undoubtedly reflected, as we shall see, in the program at the time.

[22] See statement by Mott, J. R., "Recent Developments in the Relationships of the Student Young Men's Christian Association Movement to the Association Brotherhood," June 28, 1927. (Files of Student Division, Y.M.C.A.)

[23] Miscellaneous Reports, No. 67.

[24] Letter Document, No. 2.

[25] Interview Document, No. 24.

Chapter XIII. APPROACH TO SOCIAL AND WORLD PROBLEMS

A. DEVELOPING INTEREST IN INTERNATIONAL AND SOCIAL ISSUES

THE developments at the Des Moines Convention accentuated emphasis upon other problems to which the Intercollegiate Y.M.C.A. had already begun to give attention during the war.[1]

Study Texts on World Problems

The Intercollegiate organization of the Y.M.C.A. stimulated and sought to direct interest in international questions by various means. One method was by the use of special texts prepared under the direction of the Publication Department, Association Press and designed for group discussion and forums.[2]

Gifts for, and Fraternizing with, European Students

The organization also began very soon again to give attention, along with the Y.W.C.A., to problems of students in European countries. Indeed, the discovery by the World's Student Christian Federation in early 1920 that some students were on the verge of starvation in Central Europe started a new chapter on international emphases by the Y.M.C.A. Along with the Y.W.C.A. and the Christian student movements of certain other countries, the Y.M.C.A. developed a program of relief to intellectuals in Central

---

[1] Cf. Chapter X.
[2] These included such texts as the following: Latourette, K. S., *The Christian Basis of World Democracy*, 1919; Fleming, D. J., *Marks of a World Christian*, 1919; Fahs, C. H., *America's Stake in the Far East*, 1920; Fahs, C. H., *America's Stake in Europe*, 1921.

146

Europe and the Near East. These included students and professors, men and women in need, in former "enemy" countries no less than others, and without reference to race, nationality, or religious affiliation. This was promoted under the auspices of the World's Student Christian Federation and through a specially-created agency, the "European Student Relief." [3] Large sums of money were secured in America for this work during the years immediately succeeding 1919. In Europe, annual conferences, started under the auspices of the European Student Relief, brought together students from various countries (including the United States) for discussion of means of relief, of international fraternity, of student welfare, and of other problems of student life.[4] The sense of solidarity with intellectuals without reference to nationality, race, or creed, which these activities developed, was further stimulated by other events. Leaders of the Intercollegiate Y.M.C.A. were sent to Europe to see at first-hand the conditions, to meet with students, and to report on these conditions to American students upon their return.[5] By 1922, these groups were composed largely of students, who went on "pilgrimages of friendship." With the departure of these "pilgrims" from various sections of the country, they were frequently "commissioned" officially by the summer gatherings of students to carry greetings and good-will.[6] Soon the "pilgrimages" were extended to Mexico and Japan.[7] From time to time, also, small groups of students from Europe toured among American colleges and discussed problems of common concern.[8]

[3] *The Intercollegian,* Vol. 37, No. 7, April, 1920, p. 1.
[4] This relief agency was succeeded in 1925 by the "International Student Service." For the developments in the work and their significance, *see* Rouse, Ruth, *The Rebuilding of Europe,* 1925.
[5] Miscellaneous Reports, No. 61-A.
[6] *The Intercollegian,* Vol. 40, No. 1, Oct., 1922, pp. 3, 12; Miscellaneous Reports, Nos. 62 and 62-A.
[7] *Ibid.:* Vol. 40, No. 9, June, 1923, p. 28; Vol. 42, No. 1, Oct., 1924, p. 32; Vol. 45, No. 6, Mar., 1928, p. 171.
[8] *Ibid.:* Vol. 36, No. 4, June, 1919; p. 14; Vol. 40, No. 9, May, 1923, p. 20.

Criticism of Christianity by Oriental Students

Simultaneously with these events, which were furnishing the basis for reflection on a new internationalism, was developing another factor affecting student thought and feeling. Beginning soon after the war, Oriental students in America had started to challenge Christianity on account of the war; it had preached peace, they said, yet Christian nations had waged the war.[9] This criticism made American students more skeptical of the validity of fastening "on Orientals a religious system which had failed here." They came to feel also that there should be self-determination in religion no less than in politics. This attitude had already been manifested in some degree at the Des Moines Convention of the Student Volunteer Movement; it was now being felt more and more. To the criticism of Christianity was added appreciation of Orientals by Americans. Paul Hutchinson, in speaking to a group of American students in 1924, said:

"As long as we stand in front of a civilization that has been as thoroughly discredited in the eyes of the . . . . East as our civilization has been, we cannot, with complacency, feel that we have solved the problem that the missionaries face when we merely commission folks to go and preach the gospel. . . . The battle is not going to be won . . . . anywhere until it is won everywhere." . . . Let us press on, but "let us understand, in deep humility of spirit, knowing that we will walk on shores where some of the noblest in the long spiritual pilgrimage of our race have walked before us; that, in the end . . . . these to whom we go will have as much, or more, to give to the common store of humanity's spiritual possessions as those from whom we come." [10]

[9] Interview Document, No. 15.
[10] Luccock, H. E., Ed., *Through the Eyes of Youth*, pp. 91, 95.

Resolutions by World's Student Christian Federation on International and Social Issues

This challenge was strengthened by developments in a meeting of the Committee of the World's Student Christian Federation held in China, April 1 to 12, 1922. A strong demand within the Federation itself for commitment on war and race, together with criticism from anti-Christian students in China, led to the adoption by the Federation of firm resolutions on these issues.[11] Participation by students since the beginning of the war in causes fostered by the Federation had heightened their consciousness, not only of the existence of this organization, but also of its significance. The action, therefore, of the Federation greatly influenced the thinking of students in the Y.M.C.A. This is reflected in the fact that two of the summer conferences of the Intercollegiate Y.M.C.A. which followed passed resolutions emphasizing international obligations of Christian nations, condemning war and armaments, and demanding justice for all races.[12]

Use of Speakers with a Radical Point of View on Social and Industrial Issues

Meanwhile, other forces were developed by the Intercollegiate Y.M.C.A. to influence the thinking of students. In early 1919, Mr. Stitt Wilson, a prominent labor leader, delivered a series of five lectures on "Constructive Christian Democracy." Very soon afterwards he was pressed into service in speaking to college communities and has continued from time to time over a period of years. Mr. Wilson's message represents a call for reconstruction in our economic system.[13] Strikingly indicative also of the new social and industrial emphasis in the program was the new note brought by Mr. Sher-

[11] The Intercollegian, Vol. 39, No. 9, June, 1922, p. 3; Report by the World's Student Christian Federation of the Conference, pp. 26 f.
[12] Miscellaneous Reports, No. 62.
[13] Luccock, H. E., op. cit., p. 61.

wood Eddy, a constant speaker for the Intercollegiate Y.M.C.A. Within a short while after the Des Moines Convention [14] of the Student Volunteer Movement, Mr. Eddy revised his own message, so as to include criticism of war and the institutions being developed for its promotion, as well as a call for a new social order.[15] The list of speakers on social and industrial issues soon came to include also, among others, Mr. Kirby Page, Mr. Norman Thomas, and Mr. Reinhold Niebuhr. By continued use of such outstanding figures in the colleges, in its summer conferences, and in its other gatherings, the Intercollegiate Y.M.C.A. has presented to students a radical point of view on industrial, economic, social, and international issues.

Summer Research Groups in Social and Industrial Problems

Another approach to social and industrial problems was also started. To the summer service group, begun in New York City in 1916,[16] were added similar groups in other cities for the first-hand study of industrial problems. The first of these was held in Denver, Colorado, in 1920, under the direction of Mr. B. M. Cherrington, one of the secretaries of the intercollegiate organization. The twenty students who participated sought their own jobs as unskilled laborers; they lodged and boarded with the workers, and lived on their own wages. A seminar was held four times a week after work hours to discuss problems. The movement was soon extended by the organization to other points; the length of the periods was also extended from six to eight weeks.[17]

[14] In 1919.
[15] See Eddy, S., Religion and Social Justice, pp. 11 ff.; also Letter Document, No. 5.
[16] Cf. pp. 92 f.
[17] The Student World, Vol. 18, Oct., 1927, pp. 370 f.

New Attitude to the Missionary Program

These developments were reflected in the demand for a new social content for foreign missions, validated by a new social order at home.[18] They were reflected also in a decreasing student response to the more traditional emphases, a fact strikingly evidenced by the decline of the number of students volunteering for foreign service. Although larger numbers than usual volunteered in the immediate post-war period, there was a rapid decrease after 1921.[19] The consequences of this decline of interest in the more traditional missionary programs were reflected in the Student Volunteer Movement. Following the Des Moines Convention, the Movement started on a process of reorganization which, through a Council similar to that of the Y.M.C.A., brought students more largely into control of its policies. Nevertheless, there was quickly evident a diminishing support of the Movement. During the year following the Des Moines Convention (1920-21), students contributed to the budget of the Movement only one-third as much as formerly.[20] As a consequence, the staff was reduced from sixteen in 1924 to four full-time and three part-time workers in 1926.[21] The question was even raised of whether, in view of developments throughout the world, there was any longer a need for the Student Volunteer Movement.[22]

Development of Committee on Christian World Education

These factors spurred the Intercollegiate Y.M.C.A. to seek a more satisfactory means of dealing with the missionary emphasis.

[18] An instance is found in developments at a conference of student volunteers from the colleges of Alabama. The delegates expressed their "firm belief that there can be no successful continuance of foreign missions unless it comes from the heart of the Christian order at home."—*The Intercollegian*, Vol. 43, No. 8, May, 1926, p. 251.

[19] *See* Chart II, p. 152, based on data assembled by the Student Volunteer Movement.

[20] Miscellaneous Reports, No. 70.

[21] Miscellaneous Reports, No. 71.

[22] *See*, e.g., *The Intercollegian*, Vol. 41, No. 5, Feb., 1924, p. 30.

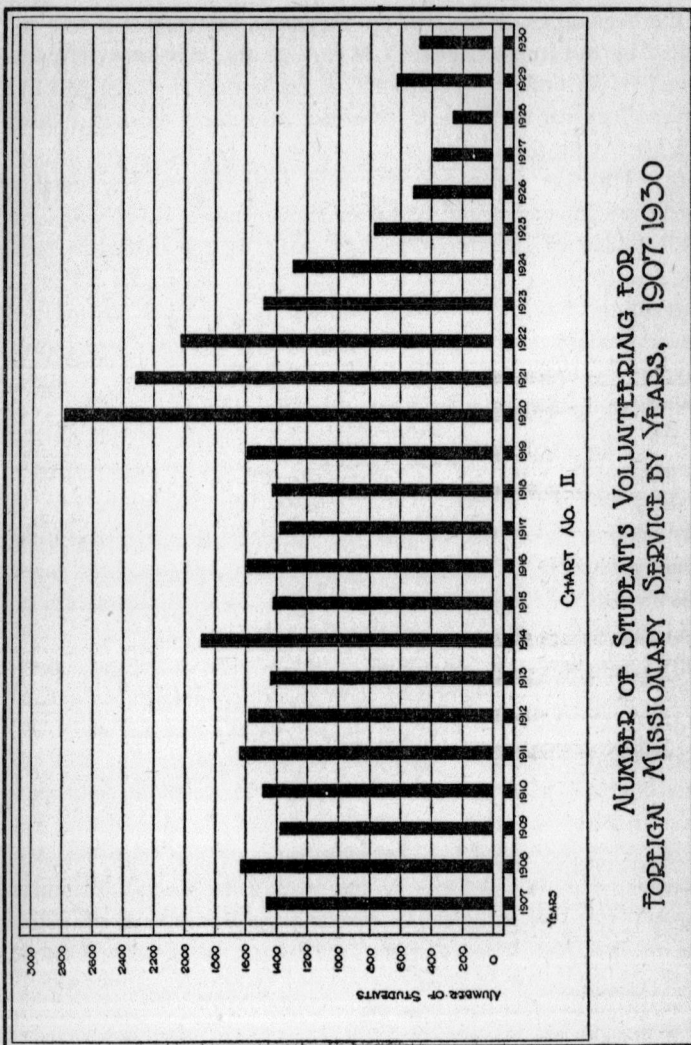

CHART No. II

NUMBER OF STUDENTS VOLUNTEERING FOR
FOREIGN MISSIONARY SERVICE BY YEARS, 1907-1930

In the beginnings of the Student Volunteer Movement, it was regarded by the Intercollegiate Y.M.C.A. as its "missionary department." [23] In time, however, some of the leaders in the Y.M.C.A. came to feel that the Student Volunteer Movement did not counsel sufficiently with them in order to develop the best programs for the work. This was a matter of discussion from time to time, notably among the Intercollegiate Y.M.C.A. staff members in 1911.[24] By 1917, leaders of the Intercollegiate Y.M.C.A. felt that there was grave danger in turning over too much "of the missionary responsibility to the Student Volunteer Movement. . . . The life of the general student work will suffer irreparably in depth and power unless every leader [of the Intercollegiate Y.M.C.A.] feels a responsibility for mission study and recruiting. . . ." [25]

Although it was generally recognized that the Y.M.C.A. depended on the Volunteer Movement for its policies with reference to the missionary aspects of the program, the Movement existed only nationally: on the campus the unit was primarily the individual volunteer. A unified program—at the top—had been made possible largely through the fact that Mr. Mott, in becoming related to the staff of the Intercollegiate Y.M.C.A., was made chairman of the Executive Committee of the Student Volunteer Movement. A similar relation held with the Intercollegiate Y.W.C.A. through the executive secretary of the latter organization. Mr. Mott's long relationship with the Volunteer Movement and the Intercollegiate Y.M.C.A. in the capacities indicated made it possible for this somewhat anomalous situation to continue over the years. Very soon after the Des Moines Convention, however, Mr. Mott tendered his resignation as chairman of the Student Volunteer Committee.[26] He had resigned several years before from the direction of the Intercollegiate Y.M.C.A. in order to become General

23 Miscellaneous Reports, No. 51.
24 Miscellaneous Reports, No. 49.
25 Miscellaneous Reports, No. 59.
26 *The Intercollegian*, Vol. 37, No. 8, May, 1920, p. 8.

Secretary of the general Y.M.C.A. Thus was discontinued a relationship which for so long had interlinked the programs of the Intercollegiate Y.M.C.A. and another organization which determined its missionary policies.

With the reorganization of the Volunteer Movement, following the Des Moines Convention, an effort was made to clear the question of its relationship with the Y.M.C.A. and Y.W.C.A. By 1925, it was stated by one of the leaders in the Intercollegiate Y.M.C.A. that the Volunteer Movement was "not . . . . a co-ordinating organization but . . . . a supplementary movement, free and uncontrolled but not independent, separate but correlated in one comprehensive task!" [27] In the meantime, the Volunteer Movement had revised its policy, concentrating thereafter on a more intensive type of educational program for those interested in missions as a possible life work, leaving the more general work to the Y.M.C.A. and Y.W.C.A.[28]

In order to deal with these various factors and more effectively to care for the new interests in world affairs and social questions, the Y.M.C.A. and Y.W.C.A. effected through the Council of Christian Associations ("C.C.A."),[29] the organization of a committee on Christian World Education (known as the "C.W.E." Committee).[30] This committee was composed of representatives of the staffs and

[27] Miscellaneous Reports, No. 28.
[28] Letter Document, No. 12. The Movement also began to encourage only such vocational decisions as were based on thorough study of what was involved in Christian missionary service and of the particular needs of the fields since the war. Christian nationals of other lands were used increasingly to interpret to American students the situation in their counries. The Movement also took a forward step on vocational direction in insisting that applicants for membership in the Movement first pass a medical examination under the mission boards. Further, declaration cards were no longer distributed at conferences or conventions; the Movement insisted that any one interested should make application for the card.
[29] This council had been developed by staff members of the two organizations to deal with problems and programs of common concern.—Interview Document, No. 28.
[30] Miscellaneous Reports, No. 62-A.

councils of the two Associations, with additional representatives from the Student Volunteer Movement and the Fellowship for Christian Life Service.[31] The program of this committee came to be stated more specifically later as "the cultivation of friendship with foreign students, ... the study of international issues, ... the appreciation of the worth of other peoples, ... the establishment of better race relations in our own land," raising funds for certain projects in other countries, and "an intelligent participation in the world-wide program of the Church."[32] Thus do we find not only new interests but a new organizational approach to interests which were formerly expressed almost entirely through the missionary programs of the Student Volunteer Movement.

B. Democratic Student Discussion of Social and World Problems: Indianapolis Convention

Another stage in dealing with social and world problems was registered through a convention held at Indianapolis, December 28, 1923 to January 1, 1924. On the invitation of the Student Volunteer Movement, the Y.M.C.A. and Y.W.C.A. shared equally in the program, making it one representing the three organizations.[33] Two decidedly advanced steps were taken in this convention over the one four years before at Des Moines. These are found in relation to the kinds of subjects discussed and the method of handling them, both largely determined by the attitude of the students. The committee on plans for the convention "early realized a marked change in the attitude of students, owing to altered world conditions. . . .

[31] The last-named organization (known as "F.C.L.S.") had been started in 1922 on behalf of students intending to do professional Christian work in America. It was discontinued a few years later.—Interview Document, No. 24.

[32] Christian World Education Committee, "Scrap Book," 1929, p. 2. One of the first tasks undertaken by this committee was the development of literature on such interests, as well as suggestions for forums, discussion groups, etc. For some of its early publications, see p. 156, Note 35.

[33] Cf. Report of the Student Volunteer Convention, 1924, p. 426.

The youth movements in Europe, Asia, and South America had profoundly influenced North American youths. International and interracial problems were being widely discussed . . . ." along with modern industrial conditions.[34]

The program of the first day of the convention was devoted to consideration of modern industrial conditions; racial relations; international problems; and social and intellectual unrest. On the following forenoon the delegates assembled in forty-nine discussion groups planned for the frank consideration of questions of mutual and vital concern to the members of the different groups.[35] They were designed to help students in an "attempt not to compromise but to integrate their experience and their convictions in a new and better group will, which may be for this group of students really the Will of God." At the same time it was believed that the greatest result would "be the stimulus to consider these questions further after students return to their respective campuses." In order to give students the greatest possible freedom, faculty representatives, missionaries, and other non-student delegates were invited to attend the discussional groups, with the understanding that they would "not participate in the discussions unless requested to do so by the leader." [36]

[34] *Ibid.,* Introduction, pp. iv f.

[35] This represented an approach to problems which had been developed by the Y.M.C.A. prior to and during the war. It had more recently been adopted by the Student Volunteer Movement. Indeed, the old form of textbook which had been used so extensively in the Volunteer Movement prior to the war was no longer possible as a device for interesting students. Discussion courses were developed as one means of meeting this situation. —Letter Document, No. 12.

Discussion outlines in preparation for the convention had been prepared by the "C.W.E." Committee (see pp. 151, 153 f.) and the Volunteer Movement, and made available for use some time beforehand. These included such outline courses as the following:

International Problems and the Christian Way of Life; Racial Relations and the Christian Ideal; Economic Problems and the Christian Ideal, M. T. Stauffer; *Youth and Renaissance Movements,* M. T. Stauffer.

[36] *Report of the Student Volunteer Convention,* 1924, pp. 225 ff.

The first meeting of the discussion groups revealed that questions concerning race and war would be the chief ones to be considered by the students. In the second meeting of the groups, the students carried the discussions further, arriving so far as possible, at tentative proposals and conclusions. A third meeting—in charge of students, and this time an open meeting—was given over to eight statements by students on war and race. The speakers had been picked by the group leaders and student representatives from the groups with a view to presenting varying proposals of different groups.[37]

Once the discussion groups were started, however, the convention began to give simultaneous attention to the more traditional emphasis of the Volunteer Movement. For it was "desired to sacrifice nothing of the valuable deposit received from past Student Volunteer conventions, such as the strength of a direct appeal and the emphasis upon the need of Christ for the redemption of the individual. . . . Unless He transforms a sufficient number of individuals, how can He transform society, which is made up of individuals?"[38] The more traditional emphasis, it is true, was confined to a smaller proportion of the convention program than formerly. Moreover, decided changes are found here. A series of addresses on Christian faith was given by one man, and there was a presentation through twenty-two simultaneous forums of different kinds of work abroad.

Nevertheless, the fundamental interest of the Volunteer Movement and that of the Christian Associations (represented especially in the discussion groups) called for such different emphases and such different approaches that they could not be integrated into a unity. Moreover, neither group was satisfied that the emphasis for which it felt primary responsibility secured sufficient attention. The Volunteer Movement decided later to return to the more definitely mis-

[37] *Ibid.*, pp. 225 ff.
[38] *Ibid.*, Introduction, p. iv.

sionary conference and four years later held a convention on that basis. The Y.M.C.A. and Y.W.C.A. continued to include in their programs the other emphases, a development which, along with other factors, led to a convention of the Y.M.C.A. and Y.W.C.A. at Milwaukee later.[39]

C. Procedure in Dealing with Controversial Issues

Another stage may be seen in the program of the Intercollegiate Y.M.C.A. at this time. The convention at Indianapolis, following the early post-war program developments, quickened the interest on the part of students in social and world problems. The delegates went from the convention eager to do something about them. We must note another program factor which entered to determine attitudes, as well as some of the ways in which these were expressed.

Developing Social Attitudes through Bible Study

A significant factor in stimulating conviction of students at this time was the Bible-study program promoted by the Y.M.C.A. and Y.W.C.A. It will be recalled that, at the beginning of the war, the Intercollegiate Y.M.C.A., along with other interested agencies, was promoting a series of studies developed on a graded basis and in the light of varying situations, or "problems," facing the student from his freshman to his senior year.[40] This approach was carried over into the war and the early post-war period.[41] As these discussions developed, however, the problems and interests of the students came to be magnified more and more at the expense of Bible study as an end in itself.[42] In some cases, the attitude of students led to the development of forums to the exclusion of Bible

[39] Cf. p. 177.
[40] Cf. pp. 112 ff.
[41] There continued to be the emphasis at the same time on personal evangelism, as found for example in the text prepared in 1920 by Stewart-Wright, *Personal Evangelism Among Students.*
[42] Interview Document, No. 6.

study.[43] Such an approach to vital issues seemed to some of the Intercollegiate Y.M.C.A. leaders not to offer sufficiently clear-cut proposals of action, as well as dynamic for carrying these out. There was a feeling that these needs could be met by studies which would magnify the Bible as such, and particularly the life and principles of Jesus.[44] This point of view was voiced in the early post-war period by a leader who said that the central aim of the organization should be "an increasing effort to promote the fertilizing practice of systematic, daily, Bible study. Men must learn to apply the principles of Jesus to their own conduct and to their relation to all men and women everywhere. . . ."[45]

Congenial to this point of view was an emphasis developed after the war by Professor Bruce Curry, whose help was secured in giving special attention to Bible study. As a student of Professor W. W. White and later a teacher on his staff, Professor Curry had been trained in the method of Bible study used by the former and also developed by him in the early Bible studies of the Intercollegiate Y.M.C.A. The method placed primary emphasis upon examination of the Biblical material, and upon values believed to be gained by the student when exposed to the Bible and stimulated to make his own interpretation of the material found there. It was believed that through such means there would come illumination and prophetic insight.[46]

During the war, Professor Curry had carried responsibility in connection with Bible study for men in the army and navy. Finding that these men were not interested in Bible study as such, he adopted the method of the "problem" or "situation" approach, as it had been developed in the College Voluntary Study Courses.[47] Taking the situation of the soldiers, he furnished Bible references

[43] Miscellaneous Reports, No. 63,
[44] Ibid.
[45] The Intercollegian, Vol. 37, No. 1, Oct., 1919, p. 11.
[46] Interview Document, No. 6.
[47] See pp. 112 ff.

for discussion of their problems, and trained leaders on that basis. Along with Mr. Harrison S. Elliott, he developed a series of Bible studies on the problem approach with daily readings for a year and suggestions for group discussion on each week's topic.[48] This represented a shift of emphasis from subject matter to be mastered to the problem of the individual, or the group, as the determinant. Feeling, however, that the two emphases should be combined, Professor Curry developed in the post-war period a procedure looking to that end. The method originally employed for the study of the biblical material emphasized these steps in the large: 1. analysis of the material, guided by the question, "What is here?"; 2. interpretation of the material—"What does it mean?" Inspired by the main steps in the "problem" approach,[49] Professor Curry now added: 3. analysis of the problem dealt with in the biblical material—"What was the problem then?" "What is the similar problem now?"; 4. examination of the solution proposed—"What solution did Jesus propose?"; 5. evaluation of the solution—"What is the value today?"[50] The foregoing method, however, presupposes interest in the Bible. To meet the practical problem involved where there is not such an interest and to get a hearing for Bible study, Professor Curry frequently developed discussions on the basis of the "problem" approach.[51]

More significant, however, than the method developed by Pro-

[48] *New Testament Ideals for the Present World Task,* by Harrison S. Elliott and A. Bruce Curry. A number of other "problem" Bible studies for soldiers were brought out during the war period.

[49] This consists essentially of the following: (a) statement and analysis of the problem; (b) marshaling of resources (including the Bible) to help on the solution; (c) drawing up tentative conclusions and plans for experimentation.

[50] Interview Document, No. 6. This procedure is developed by Professor Curry in his text, *Jesus and His Cause* (1920). Cf. revised and enlarged form (1925), Association Press. A parallel effort to combine a problem approach with a more systematic study of the biblical material is found in *How Jesus Met Life Questions,* by Harrison S. Elliott, published in the same period.

[51] Curry, B., *Facing Student Problems.*

fessor Curry was his point of view. He had come to feel that what was needed was a rediscovery of the "mind and method" of Jesus in order to apply courageously his principles to the vital problems of students.[52] The principles of Jesus represented for him a revolt against the "materialistic, selfish superstructure of tradition in religion, science, politics, industry." He continued:

"The revolt of which I am thinking is not negative or schismatic. It is to be a 'Revolt of Reconciliation,' an attempt to vitalize and respiritualize the Christian movement. Its method must be the method of Jesus—reason, good-will, and non-resistance. Discussion is the crucible in which both the new and the old ways must be tested. A courageous attempt to live the new way of life must accompany even the discussion. . . . The first step needed is a return to the New Testament records for a clear-cut, scholarly, sympathetic rediscovery of the mind, the method, the conscience, the Spirit of Jesus and his early followers. They got hold of something which turned the world upside down. . . . There would next come a demand for consecration, such as the cause of Jesus has not felt for centuries." [53]

In discussing the question, "How radical shall we be?" Professor Curry said:

". . . . If Jesus were here today he would be . . . . some of us would . . . . say . . . . a Communist. . . . There are too many ungodlike elements in state, church, and social order to leave place for anything short of protest and 'constructive revolution' in a spirit such as his."

By such a movement, Professor Curry called for "radicals according to Jesus." [54] Working in the colleges, under the auspices of the Y.M.C.A. and Y.W.C.A., he gave the two years, 1923-24 and 1924-25 and week-ends from time to time in the immediately suc-

[52] *Ibid.*, Foreword, p. x.
[53] *The Intercollegian*, Vol. 42, No. 4, Jan., 1925, pp. 120 f.
[54] *Ibid.*, Vol. 42, No. 9, June, 1925, pp. 273 f.

ceeding years to developing Bible study in which this point of view prevailed.   It constituted a significant factor in determining attitudes on social and international issues.[55]

Interracial Activities

Significant developments took place on race, especially in the South.   The work of the Intercollegiate Y.M.C.A. in that section prior to the war was a large factor in the development during the post-war period of an "Interracial Commission" to deal with problems which became acute at that time.[56]   The two organizations, as well as the Y.W.C.A., worked closely together in dealing with interracial problems which pertained to the student field, all of the contacts of the Interracial Commission with students being made through the Intercollegiate Y.M.C.A. and Y.W.C.A.[57]   Other developments followed later in the program of the Y.M.C.A. itself. Special literature was produced on the question of interracial relations.[58]   Prominent Negro educators were brought in to speak to students at the summer conference at Blue Ridge, North Carolina. Beginning in 1924, there was developed also and maintained for a while an exchange of fraternal delegates between this conference and one for Negro students at King's Mountain, North Carolina.[59] Fraternal delegates were also invited later to a conference of student volunteers in southern Texas in which the Y.M.C.A. and Y.W.C.A. coöperated; at this conference, moreover, one of the group leaders was a Negro minister.[60]   Professor George W. Carver, of Tuskegee Institute, was used as a lecturer in colleges of Tennessee and Vir-

[55] Miscellaneous Reports, Nos. 63, 64, 65.
[56] *See* article by President R. R. Moton, in *The Student World,* Vol. 14, July, 1921, p. 131.
[57] *The Intercollegian,* Vol. 43, No. 4, Jan., 1926, p. 118.
[58] E.g., Bergthold, J. W., *et al., Christian Principles and Race Relations,* 1926.
[59] Miscellaneous Reports, No. 63.
[60] Miscellaneous Reports, No. 39.

ginia.[61] Small interracial student gatherings were also developed.[62]
Interracial groups were formed at various points in the South: in
Atlanta, Georgia; Nashville, Tennessee; and other places. In one
college in Virginia, an interracial commission of students coöperated
with the townspeople in considering the problem of better schools
for Negro children.[63] Some groups were formed of the two races
unitedly studying subjects of common interest.[64] Again, in the
South and Southwest, some of the white and Negro students who
were attending certain conventions used the same Pullman cars.[65]
In the Southwest, also, following one of the joint summer
conferences of the Intercollegiate Y.M.C.A. and Y.W.C.A. for
that area, the council representing these two groups sent to the
governors of five States letters concerning race problems. These
letters called attention to recent mob violence in that area and expressed "the conviction that race relations should be improved by
increased activity of the interracial commissions." At the same time,
the council offered its services in helping to create public opinion
against mob violence and on behalf of equal justice in the courts to
all races.[66] In several instances students manifested their convictions on racial questions at the expense of estrangements within their
own families and of criticism within their clubs.[67]

Industrial Problems

Interest in industrial questions, at first expressed largely through
the use of speakers on such issues and through summer industrial

[61] The Intercollegian, Vol. 45, No. 9, June, 1928, p. 272.
[62] For details on a significant conference of this sort, held at Chatta-
nooga, Tennessee, and made up of both sexes, see The Intercollegian,
Vol. 43, No. 4, Jan., 1926, p. 121.
[63] Miscellaneous Reports, No. 66.
[64] Ibid.
[65] Miscellaneous Reports, Nos. 30, 32.
[66] The Intercollegian, Vol. 45, No. 4, Jan., 1928, p. 111.
[67] Interview Document, No. 5.

research groups, came to manifest another emphasis also. There developed a tendency to take sides in conflict situations.[68]

International Relations and Institutions of War

In its program on international affairs, the Intercollegiate Y.M.C.A., along with the Y.W.C.A., carried forward a vigorous campaign on behalf of the World Court.[69] To the resolutions on international relations already noted [70] were added others on the institutions of war. The following strong protest against compulsory military training, passed by the National Council of the Intercollegiate Y.M.C.A. in September, 1926, is typical:

"Whereas, We view with genuine alarm the increasing activity of the forces and agencies of militarism which lead to war, retard the progress toward international good-will, and infringe upon freedom of speech and conscience; therefore be it
"Resolved, That we, the members of the 1926 National Council of Student Young Men's Christian Associations, do hereby register our emphatic protest against compulsory military training, (in other than technically military schools), as one of these agencies of militarism in our schools, colleges, and universities." [71]

A Crusading Spirit

Characteristic of such emphases was an attitude of mind in which the organization tended to become caught up quickly after the war—an attitude of struggle and crusading. An announcement

[68] For an account of the arrest of a member of the Intercollegiate Y.M.C.A. staff for this reason, see The New York Times, Vol. lxxix, No. 26,227, Nov. 14, 1929, p. 29.
[69] Cf. The Intercollegian, Vol. 43, No. 2, Nov., 1925, p. 46; also leaflet, Student Opinion and the World Court.
[70] Cf. p. 149.
[71] Miscellaneous Reports, No. 74.

for a summer conference in 1922 stated the gathering would convene with the

".... one purpose of helping college men fight through to conclusion in campus, life work, scientific, social, personal, international, and other problems which they in college and after college must solve. The call to the 1922 Hollister Conference is for men with the real spirit of the Southwest, who, as pioneers, are willing to pay great prices in order to prepare for leadership in the crusade for a Christian world." [72]

The college Y.M.C.A. secretaries in assembly in 1923 at Estes Park, Colorado, declared one of the purposes of the Association to be that of ".... making revolutionary Christians by stimulating thinking on international, social, industrial, and missionary subjects." [73] Again, the Indianapolis Convention (1923) was interpreted by some as successful because outspoken convictions developed there on military training led to an official reprimand of some students, of expulsion of some others, and a request for the resignation of several employed secretaries of college Y.M.C.A's. In one area of the country alone, it was reported in 1924 that five important local posts had to be remanned because of the local secretaries' attitude on race relations and the R.O.T.C.[74] A former employed officer of the Intercollegiate Y.M.C.A. writes,

"How often have I heard secretaries say, 'If I can but develop one revolutionary Christian this year I will be satisfied.' " [75]

With such a point of view, the emphasis in the program sometimes tended to become placed on reform, or radicalism, as such, instead of on the problem under consideration and the most effective means of bringing about change.

[72] Folder announcing the conference.
[73] *Report of National Student Secretaries Assembly,* 1923, p. 12.
[74] Miscellaneous Reports, Nos. 24 and 25.
[75] Letter Document, No. 1-A.

D. Other Developments

Movement toward United Activities of Men and Women

The experience of students working together at Indianapolis led to their desire for a continuance of a united approach by the Volunteer Movement and the Y.M.C.A. and Y.W.C.A. to the various problems. They felt that the time had come for advance through a united student movement. Students representing the councils of these three organizations met one day during the convention and voted, officially charging their leaders to effect such a movement.[76] Representatives of these three organizations, together with the "Fellowship for Christian Life Service," [77] met later to discuss means of effecting such a union. Federation, however, was deemed unwise.[78] The desire of the students largely came to naught, as one who was a student leader in the Y.M.C.A. at the time says, "with the loss of much time and money." As one result, however, the Intercollegiate Y.M.C.A. and Y.W.C.A., as well as the Volunteer Movement, soon began to hold their annual national meetings at the same place and time. Closer coöperation has also developed in other ways. Moreover, the "C.C.A." [79] was reconstructed and began to assume a much greater significance than formerly.[80]

To the joint efforts in such enterprises as the Student Friendship Fund,[81] the Bible-study program,[82] and the "C.W.E." Committee,[83] were added other activities, such as emphasis on behalf of the World Court. A very real limitation, however, to the significance of the "C.C.A." as a means for realizing the students' desire for a united organization soon became apparent. As is pointed out

[76] Interview Document, No. 25.
[77] Cf. p. 155, Note 31.
[78] *The Intercollegian*, Vol. 41, No. 9, June, 1924, p. 11.
[79] Cf. p. 154.
[80] Interview Document, No. 25.
[81] Cf. pp. 126 f.
[82] Cf. pp. 158 ff.
[83] Cf. pp. 154 f.

by Miss Jean Kennedy, a participant in the first meeting of the reconstructed "C.C.A.," this limitation lay in the fact that members of the "C.C.A." sat in the meeting as representatives of the Y.M.C.A. and Y.W.C.A. rather than as members of a united body.[84] The rôle of the members of the council accordingly became that, largely, of coördinating two programs rather than that of building a program for the two organizations as a unit.

Expansion of Denominational Activity

Immediately after the war the churches enormously expanded their work with students. In some cases they developed student summer conferences, as well as national student denominational organizations, one or two of which began to carry on their work without reference to that of the Y.M.C.A.[85] With such activities there was also a diversion of certain funds from the Y.M.C.A. This made it difficult, particularly in local units of state-supported institutions, to maintain a staff and program on the same basis as before.[86] The Intercollegiate Y.M.C.A., noting these developments, reported to the general Y.M.C.A. Convention in 1929 its conviction that ". . . . it is clearer now than formerly that there is a distinct field for such work and also for the interdenominational work" of the Y.M.C.A.[87] Findings were adopted in the convention urging that the whole task of the campus be faced by the various forces, and that there be coöperation and coördination.[88]

In 1928, the executive secretary of the Intercollegiate Y.M.C.A. said, "Whatever may or may not have been the case in the past, we can no longer carry on a vital Christian work along independent

[84] *The Intercollegian*, Vol. 42, No. 5, Feb., 1925, pp. 160 f.
[85] Miscellaneous Reports, No. 25.
[86] Interview Document, No. 8.
[87] *Report of International Committee to the International Convention of Y.M.C.A's.*, 1922, p. 56.
[88] *Report of Y.M.C.A. Convention*, 1922, pp. 242 f.

lines. . . ." [89] In keeping with this point of view, further efforts
have been made by the Y.M.C.A. leaders to effect coördination of
their forces with those of the denominational agencies. In certain
colleges, particularly in New England, some Y.M.C.A. secretaries are
employed jointly by the Y.M.C.A. and the Church Boards, and serve
in the dual capacity of association secretaries and college pastors.[90]

Reference has been made to the proposal that coöperation be
effected also through an official representation of Church Boards at
summer conferences of the Y.M.C.A.[91] Although this proposal
underwent changes, it did not on the whole prove satisfactory because church leaders did not feel that it made them an integral part
of the conferences; accordingly, the procedure has been largely
abandoned.[92] A more effective means of coöperation is found in the
fact that Church Boards were invited to elect members to the councils, charged with the responsibility of planning and directing the
Intercollegiate Y.M.C.A. work.[93] Other efforts toward coöperation
are found, as in the planning of a conference held at Milwaukee,[94]
and another on student-faculty relationships held at Detroit.[95]

One other factor needs to be noted. Emphasis on loyalty to the
Church, instead of on loyalty to the denominations, has been emphasized to some extent in recent years by certain of the Y.M.C.A.
workers with students.[96] Church leaders have urged, however, that
one cannot be loyal to the Church in general except by working

[89] Porter, D. R., *The Necessity of the Student Christian Movement*,
p. 9.
[90] Miscellaneous Reports, No. 29.
[91] See p. 125.
[92] Interview Document, No. 1; also Miscellaneous Reports, No. 76.
[93] Miscellaneous Reports, No. 25.
[94] See pp. 177 f.
[95] See pp. 194 ff. Another type of coöperative endeavor is found in a
special course of study developed in the summer school of Union Theological Seminary, New York, in the summer of 1930, for workers with
college students. This was sponsored by a committee including representatives of the Intercollegiate Y.M.C.A. and Y.W.C.A., and the Church
Boards of Education.—*See* pamphlet announcing the course.
[96] Miscellaneous Reports, No. 38.

through the denominations, and that, consequently, work of the Y.M.C.A. in which this attitude prevails makes for another denomination.[97]

Developments by Administrative Officers of Universities

Soon after the war university administrative officers also began to manifest greater interest in the extra-curricular life of students, reflecting the changed conditions in colleges and universities and the new educational emphases found in the post-war period. In some cases disappointment has been expressed in the existing religious agencies from the standpoint of problems peculiar to the institution. An example is found in a statement by L. B. Hopkins:

"The building of character, it is thought, is the duty of the home and the Church. But when organized religion breaks down, as it now has in the case of many students, the conditions are changed. The college is then confronted with a new problem, namely, that of enabling the student to work out a rational view of life which accords with the teachings of science but which also takes into account those higher truths of character which science cannot teach." [98]

Further,

"there is . . . . some difference of opinion as to precisely what it is hoped to accomplish. This difference of opinion frequently comes about because those who are the leaders in the religious organizations, while working for a common cause, strive also for the glory of the organization which they represent. . . . This error in emphasis of religious workers on college campuses has sometimes seemed to be so unfortunate as to demand some action on the part of the institution. . . ." [99]

[97] Interview Document, No. 1.
[98] Hopkins, L. B., "Personnel Procedure in Education," *The Educational Record Supplement*, No. 3, Oct., 1926, p. 63.
[99] *Ibid.*, pp. 92 f.

In not a few cases, the institutions have manifested this new interest in extra-curricular life by taking over certain service programs which were being promoted by the Y.M.C.A.[100] There has also been a further development with reference to the Y.M.C.A. Although its criticism of college and university life has called out appreciation on the part of some, occasionally it has been censured because of the issues which it was stressing and because of its manner of dealing with them. In the minds of many, the Intercollegiate Y.M.C.A. became "synonymous with race-equality, World Court, and anti-militarism." [101] In some cases the censure concerned the apparent fact that new convictions gained by students on controversial issues outran the development at the same time of skill in making their convictions effective without endangering the harmony and unity of campus life.[102]

Moreover, men have been added to the faculty of certain institutions with responsibility for developing their religious life—chaplains, deans of religion, or directors of religious activities. In some instances departments of religion have been created in which the history and literature of Christianity are being taught. In others, especially in state institutions, an effort has been made to meet these needs through closer coöperation with the forces of organized religion. Indicative of these general developments was a conference called by the University of Chicago Board of Social Service and Religion in May, 1928; for two days representatives of the "Big Ten" universities of the middle West discussed more satisfactory ways of developing the religious life in an educational community.[103]

Trend toward Smaller Membership

With these developments, there was at the same time a decreasing number of students participating in certain of the more tradi-

[100] Interview Document, No. 19-A.
[101] Interview Document, No. 8; Miscellaneous Reports, No. 33.
[102] Interview Document, No. 17.
[103] Miscellaneous Reports, No. 35-A.

tional program emphases of the Intercollegiate Y.M.C.A. As is generally known, evangelistic campaigns have been practically discontinued, particularly in the larger institutions. Charts show a decline in the Bible-study groups,[104] in the observance of the "Morning Watch," [105] in decisions for Christian life and church membership,[106] and in attendance at the summer conferences.[107]

Various factors contributed to this decrease of participation in the more traditional activities. Among these must be included the general disillusionment in the post-war period and the multiplicity of extra-curricular organizations developed after the war which absorbed the students' interests,[108] as well as the development by the Y.M.C.A. and Y.W.C.A. of "retreats" and small week-end conferences. The last-named have dealt with various themes, and have fulfilled to some extent the functions formerly discharged by the summer conferences.[109] Again, the fact that the Intercollegiate Y.M.C.A. membership came to be thought of in terms of commitment to certain "radical" ideas on controversial issues tended to

[104] See Chart III, p. 172. This chart is based on data assembled by the Bureau of Records, National Council of Y.M.C.A's. and from the Y.M.C.A. Year Books. The number of students in Bible study is recorded from 1885 to 1930; the number deciding for the Christian life from 1905 to the same date; the number observing the Morning Watch from 1917 to 1927, after which data on this practice were no longer requested. Although reports from several preparatory schools and professional institutions are included, the general picture is fairly indicative of developments in these activities with undergraduates, because the same sorts of institutions were included in the data for the years indicated in each graph. Data from the Canadian branch of the Intercollegiate Y.M.C.A. were included in the reports through 1921, but not afterwards.

[105] Ibid.

[106] Ibid.

[107] See Charts IV-A, IV-B, and V, based on data assembled from different sources (pp. 174-5-6). The decline in attendance at the summer conferences in the period prior to the economic depression is most marked in the Southern Conference at Blue Ridge, North Carolina, where the attendance dropped from 453 in 1922 to 163 in 1927.

[108] A survey of campus organizations and groups at Northwestern University in 1927 revealed a total of 125.—Miscellaneous Report, No. 30-A.

[109] Miscellaneous Reports, No. 66.

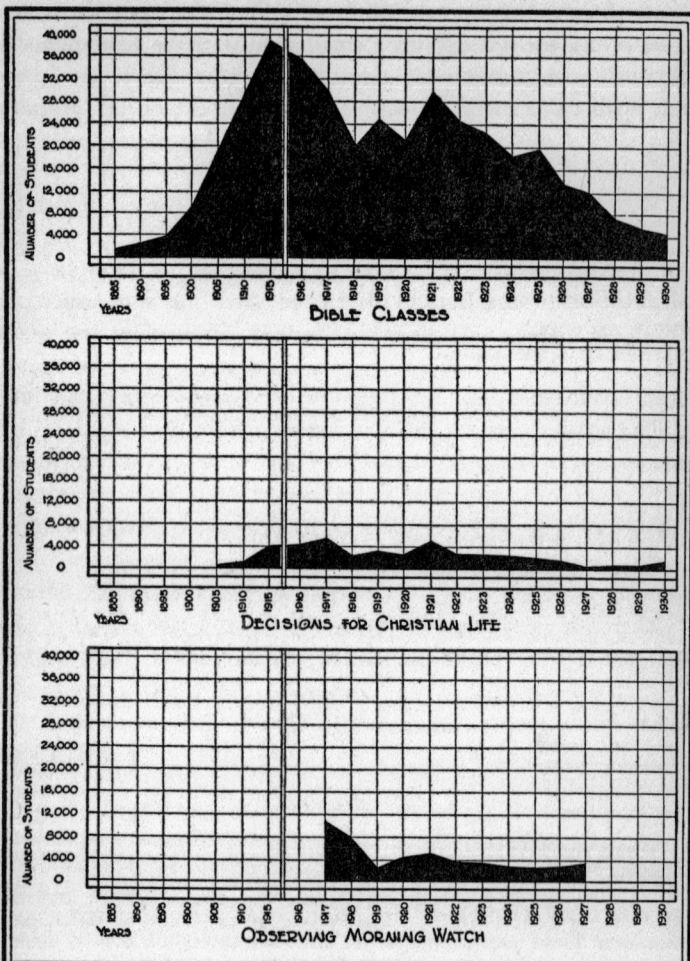

CHART No. III
PARTICIPATION IN CERTAIN ACTIVITIES
OF THE INTERCOLLEGIATE Y.M.C.A.

reduce the membership to small groups.[110] Indeed, emphasis came to be placed increasingly upon small groups as the best means of effecting social change. One leader in the Association formulated such a point of view as follows:

". . . . Concentrate on an intensive program and membership, in the hope that thus a quality of life will be built up in the fellowship of the local group whose contrast with, and superiority to, the common life of the campus will appeal to the more virile and able non-Christian student. . . ." Such a fellowship group will be radical in the sense that Jesus is for the members "the supreme fact of human experience. . . . It would be more interested in ideas than activities or organizations. . . .

". . . . Fellowship in the group would demonstrate a new basis for social relations—transcending race barriers, college cliques, caste lines created by fraternities, etc. . . .

"The group would serve as the center for creating a public opinion on the campus against unchristian practices and in favor of those which seem to reflect the mind of Jesus." [111]

There has been criticism within the organization of such a proposal for creating public opinion on the campus.[112] Nevertheless, the proposal represents a policy which has been greatly stressed by leaders of the Intercollegiate Y.M.C.A. in the post-war period.

Rôle on Campus

These various developments led to the question of whether the Y.M.C.A. any longer had a vital place on the campus. This issue was one factor leading to the planning of a national conference

[110] Interview Document, No. 17.
[111] *The Intercollegian,* Vol. 44, No. 2, Nov., 1926, pp. 48 ff.
[112] For example, see articles by H. E. Wilson and K. P. Zerfoss, *The Intercollegian,* Vol. 44, No. 2, pp. 47 and 48 respectively, Nov., 1926.

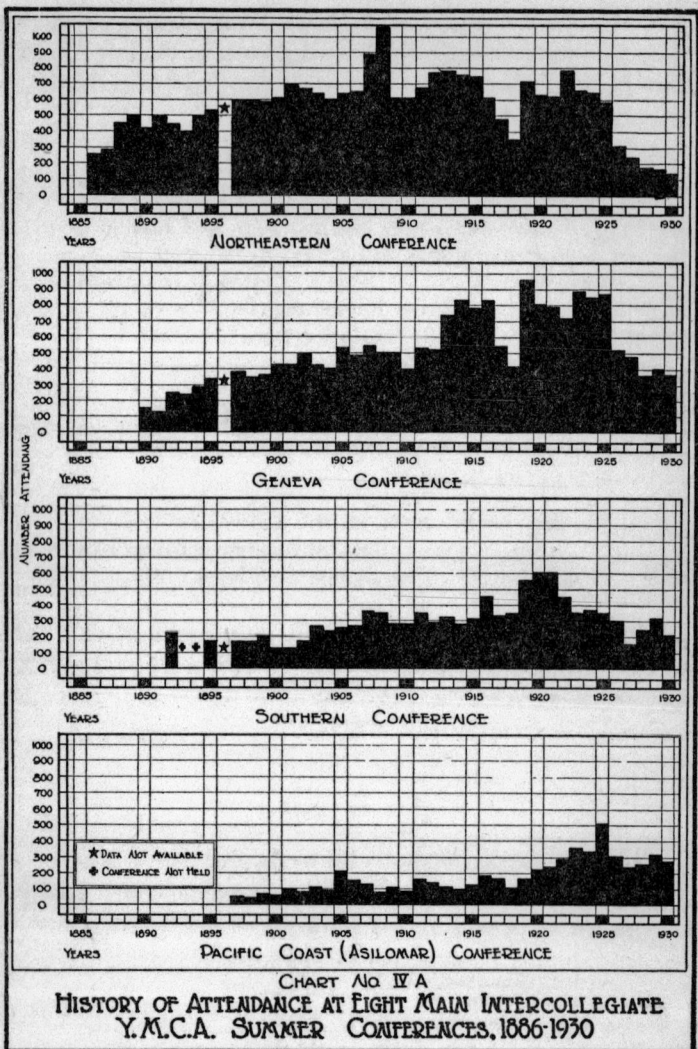

CHART No. IV A
HISTORY OF ATTENDANCE AT EIGHT MAIN INTERCOLLEGIATE
Y.M.C.A. SUMMER CONFERENCES, 1886-1930

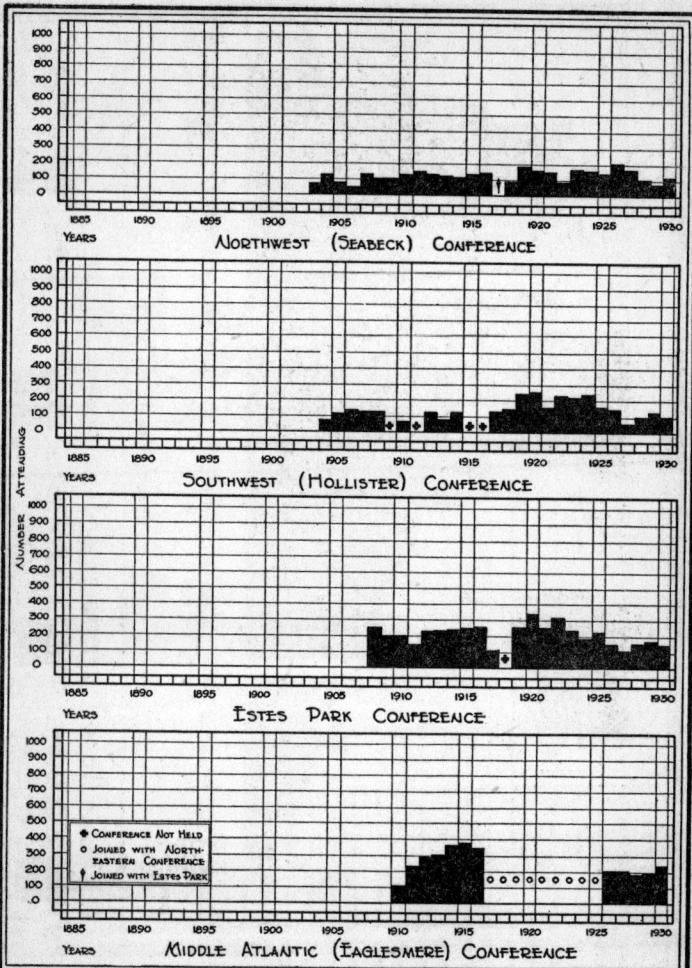

CHART No. IV B (CONTINUED)
HISTORY OF ATTENDANCE AT EIGHT MAIN INTERCOLLEGIATE
Y.M.C.A. SUMMER CONFERENCES, 1886-1930

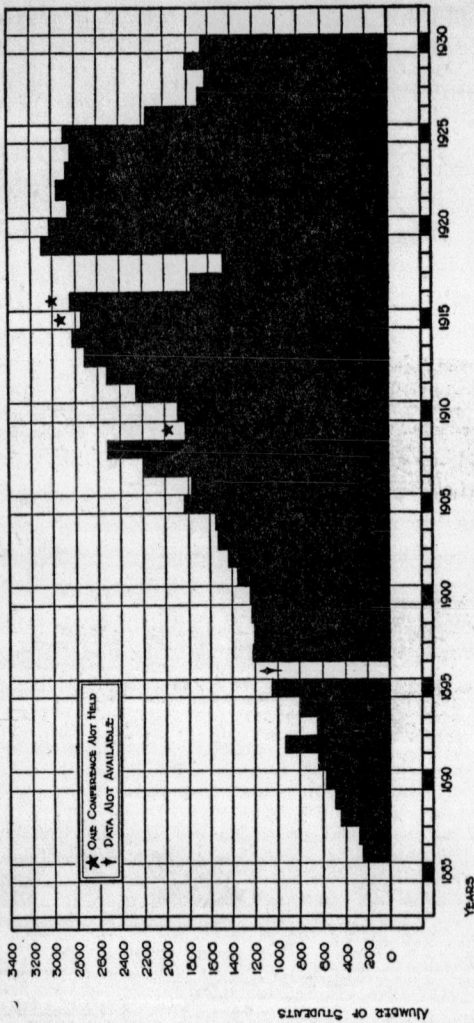

CHART No. V

TOTAL ATTENDANCE AT EIGHT MAIN
INTERCOLLEGIATE Y.M.C.A. SUMMER CONFERENCES, 1886-1930

at Milwaukee and it has received attention from time to time since then.[113]

First National Y.M.C.A.-Y.W.C.A. Student Conference: Milwaukee

In these various post-war conditions there was developed a conference [114] to carry two major functions. One was that of dramatizing the programs of the Intercollegiate Y.M.C.A. and Y.W.C.A., of their work together through their joint council, and of their united relationship to the organized work of the churches. The other function was that of furnishing a spiritual view of life at a time of scientific pre-occupation.[115] The latter purpose came to be expressed more and more, however, as an effort to furnish spiritual resources for "tired radicals." [116] This was attempted through addresses around three main cycles: "the accessibility of God," [117] "God the Father of all mankind," [118] and "divine possibilities of human life"; [119] supplemented by discussion groups following the addresses which were intended to carry each theme further; by exercises in corporate worship; by forums on such questions as science and religion, intellectual problems of faith, relations of men and women, military training in educational institutions, campus attitudes, and the meaning of prayer; [120] and by trips to industrial, civic, and social centers.

[113] Cf. Porter, D. R., *op. cit.* The question is also discussed in a pamphlet, *The Place and Function of Christian Associations in the Present University Situation,* this being the report of a commission appointed on behalf of the Y.M.C.A. and Y.W.C.A. to study the question.

[114] This gathering was held at Milwaukee, Dec. 28, 1926–Jan. 1, 1927, with a total attendance of 2500. See F. P. Miller *Religion on the Campus,* p. 131. In the statement which follows, however, the author has drawn principally upon his own experience as a participant in the conference.

[115] Miscellaneous Reports, No. 66.

[116] Interview Document, No. 21.

[117] Miller, F. P., *op. cit.,* pp. 11 ff.

[118] *Ibid.,* pp. 55 ff.

[119] *Ibid.,* pp. 117 ff.

[120] *Ibid.,* pp. 188 ff.

The discussion groups were generally considered a disappointment, especially so when it had been hoped that they would play a
"large part in stimulating creative thinking." [121]   In preparation
for the Indianapolis Convention, three years before, time and attention had been given to developing skill on the part of the leaders
in locating and considering problems of vital interest to students.
As a result, discussions ensued which created great interest and conviction. Not an equal amount of attention, however, was given to
this phase of the group discussions at Milwaukee. Moreover, it was
desired that the group thinking be developed around the themes
of the lectures, a fact which handicapped the discussions, because the
first of the lectures did not on the whole prove of great interest to
the students. Once, however, the addresses from the platform began
to deal with such ethical aspects of religion as international, racial,
and industrial problems, there was an outburst of interest.[122]   Also,
the opportunity for field trips for social and industrial investigation
were of peculiar interest to students.

In the afternoons, in addition to the forums, there were other
informal events which contributed to the value of the conference.
These included opportunities to meet foreign students at tea, as well
as to participate in discussions developed quite informally around
questions of special interest.

A conspicuous rôle was played by men and women students in
presiding at sessions of the conference and in shaping the program.
The various activities of the gathering, including an exhibit room
bearing evidence of coöperation of church and related groups,[123]

---

[121] *Ibid.*, Introduction, ix.

[122] *See* article by G. A. Coe in *The Intercollegian,* Vol. 44, No. 6,
March, 1927, pp. 159 ff.

[123] The following organizations and committees were represented in the
exhibit: Student Volunteer Movement; Intercollegiate Prohibition Association; League for Industrial Democracy; National Committee for the
Prevention of War; Missionary Education Movement; Committee on Militarism in Education; Council of Women for Home Missions; Women's
International League; Federal Council of Churches of Christ in America;

contributed also to the dramatization of the Intercollegiate Y.M.C.A. and Y.W.C.A. in their varied relationships. At the same time the conference activities tended to further the emphasis upon self-determination for the Intercollegiate Y.M.C.A.[124]

Foreign Division of the Y.M.C.A.; National Board of the Y.W.C.A.; Interracial Commission.—Miller, F. P. *op. cit.*, p. 196.

[124] Miller, F. P., *op. cit.*, introduction, p. vii. In the closing meeting a challenge was thrown out to the Intercollegiate Y.M.C.A. by one of the speakers to carry on its struggle for an autonomous movement. As we have seen, this was achieved some months later. *See* Chapter XII.

Chapter XIV.   NEW PROGRAM EMPHASES

THE foregoing chapter deals with program emphases which developed in the organization following the war and which at Milwaukee sought resources to carry them on.   It is necessary, before concluding the discussion of the post-war period, to indicate other emphases more recently developed and largely of a tangential character.

NEWER EDUCATIONAL EMPHASES

One phase of the new emphases was stimulated by developments in educational thought in the colleges and universities during the post-war period.   The organization was approaching the social issues in a "crusading spirit."   As a result, it secured among its constituency in many cases an adherence to principles without sufficient help on the practical problems involved in their realization.   There developed on the part of some, however, the feeling that such a method was not most productive in effecting social change, as well as the conviction that more attention should be given to the means of guiding the interests and idealism of youth into channels making possible more fruitful activity, with sufficient achievement and satisfaction to lead on to further significant activity.   Among factors making for such an attitude were not only the practical difficulties encountered, but also an emphasis in educational thought upon respect for the individual and his fundamental interests and purposes [1] —a principle which the Intercollegiate Y.M.C.A. stressed as "Voluntarism."   The significance of this point of view in relation to controversial issues was interpreted in a statement by Mr. M. H.

[1] For some of these developments, see the *Report on Undergraduate Education* of the Dartmouth College Senior Committee, 1924; and files of the paper, *The New Student*, started in 1922 and continued until 1929.

Bickham, at the time a leader in the college Y.M.C.A. work in the Central West:

"Student life in America has turned a corner. There is a developing reaction against propaganda. Students are showing a disposition to scrutinize all attempts to secure fixation of ideas through the use of propaganda methods. . . ." [The Association] "in the years since the war has been in a highly controversial atmosphere. . . . . Some have held tenaciously to certain convictions and have not scrutinized any too carefully the instruments by which these ideas were foisted upon others. . . ." [Some others in the Association have] "been blazing a pathway to the use of creative methods of sharing our Christian faith with others. . . . The educational process, in its true form, starts with respect for the personality of the student. Thus it is directly opposed to propaganda. . . ." [2]

APPROACH TO THE LOCAL ASSOCIATION'S PROGRAM

The implications for the Y.M.C.A. of this new educational emphasis were developed by certain leaders of local Associations and others in the "field." A committee of secretaries working with students in the Central West made an inquiry in 1925 into the distinctive function of the college Y.M.C.A. in relation to the total educational process.[3] The committee placed great emphasis upon "voluntarism" as the distinctive character of the Association from an educational point of view, and sought to establish criteria for evaluating the educational effectiveness of the local college association, as well as means for appraising its program in the light of these criteria.[4]

How this new educational approach took shape in one Association [5] is indicated in part by its employed secretary:

[2] *The Intercollegian*, Vol. 43, No. 5, Dec., 1927; p. 68.
[3] Hinckley, E, R., *et al.*, *A Study of the Present Position of the Student Y.M.C.A. in Relation to Higher Education*, p. 5.
[4] *Ibid.*, pp. 50 ff.
[5] Northwestern University.

[About 1924, the Association found itself unequal to] "the new ideas, the new ways, the new life that flooded the university. Oddly enough, our statistics had been steadily improving. Each year we took in more money, more members. . . . 'More' was our slogan. . . . . Meanwhile, university authorities inaugurated a series of educational studies to evaluate the curriculum and teaching methods. Educational experts were talking in terms of 'specific objectives,' 'student interests,' and 'purposeful activities.' Students and professors began asking embarrassing questions about campus organizations. . . . The Association had mastered the psychology of persuasion but not learned the psychology of participation. . . ." [The Association set as its goal] "the development of creative Christian personalities." [It defined its task as that of] "leading men through a series of such experiences or to engage in such projects as will develop in them the attitude, knowledge and capacity to meet life situations in the spirit and way of Jesus." [By means of a series of discussional or training periods, the Association determined on more effective means for studying, planning, and appraising the work. Thus did this Association seek to substitute for] "promotional methods . . . . sound, educational procedure." [6]

WORK OF THE "C.W.E." COMMITTEE

An expression of such a point of view in the national program is found in the more recent programs of the Committee on Christian World Education. The early emphasis of this committee was typified by the effort to create opinion favorable to the World Court.[7] More recently, however, the committee has sought to expose students to larger problems in which it believes they ought to become interested, at the same time bringing to their attention pertinent facts bearing on such issues; it has urged students to give expression to their interests and their convictions in some definite way, but it has not continued to insist on any one procedure.[8]

[6] *The Intercollegian*, Vol. 45, No. 1, Oct., 1927, p. 20.
[7] Cf. p. 164.
[8] Interview Document No. 5. See leaflet, *Christian World Education Service*, Jan., 1929. Other activities pertaining to international affairs promoted by the "C.W.E." Committee include model League of Nation assem-

Special attention has been given to institutes on "Christian world education." A conspicuous development of such a type of program occurred in February, 1928, in colleges of Virginia in sixteen institutes of two days each and in four shorter ones. These were developed with the purpose of helping students think through what it means to live as a Christian in the modern complex civilization; to start them thinking on new issues; and to supplement the work done in the college curriculum. The topics included international relations and foreign policy, missions, race relations, industry, prohibition, and modern interpretations of religion. These were discussed through regular classes offered for the purpose, through assemblies and chapels, and through voluntary meetings. Supplementary means included exhibits and displays of books and other literature. Some twenty persons from twelve organizations assisted. Four or five speakers were on a campus at one time and were often followed by a quartet of Negro students or a prominent Negro educator.[9] Although controversial issues were dealt with very frankly, the outcome was considered quite successful and acceptable, due largely to the participation in the planning on the part of students, faculties, and administrative officers.[10]

The "C.W.E." Committee has given attention also to missionary emphases as revealed in the development of a Joint Committee on Missions representing the "C.W.E." Committee and the Student Volunteer Movement. In this connection the "C.W.E." Committee has supplmented the work of the Student Volunteer Movement in helping to recruit students for foreign service; but it has done so only by presenting the specific jobs to be filled, not by soliciting volunteering in general for foreign service.[11] Along with the Stu-

blies (fifteen were sponsored by the committee in 1928-29) and the publishing of a monthly digest for students of pertinent international news, including special numbers on such issues as the Cruiser Bill and the Kellogg Pact.—Miscellaneous Reports, No. 28.

[9] Miscellaneous Reports, No. 34.
[10] Miscellaneous Reports, No. 35.
[11] Interview Document, No. 5.

dent Volunteer Movement, the "C.W.E." Committee has sought also to develop a better approach to the means of locating desirable candidates for foreign posts by soliciting the help of personnel agencies in colleges and universities.[12]   Again, efforts have been made to stimulate gifts of funds for foreign mission projects of the churches and of the Y.M.C.A. and Y.W.C.A., as well as for special interests represented by the World's Student Christian Federation. Moreover, the missionary interest has been borne in mind by the "C.W.E." Committee in its preparation of special study texts.[13]   Indeed, as is generally known, some of the most influential leaders in the Intercollegiate Y.M.C.A. would have the missionary emphasis the dominant one of the committee.   In contradiction to the point of view represented by other emphases in the program of the committee, they urge that the Intercollegiate Y.M.C.A. can be most vital or can call itself a "Christian" movement only by projecting a pronouncedly missionary program.[14]   The extent, therefore, to which the newer approach represented by the committee will become operative at this point remains to be seen.

ECONOMIC QUESTIONS

The new emphasis in the method of dealing with controversial issues has been found also in the approach to the economic problems. At the summer conference at Blue Ridge, North Carolina, in 1929, two points of view in the conflict on the textile situation were presented.   One of the speakers was a representative of the Brookwood Labor College, and the other, a cotton-mill operator.[15]   Again,

[12] *Ibid.*
[13] These include the following:

Fleming, D. J., *Whither Bound in Missions,* 1925; Wrong, M., *Ideals and Realities in Europe,* 1925; *Christian Principles and the Problems of the Pacific,* 1926; Fleming, D. J., *Attitudes Toward Other Faiths,* 1928; and Fleming, D. J., *Ways of Sharing Other Faiths,* 1929.

[14] Interview Document, No. 11.
[15] *Report of the General Board to the Meeting of the National Council, Y.M.C.A's.,* 1929, p. 29.

a significant contribution has been made by a commission [16] appointed by the council of the two associations to study the question of a Christian student's attitude "toward his own personal economic life and toward the entire present economic order." [17]

The study seeks to make available some of the areas in which students may effect social and economic changes. It is offered, however, as a source book, with the thought of raising "many questions, each requiring genuine thinking and honest research," [18] and of stimulating discussion of such questions as its six chapters suggest: "Economic Implications of Being a Student"; "Individual Spending, Income, and Ownerhip"; "Economic Aspects of Vocational Choice and Planning"; "Students and Modern Industry"; "The Contribution of the Coöperative Movement"; and "Toward a New Economic Order."

RACE RELATIONS

Another area in which a changed approach is found is in the manner of dealing with the question of race relations, particularly in the South. It was realized that the development of a right attitude on the part of all involved a slow, educational process. The interracial emphasis, accordingly, was taken up with smaller groups of interested students; in some cases both white and Negro students meeting together to discuss ways and means of furthering such a program. Another type of development is seen in the holding of a summer camp, where an equal number each of interested Negro and white students met in comradeship. In this case, they came together not to discuss the race question, but other questions of common concern to both. "We found," said one in reporting this event, "that the most important contribution to interracial emphases

[16] See the results of the commission's study, Francis Henson, editor, *Toward a New Economic Society,* 1931.
[17] *Ibid.,* p. 6.
[18] *Ibid.,* p. 7.

is made by efforts of this sort rather than by dealing directly with
the race question itself." [19]

Work With Individuals

Again, a new approach is found in work with individuals. The
force of this emphasis was sufficiently strong by the time of the
Milwaukee Conference to call out an interpretation of its character
in an address at the gathering.[20] Discussing "The Findings of
Modern Psychology and the Potentiality of Human Life," Professor
Harrison S. Elliott emphasized the significance, not only of the bio-
logical inheritance, but also of one's experience in life as an important factor in shaping one's personality. "A free, growing,
healthy personality is an achievement, dependent upon a proper kind
of experience." [21] Human characteristics are modifiable and specialists are now available to help as consultants on how to develop sane,
normal personality. Accordingly, various sorts of personal problems
—marital difficulties, nervous disorders, problems of temper—are
now being treated in a scientific manner.[22] Individuals have possibilities of growth and development far beyond their present attain-
ment.[23] Moreover, human beings have within themselves the
capacities for their own improvement.[24] ". . . . The science of
psychology, dealing as it does with human personality, of course,
necessitates a re-thinking of religion. . . ." [Yet] "no scientist
claims to create the resources for human life and endeavor. He
discovers them and finds the conditions for their release. . . ." [25]

An example of how this emphasis has found expression in the
work is seen in the program of the summer conference at Geneva,

[19] Interview Document, No. 17.
[20] *See* Miller, F. P., *op. cit.*, pp. 143 ff.
[21] *Ibid.*, p. 150.
[22] *Ibid.*, p. 151.
[23] *Ibid.*, p. 153.
[24] *Ibid.*, p. 154.
[25] *Ibid.*, p. 158.

Wisconsin, in 1929, when a psychiatrist and specialists in psychology were used to present the point of view and to counsel with students.[26]   It is seen also in other phases of the program which follow.

RELATIONS OF MEN AND WOMEN

The relations of men and women constitute another area revealing changes.   Following the war, there was a marked challenge by youth of old standards concerning sex.   The new spirit of freedom, the growing attention to the sex life of women, and the emphasis upon the need of one sex for the other in comradeship and labor—these factors led to notable changes in relationships of men and women.[27]

Such changes in attitudes and interests of students are registered in the summer conferences of the Y.M.C.A.   Beginning in 1919, questions of race, industry, and international relations were considered in the summer gatherings and remained prominent for the next six years.   During this period in one of these conferences (at Silver Bay, New York), some 300 of the delegates each year elected these questions for special consideration.   In 1930, however, in the conference which succeeded that one, only a total of 20 out of 525 elected groups on war and industry and race relations, while discussions at the same time on the relations of men and women drew 80.[28]

The Intercollegiate Y.M.C.A. made a very real contribution in connection with this new interest by publishing in 1923 a text by A. Herbert Gray,[29] who was greatly influenced by the new psychological emphases.   Later, in response to requests from the field, the Y.M.C.A. and Y.W.C.A. appointed a commission to study

[26] Interview Document, No. 14.
[27] See Eddy, S., Sex and Youth, tentative edition, Doubleday, Doran & Co., 1928, p. 9; also, Gray, A. H., Men, Women and God, Chap II.
[28] Interview Document, No. 24.
[29] Gray, A. H., op. cit.

the whole question. As a result another text [30] was published in 1929, showing further advance. An effort has been made to guide the sexual urge into its wider significance. The new term which came to be used—"men-women relations"—connotes in itself a changed point of view. It is significant also that a woman, Dean Irma E. Voight, of Ohio University, led the discussions at the Geneva summer conference in 1925 for men on the question of the relations of men and women.[31] The same year a joint summer conference of men and women, the first of its kind, was held at Estes Park, Colorado,[32] and others were soon started in the Southwest and in the middle Atlantic area. These grew up from close coöperation of the men's and women's student councils in their respective areas—a development motivated by the conviction that the problems common to men and women are more important than those restricted to either group alone. In addition, there were small joint conferences of men and women which began in New England in 1924 for the discussion of religious problems.[33]

VOCATIONAL EMPHASES

Special attention has been given to vocational problems also. It will be recalled that prior to the war the Intercollegiate Y.M.C.A. had, under the force of the social gospel, come to emphasize the dignity of all work and to urge that all vocations be approached with the same earnestness.[34] During and immediately following the war great stress came to be laid again upon recruiting for foreign-missionary and other Christian callings.[35] More recently, however, the emphasis enunciated prior to the war has been taken up increasingly

[30] *The Sex Life of Youth,* by Grace Loucks Elliott and Harry Bone, Association Press.
[31] Miscellaneous Reports, No. 29-A.
[32] Interview Document, No. 20.
[33] Miscellaneous Reports, No. 26.
[34] *See* pp. 93 ff.
[35] *See* pp. 129 ff.

again and supplemented by specific means for the study of the individual. A pamphlet published in 1922 by the Intercollegiate Y.M.C.A., although still influenced by stress on recruiting primarily for Christian callings, revealed new approaches. Emphasis now came to be placed more on helping students find themselves and the vocation for which they were fitted, to that end using tests, analysis blanks, personal interviews, and "laboratory conferences." [36]

The interpretation of divine guidance, which for a long time included stress upon a particular type of emotional experience, was given a new content in 1925 by one of the employed secretaries in the field:

"Finding that form and place of life-service in which one's true capacity, society's real need, and the fullest development of one's own personality unite—that is God's will." [37]

Moreover, it was recognized that the vocational question "is inextricably interwoven with the other great problem areas which a student has, and must be met by some united approach." [38] The question was approached more and more from the same point of view by the employed college secretaries in their assemblies. In 1929 the assembly adopted a program for the local Association to include occupational information, lectures for freshmen, campus surveys to discover student needs, interviews, personal history records, and bibliographies.[39]

In some of the summer conferences, also, there has been a conspicuous development of this emphasis. This began with an experiment in 1925 at the Geneva summer conference, when a plan for more thorough-going interviewing on vocations was carried through. Experts on personnel coached a group of vocational counselors, who

[36] See Tinker, W. H., Life Work (pamphlet).
[37] Pence, O. F., The Intercollegian, Vol. 42, No. 7, April, 1925, pp. 253 f.
[38] Ibid., Vol. 42, No. 6, March, 1925, pp. 175 f.
[39] Report of The National Assembly of Student Secretaries, 1929, pp. 13 f.

in turn interviewed the students desiring such help.[40]   Two years later, at the same conference, a more elaborate plan was developed under specially-trained leadership; fifteen university counselors advised sixty-eight students during the period of the conference. The average number of interviews per student was five; and the average number of hours given to each of the sixty-eight students was four and two-tenths. The work of each counselor was carried forward in the following sequence: acquaintance interview, careful study of personal history record (which had been prepared in advance), interest analysis, special readings, and final suggestions for inquiry. This was followed up in some cases by referring the counselees to particular persons for further consultation. Underlying the effort was strong emphasis upon the principle of vocational self-determination.[41]

In 1928 this plan was greatly extended at the conference at Blue Ridge, North Carolina. Some twenty-five counselors were secured from among the faculties in the South who were regarded as "the nucleus of the conference emphasis upon a Christian personnel service" in that area. Along with attempts to present to the entire gathering a more progressive view of vocation, including the elements of a sound vocational philosophy, steps were taken, as at Geneva, for individual counseling of students. Sixty-one students received such individualized attention. An effort was made in some of the general conference sessions to stimulate an aggressive attitude of search on the part of the student. Precaution was taken, however, to guard against early decisions and, most of all, decisions at the conference itself.[42]

---

[40] Miscellaneous Reports, No. 27.
[41] Pence, O. E., "A report of a vocational emphasis in the 1927 Lake Geneva Student Conference" (Unpublished statement).
[42] Leaflet, *Life Guidance Project,* announcing the 1929 Conference at Blue Ridge, North Carolina; also Letter Document, No. 11.

APPROACHES TO RELIGIOUS EXPERIENCE

Accompanying these developments and the decline of certain of the more traditional program activities of the organization,[43] there have been increasingly perceptible new approaches to religious values. In the early days the Intercollegiate Y.M.C.A. was developed strictly within the stream of Protestant life, but that no longer holds true, for reasons pointed out by Professor H. P. Van Dusen:

". . . . Many of the most arresting and possibly the most significant movements of Christian life are on the far fringes of the main stream of Protestant life. If the college student is . . . . gripped by religion, it is quite likely to be by some movement quite out of the current of conventional Christianity. . . ." [But there is a] "steadily growing interest among students" [in a rational interpretation of life's meaning; others are interested in a] "richer experience of life, especially an experience of beauty and wholeness and self-realization." [44]

An example of this fact is found in a small conference of the Intercollegiate Y.M.C.A. which set for itself the task of "seeking what discipline of life is needed in order to bring about the integration of personality which results eventually in the only satisfactory freedom in life." [45] It is found in other small conferences developed with such themes as the "Christian technique of living," [46] and "Finding One's Self in the Modern World," [47] as well as in the theme of the 1930 summer conference at Asilomar, California, "The Good—The True—The Beautiful," and in new and varied types of worship programs at the same conference.[48] Again, in the united men's-women's conferences at Estes Park, Colorado, and Hollister,

[43] *See* pp. 170 ff.
[44] *The Student World,* Vol. 22, April, 1929, p. 163.
[45] Miscellaneous Reports, No. 40.
[46] Miscellaneous Reports, No. 36.
[47] *Ibid.,* No. 36-A.
[48] Leaflet announcing the conference.

Missouri, worship services have been developed around the problems and situations which the students were facing.

The changing attitude of students with reference to religious experience is seen further in a questioning of the more traditional assumptions. Of the summer conference held in 1925 at Estes Park, one of the students who helped to plan it said:

"Nothing was assumed except that, faced with the facts and given an opportunity to discuss them, a group of students came to sound conclusions. . . . Not even Christ or God was taken for granted. . . ." [49]

With this attitude has gone one of inquiry and a trend toward a new vocabulary of religion, as seen in criticism by students of the basis of membershhip which was last adopted.[50]   On this point the field council of the Intercollegiate Y.M.C.A. in the Central area said in 1928:

"The present statement of purpose creates a bad . . . . reaction.   The verbs 'lead,' 'promote,' 'influence,' imply that the Y.M.C.A. members are better, have arrived, and know how to show others the way.   Members do not want to be put in such a hypocritical or a holier-than-thou relationship.   [What is desired is mutual sharing.]

"Students object to the theological language. . . . 'Faith,' 'the will of Christ,' and 'Kingdom of God' are not found in the vocabulary of the present student generation.   These phrases are reminiscent of a formula of salvation which has had its vogue . . . . but which is decidedly distasteful. . . .

"It gives . . . . the impression . . . . that the Y.M.C.A. exists chiefly for the purpose of getting students to go to church, read their Bibles and to pray. . . . Students are tremendously interested in, and challenged by, the issues of life.   They are not much . . . . concerned about the traditional 'means of grace.' . . ." [51]

[49] Hanson, R., The Intercollegian, Vol. 43, No. 1, Oct., 1925, p. 21.
[50] This was in 1922. See p. 141, Note 7.
[51] Miscellaneous Reports, No. 75.

The same statement indicates also a tendency to make the membership less exclusive and more inclusive. Nor is this attitude confined
to students. A member of the Intercollegiate Y.M.C.A. staff on
the Pacific Coast would have the membership include all who "are
drawn by the principles of Jesus, whether they be Protestant, Catho-
lic, Morman, or Jew!" [52]

ATTENTION TO CORPORATE LIFE

The new emphases in program have also led to increasing recognition of the importance of the corporate life of the institution in
moulding the personalities of students. Accordingly, as suggested
by Mr. W. W. Mendenhall, formerly related to the college
Y.M.C.A. work in the state of Indiana, the college Y.M.C.A. has
been urged to rethink its rôle on the campus in terms of the total
life of the institution.[53] Mr. Mendenhall goes on to recommend
coöperative endeavor between the Association and the faculty and
administrative officers:

". . . . To gear the Association's contribution into the complex
program of college life demands more educational and moral perspective than is possessed by most undergraduates. Unfortunately
our practice in too many institutions . . . . has been to exclude
our administrative friends from useful participation. . . . The Association becomes isolated, a section of an 'outside' movement."
[Yet] . . . . "when the college Association ceases to be a 'movement of students and faculty' it ceases to be 'an indigenous campus
movement.' . . . The administration greatly needs the coöperating
help of any organization that develops a true philosophy for all of
life's relationships and gives channel and direction to the voluntary
attitudes which sustain educational ideals. . . ." [54]

Association leaders themselves in the Central West developed
a program of research into the complex life of the college commu-

[52] Miscellaneous Reports, No. 37.
[53] The Intercollegian, Vol. 42, No. 8, May, 1925, pp. 253 f.
[54] Ibid.

nity. This was carried forward by a sociologist, who made a social analysis of the forces playing upon student life in a number of institutions, with a view particularly to making available to the leaders of each local Association visited, a more intelligent approach to their programs.[55]

The significance to be attached to the corporate life was to the fore as a vital issue in the meeting of the National Council in September, 1927. As a visitor at the meeting the author was impressed that a sharp difference in point of view was present between those who continued to emphasize "personal work," Bible study, and other more traditional approaches to personality development and a small minority from the Central West, who urged a program of "social engineering." Very soon afterwards, however, the Intercollegiate Y.M.C.A. began to develop a series of faculty conferences.[56] Although these were originated primarily with a view to securing recognition of the significance of the Association on the campus,[57] they also helped to make possible greater coöperative endeavor on the part of faculty members.

STUDENT-FACULTY CONFERENCE AT DETROIT

These developments were carried further in a conference of students and faculty held at Detroit [58] for the purpose of examining

[55] *See* Bickham, M. H., *Student Service Projects.* This development represents also a return to the problems of the campus as the field of major attention. In the South, "The Tool Kit," a special monthly bulletin, was started, furnishing resource material for the local Association leaders in developing their programs. The national headquarters followed soon afterwards with "Intercollegian Program Service" papers to help in a similar way throughout the country.

[56] Notable among these was a conference of some two hundred college presidents and professors held at Princeton, New Jersey, in 1928. Nominally at the call of a committee of college officials, the conference was initiated and developed by the Intercollegiate Y.M.C.A.—Miscellaneous Reports, No. 67. *See* report of the conference, Fisher, G. M. (editor), *Religion in the Colleges.*

[57] Interview Document, No. 25.

[58] December 27-31, 1930. Cf. Council of Christian Associations, *Education Adequate for Modern Times.*

American education and the implications of Christian faith in the modern world. The program was developed through a series of addresses on present-day interpretation of Christianity, as well as aims and procedures of higher education; through corporate worship; and through the work of seven commissions on "the administrative policy," "the educational system," "the social and organized life on the campus," "morals in a day of relativity," "social attitudes and responsibilities," "student counseling," and "the place of religion and religious agencies in student life today." [59] In the work of the last-named commission various religious agencies active on the campus were considered. The chairman, along with other members of the commission, was a representative of organized religious forces on the campus. The work of these commissions was significant. Although the time of preparation was undoubtedly too brief —only a few months in the colleges—preliminary discussions had been carried on in a large number of institutions. A preliminary inquiry had been made, gathering data from various colleges and universities about actual situations being faced on the campus. The procedure of the various commissions was determined largely by an analysis of such material from 150 institutions reporting.[60]

The distinctive values of the conference were not in any conclusions reached in its sessions, but in questions which were raised, in the spirit of coöperative inquiry and endeavor started, and in insight gained as to the possibility of new approaches to the life of the campus.[61] Indeed, in the Detroit Conference we see a return of the Intercollegiate Y.M.C.A. to a program involving in a large

[59] *Ibid.*, pp. 91 ff.
[60] *Ibid.*, p. 11.
[61] This is seen strikingly in one problem which became acute at the conference and which evidenced great confusion in dealing with it. Racial discrimination was manifested in the hotel which was host to the gathering. Consideration of the situation by the entire conference forced the delegates to appreciate more thoroughly the existence of such an evil, as well as the complexity of values involved in bringing about desired change, and challenged them to begin work on the issue in their own communities.

measure the issues of the college community with their wider implications; we see a return from an ultra-student emphasis to one in which the faculty not only participate but share equally with the students; and we see a program developed more largely in the spirit of inquiry, of sharing experience, as a means of realizing religion in life. Moreover, we see a program in which the forces of organized religion are active.

As a participant in the conference, the author felt the presence, however, of two essentially different points of view, which, although less marked than in previous gatherings, were still not entirely integrated. The addresses on religion dealt primarily with the Christian heritage, with an attempt to reinterpret its meaning today, and with means for maintaining and realizing that heritage in the individual and corporate life. On the other hand, there was underlying practically all the commissions the assumption "that there is a way of being intelligent that can be worship; that there is a way of looking even at tangled goals and tangled problems, so that the looking at them is religious; that there is a way of feeling other people's emotions that is religious; that there is a way of entering into the life of the world and the people around us that is in essence religious." That way is found in "the present generation," in "the honesty, in the fearlessness, in the courage, in the way in which it is tackling life." [62]

[62] *Ibid.*, p. 257.

Chapter XV. CONCLUSION

IT now remains to summarize the principal developments in programs and policies of the Intercollegiate Y.M.C.A., and to point out in conclusion the more important recurring and continuing issues in relation to these.

RÉSUMÉ OF DEVELOPMENTS IN PROGRAMS AND POLICIES

1. Period of Informal Beginnings, 1877-1890.

The general Y.M.C.A. was started by a small group of young men in an effort to help one another on the practical problems involved in living the Christian life. The same objective characterized the early development of the intercollegiate branch, begun in the United States in 1877. With its units starting in each case as a small, intimate group of students, the organization fostered mutual helpfulness, growth in leadership within the group, and expression of religious life in service toward others. These things were carried out in terms primarily of the prevailing points of emphasis of personal religion within which the organization developed—Bible reading, prayer, revivals, and personal evangelism. At the same time they were directed to very practical ends: the Bible was used as an aid in enlarging the group of professing Christians among students, and in an effort to stimulate a devotional life helpful on personal problems; the discussions in the Bible-study groups, as well as in the general "meetings" of the members, consisted largely of mutual testimony.

Underlying these activities was the primary objective to secure commitment to the Christian life. Although the point of approach was a particular problem, it was assumed that through "conversion" one was transformed in a general sense. It was from this point of view that personal problems were envisaged. The question of sex, for example, was approached in a way intended to secure renouncement of what was considered undesirable practice and to lead the individual to accept the will of God for his life. Moreover, it was assumed that such renunciation and commitment were indicative of a more general transformation which would carry over into other areas of life. Somewhat later the question of sex was often singled out for primary consideration, and frequently in a way which tended to imply condemnation of the natural impulses of adolescence no less than of overt acts.

The goal of securing commitment to the Christian ideal was determinative of the life objective of the Christian student. A pronounced emphasis was placed upon the "evangelization of the world" as the supreme vocation, and one's readiness to be a foreign missionary was deemed to be an essential and sufficient evidence of consecration, since this presumably involved the highest and most sacrificial decision a student could make. Accordingly, the organization participated actively in founding and developing the Student Volunteer Movement for foreign missions.

To aid in promoting the points of emphasis outlined above, young men were employed just as they were graduated from college to serve for a year or two as "secretaries" of the organization in several of the larger institutions.

2. Period of Expansion and Mass Impact, 1890-1910.

In the second general period of some two decades, beginning about 1890, the organization, under a staff of strong personalities, effectively standardized and expanded its program. To meet the practical problem involved in such development of the work, the organization departed in several respects from earlier procedures. With criticism that the work in the Bible-study circles was lacking in academic thoroughness, new studies of a more scholarly character were developed. Somewhat later, the Bible-study program was projected around a systematic exploration of the Gospels, providing at the same time for daily study, with the idea of securing in that way general illumination and dynamic for living. An effort was also made to popularize the Bible-study program in order to appeal to much larger numbers of students.

The desire to reach more students called out much greater emphasis upon mass evangelism, this method of work also being highly developed to secure decisions for Christian life. Through missionary conventions and summer conferences emphasis was placed upon mass recruiting for foreign-mission service and for other professional callings, which the organization began also to bring to the attention of students.

The rapid growth of the movement led to the idea that it provided a life work for the employed officers. Accordingly, maturer men were chosen as secretaries and processes were established for their training.

With the development and expansion of the work, however, a number of problems also became acute. One concerned the relationship with the general Y.M.C.A. Many of the Associations which were organized in the colleges in the early days had been made up of men and women; these had been reorganized with men alone because of requirements by the parent movement. Now other factors contributed to problems of relationship in this area. Difficulties arose from the fact that both the national and state agencies of the Y.M.C.A. were interested in the college work and that both were seeking to supervise it. There was also the feeling on the part of some that the distinctive student program was made subservient to that of other kinds of Y.M.C.A. work. Again, difficulties encountered by students and professors in securing commitment to the religious requirements of the general Y.M.C.A. led the college group for the first time to ask for a special membership basis which represented a more liberal theological approach to religious questions. The request was granted, but not without opposition within the general Y.M.C.A.

Relationships with denominational agencies presented another difficulty. While the Intercollegiate Y.M.C.A. sought to relate students to the parish church of the college town, it developed its own program on the assumption that the college constituted a community of its own and that the student grouping was the fundamental one. Denominational leaders felt that this broke the continuity of relationship which students had with their churches, and the question arose as to whether the student group approach or the church approach should be used. Various attempts were made to meet this problem. The leaders of the Y.M.C.A. (and of the Y.W.C.A.) maintained the basic position, however, that the religious life of students should be approached as a unit and that the Associations should be recognized as the organizations to make this possible. They insisted that the distinctive function of the Y.M.C.A. and Y.W.C.A. was leadership in the interdenominational field, and that in distinctively denominational matters the two organizations should coöperate with the regular parish churches; they urged that their movements be recognized as constituting the voluntary principle of student initiative.

One university Association sought to deal with the situation by unifying into one staff the employed officers of the organization and the employed representatives of the church bodies. This approach was later extended to several other university centers.

3. Period of Rising Social-Educational Emphases, 1910-1917.

The third general period, beginning about 1910 and extending until the beginning of the World War, reflected the influence of a rising social-educational consciousness. Social-service programs which had been started on the campuses in the preceding period now came to assume a primary emphasis. Attention was given also to an effort to have alumni continue their social service activities after leaving college, to the study of Negro life, to social evangelism, and to the study during the summer of social problems in city life.

Emphasis was placed upon the dignity and significance of all needed work, and it was insisted that *all* vocations be approached with no less earnest consideration than that associated with foreign-missionary service. Such a personal problem as sex was dealt with less through evangelism and more through a program of "sex education," which emphasized the possible contribution of the sex impulse to greater efficiency and character and fullness of life. The missionary program was challenged in a slight degree, but it remained for a later period to recognize the full significance of the new note.

Along with these points of emphasis there developed a new type of organizational approach to the campus. In its growth during the previous period the Association had become an all-campus movement, in many cases deviating from its small, intimate group approach and taking on the form of a mass impact in order to accomplish that purpose. As the student community became larger and more complex, however, the organization had to face the problem of how to extend its program effectively throughout the entire student body. It sought to do this through small groups of students in the residence centers—fraternities, dormitories, and boarding houses—and representatives of these different groups were selected and organized for the promotion of its program. The plan to combine the group approach with an effort to reach the mass of students was introduced also into some of the summer conferences and later into several of the larger gatherings.

Significant changes were also developed in the voluntary-study activities. These were occasioned by difficulties in maintaining interest in the Bible-study program, along with the problem of finding a place for the mission study and the rising social interest, as well as by the continuing question of relationship with the denominational agencies. Instead of continuing to teach the Bible as an end in itself on the assumption that this would thereby produce moral life, the problems and interests of students in relation to their changing experiences from their freshman to their senior years were given primary consideration, and biblical and other materials were used in so far as they were deemed to bear on the specific situations which students were facing. Moreover, the Bible, mission, and social studies were correlated into a single series of texts. Again, while these studies were prepared on the assumption that the college constituted a community with special problems for students, they were developed jointly by the Y.M.C.A., Y.W.C.A., the Student Volunteer Movement, and the Sunday School Council of Evangelical Denominations, establishing a high point in united endeavor. Coöperation among these various agencies in their work with students was carried further in special conferences beginning in 1915. Such activity, however, was arrested by the coming of the World War.

The question of relationship with the general Y.M.C.A. again asserted itself, this time in a call for "democratization" of the college work. This was expressed by the employed "field" and residence secretaries, whose rôle and quickly enlarged numbers had made them a significant force in the work. They asked from national "headquarters" a larger share in the development of policies and programs. The request quickly evolved, however, into an appeal to restore the movement to the student members. It was considered sympathetically by the general Y.M.C.A. and was destined to receive fulfilment later.

4. World War: Period of Transition, 1917-1918.

In the fourth period—that of the World War—there was a return of emphasis upon personal religion. A renewed impetus was given to the recruiting of workers for the foreign-missionary program and for other types of Christian professional leadership.

At the same time, however, the organization facilitated consideration by students of the social and world issues which the war made prominent. Moreover, from the very beginning of the struggle in Europe, emphasis was placed on sacrificial giving of funds for war sufferers. Through such means there was a quickening of social interest which was at the same time directed to the vast problems growing out of the international struggle. These emphases were destined to be felt in the succeeding years.

5. Period of Different Educational Approaches to Social Problems and Issues in Student Life, 1919-1930.

During the fifth and last period, beginning after the war and extending to 1930, the program of the organization was markedly influenced by the new conditions which the struggle occasioned, while magnifying issues already present.

With the war there grew up quickly a greater interest in the foreign-missionary cause, but the post-war disillusionment and confusion occasioned a challenge of its program. Dramatic expression of this fact was found in the Student Volunteer Movement convention held at Des Moines in 1919: some of the student delegates strongly criticized the central emphasis in the enterprise upon evangelism and demanded a more adequate basis for missions, a point of view which reached its climax at the succeeding convention four years later at Indianapolis. At the latter gathering, military training, industrial, racial, and international issues claimed major attention—so much so in fact that these issues were assigned thenceforth to the Y.M.C.A. and Y.W.C.A., while the Student Volunteer Movement continued the more definite responsibility of securing candidates for mission boards, and an intensive missionary program for interested students.

Within the Intercollegiate Y.M.C.A. attention became centered largely on social and world problems. Through textbooks on such issues; through the use of outstanding speakers with a radical point of view on social, economic, and international questions; through summer research groups on industrial issues; through interracial activities; through the Bible-study program; and through summer conferences and other gatherings the organization challenged students with the urgency of problems thrown into relief by the war.

Moreover, many of the leaders in the Intercollegiate Y.M.C.A. sought to influence the organization to become an agency for promoting specific attitudes concerning such issues. Programs maintaining a single point of view and partaking somewhat of an evangelistic or "crusading" spirit were developed with reference to them. One's personal loyalty as a follower of Jesus came to mean for many a commitment at any cost to a single point of view on social issues, as earlier volunteering for foreign missionary service had been the indication of complete consecration.

So earnest was the response that, as a result, some students were reprimanded because of their outspoken attitudes, some others suffered expulsion, and still others felt estrangement within their own families and clubs; moreover, several employed officers of the college Y.M.C.A. stationed on the campuses were discharged. Some critics felt that personal commitments on such questions as racial attitudes and compulsory military training often outran the development of skill in dealing with them, thus endangering the harmony of the campus life.

This attitude on social issues, the expansion of denominational activities, developments promoted by administrative officers of colleges and universities to meet the needs of students, and other factors led to a reduced number participating in the organization and in its more traditional activities.

Along with its program on social issues, the organization carried on at the same time a struggle of another sort. The emphasis during the war upon political self-determination accentuated an issue between the Intercollegiate Y.M.C.A. and the general Y.M.C.A. Out of the demand prior to the war for the "democratization" of the intercollegiate branch there developed a national council from within its constituency to give direction to the work. The problem, however, of autonomy for the movement again became acute with the reorganization of the general Y.M.C.A. in 1923. Threatening to withdraw from its parent movement, the intercollegiate branch in 1927 was given a status which met essentially the demands of its leaders, but not without some opposition within the general Y.M.C.A. At the same time the problem of relationship between the intercollegiate section and the state Y.M.C.A. committees remained unsolved.

The demand of the Intercollegiate Y.M.C.A. for self-determination was reinforced by the desire of men and women students to have a united movement—an interest which stimulated the organization of the "Council of Christian Associations" representing the council each of the Y.M.C.A. and Y.W.C.A. A means was thus established for clearing on enterprises of common concern to the Y.M.C.A. and Y.W.C.A., just as prior to the war the "Council of North American Student Movements" had been used by these two agencies and the Student Volunteer Movement for united programs.

These organizational developments, along with the results of the program on social issues, were brought to a focus in a conference of the Intercollegiate Y.M.C.A. and Y.W.C.A. at Milwaukee in 1926. The gathering was planned in an effort to dramatize the significance of the united endeavors of the two organizations, to strengthen their position with the Church, and to offer spiritual reinforcement for "tired radicals" on social issues.

Within the constituency of the Intercollegiate Y.M.C.A., however, were being developed other approaches to program which were found in their fullest expression during the latter part of the post-war period. Although dealing with various aspects of the work, they represent as a whole a point of view essentially different from the one just indicated. An emphasis during the period just prior to the war which directed attention to the situations facing students and which urged democratic consideration of such issues was now reinforced by developments in general educational thought. The proponents of this point of view insisted that greater respect be shown for the student's personality and interests and that techniques of participation be developed to replace techniques of persuasion. Moreover, they urged that attention be directed to the problems impinging upon the campus and upon the student, on the assumption that, if one dealt earnestly and thoroughly with these in their wider implications, one would most constructively guide the idealism of youth into a start on social reform.

More recent programs developed by the Christian World Education Committee of the Y.M.C.A. and Y.W.C.A. have reflected this attitude in the sharing of various points of view on world problems.[1]

In approaching certain industrial problems, both employer and employe have been heard. Consideration has been given also to students' use of their funds and to other campus problems in the realm of economics. In some cases in dealing with race relations, white students and Negro students who were sufficiently interested have been given the opportunity for fellowship together; in other instances various elements of the college communities—student, faculty, administration—have been invited to share in planning for constructive consideration of the question on their campuses.

Significant emphases have been expressed also with reference to personal problems. Questions of sex came to be discussed in

[1] Although the more recent program emphases of this committee have stressed current social questions pertinent to the experience of students, they have maintained an active interest in the foreign missionary program. Indeed, some leaders of the Y.M.C.A. would have the Christian missionary emphasis the dominant one of the committee. *See* page 184.

terms of "men-women" relations, implying the wider significance of the question. Problems arising out of the fact of one's being a student were stressed as more important than those of men alone or of women alone. Comradeship of the one sex with the other was emphasized as essential to desirable emotional development. Use of psychiatrists and specialists in psychology reveals also recognition of the inter-relation of all personal problems, or personality difficulties, as well as the need of seeking a more adequate basis for the remaking of personal life.

In vocations emphasis was placed on the autonomy of the individual and on such a program of guidance as would enable the student most intelligently to choose his vocation. In some of the summer conferences expert vocational counselors worked with other adult leaders in carrying through a program on this basis.

Less conventional approaches were made to religious values. For many the authority of the Christian heritage, with emphasis upon the more traditional expressions of Christian life, no longer continued to have vital significance; but religious value was attached to the mutual sharing of experience in dealing with vital issues in order to gain perspective, and to the exploration of vital resources in order to live more effectively.

Moreover, attention was directed to the complexity of the corporate life of the student and to the need of dealing more effectively with the factors involved in his situation in order to influence his personality and character.

Emphases related to this second general point of view were conspicuous within a student-faculty conference held by the Y.M.C.A. and Y.W.C.A. at Detroit in 1930. These are found in the development of a program concerned largely with the prevailing complex conditions on the campuses; with an examination of the moral assumptions underlying student behavior; with democratic processes for counseling students on personal questions; with a democratic approach to the changing of social attitudes, an effort which was brought to a focus in dealing with a specific problem of racial discrimination which arose at the conference; and with a coöperative effort on the part of men and women, students, faculty, and church leaders critically to examine the educational and religious values of campus life.

RECURRING AND CONTINUING ISSUES

There emerge from these developments certain fundamental questions which have been recurring and which continue as issues today.

1. Continuing an Intimate, Participating Group

One of these relates to the possibility of continuing on the campus an organization with such a method of approach as historically has been most characteristic of the college Y.M.C.A. Starting in each of its units as a small, intimate group of students marked by fellowship, democratic participation, and mutual helpfulness on the practical issues of the Christian life, it has had to confront difficulties in maintaining the organization on that basis. It has had to face the question of whether it would continue its earlier approach or whether for the sake of its adjustment to the Church it would give up its distinctive student or campus groupings; whether for the sake of its relation to the general Y.M.C.A. it would rule out those who could not commit themselves to the more rigid test of membership; whether for the sake of reaching larger numbers it would adopt a mass psychology; whether for the sake of continuous and efficient leadership it would transfer the volunteer workers' functions to an employed staff; and whether for the sake of accepting a place in the official expression of religion on the campus it would relinquish its emphasis upon its independent, voluntary character. Again, it has had to consider the question of whether it would maintain its original type or become a new sort of agency for promoting definite points of view on social issues.

In dealing with such problems the Intercollegiate Y.M.C.A. has been concerned with an issue now recognized to be of major significance in religious education. The possibility of development on the part of the immature demands a social fellowship where there can be sharing of experiences, of purposes, of aspirations, of values, and of responsibilities.[2] This necessitates a group relationship intimate and small enough so that one may really participate in it and at the same time grow in capacity to deal with the complex life of which one is a part.

This question becomes all the more acute today in view of the complex life in the colleges and universities. When the Y.M.C.A. was started, life on the campus was comparatively simple, and there were very few student societies. The organization served as a medium through which its members shared a wide range of interests and dealt with a variety of questions; it bore a corresponding significance in the student community. Today, however, the undergraduate student life is highly departmentalized, with special clubs and societies to respond to extra-curricular interests. A striking illustration of one phase of this development is found in increasing specialized promotion of interest in such issues as prohibition, interracial relations, international understanding, and industrial problems. This fact raises the question of the extent to which such promotion grows out of conditions inhering in present-day campus life, and accordingly whether specialized issues of this sort should be handled by the Intercollegiate Y.M.C.A. or entrusted exclusively to such more recently developed agencies for dealing with them as the Intercollegiate Association for the Study of the Alcohol Problem, the Interracial Commission, the Foreign Policy Association, and the League for Industrial Democracy. It suggests also the problem of the function of the Y.M.C.A. as compared with that of these more specialized agencies.

[2] *See,* for example, Bower, W. C., *Character Through Creative Experience,* Chap. III.

Pertinent to these questions is the further one of the extent to which the campus may continue to be regarded as a community making possible small, intimate groups in which ideals can be determined and life can be helpfully shared. The present-day problems and complexities of student life undoubtedly demand the help of adult guidance more than before; but in order that such aid may most effectively contribute to the growth of students, it must be made available in such a way as to enable them through exploration, experimentation, and evaluation of life better to understand the significance of their own experience. That necessitates the sharing democratically of mature experience by an adult leader with a group working coöperatively,[3] a point of view characteristic of the Intercollegiate Y.M.C.A.

At the same time, however, the very complexity of student life militates against a democratic approach to the campus. Moreover, the college and university communities cannot escape the implications of such challenges to democracy in our political institutions as are found in the dictatorial forms of government which have been set up in other nations and the feeling on the part of many that a similar type of government should be developed in our own country. Whether a solution for the campus life may be sought in the adoption of some form of mass psychology becomes a vital question.

How, then, under the complex conditions of college and university life it is possible to secure in the program of religious education the approach essential to the development of its youth is a major question with which the Intercollegiate Y.M.C.A. has really been dealing throughout the years; it continues as a vital issue today.

2. Relation to Work with Women Students

A second and related issue grows out of recent developments of programs jointly by the Y.M.C.A., and Y.W.C.A., and concerns the question of whether the campus groups should be co-educational.

[3] *Ibid.*, pp. 182-183.

The insistence by the general Y.M.C.A. in the early days that the mixed college Associations be reorganized with men alone was based on the assumption that the moral and spiritual problems of young men were of such a nature as to require segregation of the sexes. Moreover, women leaders were interested in developing separate associations for women students on the ground that they had a special work with women. This point of view came to be incorporated in the development of a general women's movement and in the desire of women to stimulate articulation and self-expression by members of their sex. It is still a force in maintaining an association exclusively for women. On this point a prominent Y.W.C.A. leader writes:

"It is my experience . . . . that meetings in which men and women assemble are without exception dominated by men. . . . Fine women thinkers . . . . because of the masculine atmosphere . . . . sit silently throughout the whole performance even though they demur against what might be on the docket. It seems to me impossible at this stage to overcome this fact. . . ." [4]

This is undoubtedly a factor which would need to be borne in mind in any thought looking to a closer relationship between the two organizations.

The situation with reference to the segregation of the sexes, however, has undergone radical change since the beginning of the college Y.M.C.A., and it is increasingly assumed that the development of wholesome personalities in the one sex requires comradeship with the other in more and more areas of experience. Moreover, attention has shifted from problems of an exclusively personal character to those involving social issues as well and demanding for their solution the best thought of both men and women. These changes, along with developments in co-education, have contributed to factors leading to united programs of the Y.M.C.A. and Y.W.C.A.

[4] Letter Document 8-A.

The basis of grouping in the colleges seemingly would depend primarily on whether the college Y.M.C.A. continues to organize its programs in relation to fraternity, rooming-house, and other campus groups, or around the larger social issues. Councils similar to the "Council of Christian Associations" naturally suggest themselves as means for developing united programs for the two sexes. This council, however, is made up of representatives from the governing body of each of the two organizations, and accordingly serves largely as an instrument for coördinating the program plans of each rather than as a means of building a program unitedly from the ground up. It would seem desirable to effect modifications at this point so as to provide for united initiation and development of activities of common concern to both men and women.

3. Relation to the Missionary Program

A third issue is found in the relation of the Intercollegiate Y.M.C.A. to foreign-missionary endeavor. Starting at a time of rising interest on the part of the American churches in the foreign-missionary program, the organization early extended its emphasis upon the proclaiming of a "message" for the individual to fields abroad. This emphasis was developed and given a large place in the activities of the movement until the war occasioned a challenge of the assumptions underlying the missionary program and also a desire on the part of other countries greatly to reduce the number of missionary workers. The problem, therefore, of rethinking the philosophy of missions is peculiarly pertinent to the program of the Y.M.C.A. With this, is the need also of determining the relative significance to be attached to foreign missions in the present-day program of the organization—a question on which there is difference of opinion. Although there is a general readiness within the movement to continue to relate students to the missionary program as one of the points of emphasis in dealing with world problems, some of its constituency would have most of the attention given to this area centered on missions alone, presumably believing that the degree of dynamic and vitality of the organization depend upon the degree to which it develops endeavor on behalf of this cause.

There is also the question of the organizational means by which the Intercollegiate Y.M.C.A. may project whatever missionary program it wishes to maintain. This was expressed formerly through the Student Volunteer Movement, but more recent developments within the latter organization relate its program less closely to the Y.M.C.A. (and Y.W.C.A.) than formerly; while the Y.M.C.A. and Y.W.C.A. are recognized as the general educational agencies on international issues, the Student Volunteer Movement has continued as the intensive missionary recruiting agency. Some within the Y.M.C.A. regard a closer relationship to the recruiting of missionary candidates as an essential part of its program. The problem is presented, therefore, of developing a new philosophy with reference to missions and the consequent rôle of the missionary program in the Y.M.C.A., as well as organizational means, or relationships, in order effectively to function in this regard in the future.

4. *Approach to Current Social Issues*

A fourth general issue has to do with the relation of the Intercollegiate Y.M.C.A. to social questions. The organization's stress from the beginning upon practical Christianity grew, with the development of the social gospel, into a pronounced emphasis by 1910 upon social service. Following the World War, the movement reflected an acute interest in social, economic, and international questions, together with a general change of emphasis from that upon social amelioration to that upon reconstruction of the social order.

The preceding pages indicate how earnestly the organization set to stirring students out of their lethargy with reference to such questions. It has sought also through the use of outstanding national figures as speakers to students and through other means to commit them to a radical viewpoint on social problems. These have involved such international issues as the World Court; such economic problems as conflicts between employers and employes; and other social questions such as racial attitudes and compulsory military training.

We have seen, however, how others within the organization, while claiming an equal interest in such questions, have urged that the most effective preparation of students for dealing constructively with them is found in concentrating primarily upon those current problems which impinge upon the campus or with which students are directly concerned. These would have students deal earnestly with such issues, helping them in every way possible with reference to questions on which they do take a position and for the consequences of which they must assume responsibility, to arrive intelligently at such commitments. They would stimulate students' interest in national and world problems and help them to become intelligent with reference to such questions, but they would not seek to commit students to promises of action where they are not closely enough related to the issues involved fully to understand them or the significance of commitments with reference to them. They have insisted that, in helping students to arrive at attitudes, emphasis should be placed upon the sharing of data and of various convictions with reference to issues rather than upon imparting conclusions out of one's experience and thought, and they have stressed a coöperative endeavor on the part of all in order progressively to find better solutions.

So far as ultimate goals, however, are concerned there are no fundamental differences, for all are working toward objectives which finally become the same. Differences in procedure, therefore, are confined largely to two points: viz., the question of what issues one should begin with and the method of how one should work with these. Some would start with the national and world problems on the assumption, apparently, that it is futile to deal with the immediate situations of students so long as the more inclusive ones remain unsolved. Others would begin with such campus questions as the actual class divisions within the student area, the racial issue, and the implications of military training, on the assumption that these are essentially the same in character as the more inclusive ones. As for the method of work, some would seek to stimulate primarily the acceptance of a radical point of view and the personal commitment of students to the program involved; others would endeavor to start students in an experimental process which will enable them to act with increasing intelligence and effectiveness with reference to social questions.

In view of the present economic and social crisis, the issue involving these differences in procedure becomes one of major significance and one which will undoubtedly play a large rôle in the immediate future of the organization. Unfortunately, however, the question of which of the approaches should be followed can be answered only in the light of the consequences of each over a longer period of time. It would seem that there should not be emphasis upon one type of social question to the exclusion of another, but rather that students should be enabled to see the implications for all social issues of the problems involved in any particular question with which they deal, whether it be a campus or a more inclusive one. It does seem clear, however, that attitudes with reference to any of the social problems can prove significant only in the degree that students develop skill in dealing with them; and that, inasmuch as this requires practice, it becomes essential that the individual face issues in the areas in which he can effectively take responsibility and feel the consequences of his commitments. Moreover, any passing over of campus questions in order to give attention to more inclusive issues would seemingly provide a possible means of escape from immediate responsibility.

As to the method of work, the author frankly confesses faith in a democratic, experimental procedure. He believes that where one maintains persistently a single point of view at any cost one is apt to ignore the complex factors in different situations which must be taken into account if these are to be dealt with most constructively. This is not to suggest that the Y.M.C.A. refrain from proclaiming to students social ideals of a "radical" or "prophetic" character. These are undoubtedly essential in order to challenge indifference or to present the claims for a point of view quite at variance with the prevailing one. It would seem, however, that these should be expressed as a part of a definitely experimental procedure of social education. Always the program should be appraised in the light of the results as to the understanding of the problem, skill in dealing with it, the attitude of all concerned, and the total outcome sought.

5. Development and Meaning of the Christian Life

A fifth general issue has to do with the approach to the development of Christian character and to the meaning of the Christian life. We have seen that in the Intercollegiate Y.M.C.A. program in its various aspects it was assumed that through "conversion" to the Christian life one was changed in a general sense. Personal problems were approached in a way intended to secure renouncement of practices deemed to be undesirable and to lead the individual to accept the will of God for his life. Consecration to the will of God, interpreted largely in terms of the missionary program, was deemed to be an essential and adequate objective for a vocational program as well.

Although such emphases may still be found in the Intercollegiate Y.M.C.A., the organization became a pioneer in the development of another point of view. This became formulated essentially in the recognition of the specific character of the problem of Christian living. A striking illustration of this development is found in the voluntary-study program. A decline of interest in pursuing the study of the Bible as an end in itself led to a primary emphasis upon the life-experience of students and to the use of biblical and other materials only in so far as these were deemed to bear on specific problems. This constituted a pioneer effort, at the same time, in developing a curriculum on a problem and life-experience basis and in utilizing biblical and other resource materials in the solution of these problems. Moreover, the need of a much more inclusive approach to the missionary program was recognized, with emphasis less upon evangelism and more upon the need of remaking society the world over.

Again, the earlier vocational emphases were no longer deemed adequate. Stress upon willingness to be a foreign missionary came to be accompanied by presentation of other professional callings as well. Then, with the rise of the social emphases, the Y.M.C.A. stressed the dignity of all needed work and sought increasingly to guide students into the vocations which their interests and the conditions suggested. This new approach was obscured for a while by a return immediately following the World War to a pronounced emphasis upon recruiting for missionary and other professional Christian callings, but was soon revived. The autonomy of the individual became more definitely emphasized, along with counseling procedures intended to help him most effectively to arrive at his vocation.

The approach to personal problems, also, underwent change. Emphasis was placed increasingly on directing the natural impulses into their largest possible contribution to life. More recently, recognition has been shown of the interrelation of personal problems, or personality difficulties, and of the need of seeking a more adequate basis for the remaking of personal life.

In short, the newer program emphases represent the culmination of a general point of view which was found alongside the modified form of the one with which the organization was started. These contrasting points of emphasis have been important in the development of the college Y.M.C.A. On the one hand, there have been those who have believed in such methods as evangelism, the use of the Bible, and "personal work" as effective means for producing character; on the other, those who have insisted on attacking specific problems involved in Christian living, along with an effort to deal more fundamentally with the problem of character development. On the one hand, there have been those who have emphasized specific vocations and recruiting for them; on the other, those who have urged a counseling procedure which places central emphasis upon the autonomy of the student. On the one hand, there have been those who have conceived of the missionary program in terms of evangelization of the world; on the other, those who have envisaged it as the building of a new world order. On the one hand, there have been those who would restrict the emphases of the Christian life largely to ways of validating, interpreting, and transmitting the Christian heritage; on the other, those who have thought of the Christian program in terms involving increasingly the whole gamut of personal experience and social relationships.

These differences in program emphases involve different points of view in education. The Intercollegiate Y.M.C.A. naturally adopted the educational assumptions prevalent in its early history; these centered attention on the inherited experience of the race and on means for passing it on effectively to the immature. There was the accompanying assumption that through the acquisition of knowledge concerning, and of principles growing out of, such experience an approved type of living would develop. Such a point of view was expressed by the Y.M.C.A. in its emphasis upon types of experience deemed to be standard in life, and upon modes of behavior intended to be regulatory means for duplicating such experience; in defining one's vocation in terms of such an emphasis; and in stressing factual material or principles of living—whether through Bible study, mission study or other aspects of the program—intended to insure their realization in conduct.

The voluntary character, however, of the Y.M.C.A. program,

the effort to deal in a helpful way with the issues of student life, and the practical adjustments necessitated in furthering the work have tended increasingly to shift the focal point of attention to the student himself. His attitude, his experience, in a specific situation has increasingly become the determinant of the program. Such a point of view now finds increasing validation in educational thought. The conception of learning in terms of the acquisition of knowledge is increasingly being replaced by emphasis upon learning in terms of experience. Particularly is this recognized in relation to the problem of character development. Moreover, attention is being directed increasingly to the learner and his experience at the time as the focal point in the learning process; and learning is recognized as taking place in the degree that the learner is actively related to the situation. "If a person makes a decision, in the degree that he goes into that decision . . . . he is changed and he has learned to be more responsible next time. . . . All the things he took into account made the change in him. The organization in his thinking, affected by the decision, integrates all the things that he took into account. . . . It makes a difference whether he assumes the responsibility for thinking it through or merely accepts a ready-made solution that someone sells to him. . . . In the latter case he learns to respond . . . . in more or less docile fashion to his external stirring up. . . . When we can get our young people more and more to think adequately of the meaning of what they are proposing to do, then we are building up in them, or rather they are building up in themselves, broader . . . . selves, and they are able to act more and more adequately in terms of what they think is worth while. So it comes to be a question of how we can get people to grapple with life on its merits, to find the merits and to decide for themselves. This is moral education. . . ." [5]

Learning in this sense, it becomes evident, can take place only

[5] Kilpatrick, Wm. H., "Life a Continual Novelty," *The Woman's Press*, Oct., 1931, pp. 598 and 610.

in concrete and specific situations. This conviction "is far removed from the traditional idea that learning has its beginning point in more or less abstract ideas which find their 'application' or 'expression' in some form of practical activity. It is equally far removed from the conception that an idea tends to pass over into action." [6] This is not to suggest that ideals or principles have little significance in one's behavior, but rather to point out that if they are to function in one's life, they must grow up out of, or find validation in relation to, one's experience in dealing with specific situations. "If a human being is to be honest or to have good will or to be reliable, he will do so only as he has worked out this way of action in situation after situation until it becomes a habit of life." [7] It is along the lines of such educational assumptions as these with reference to growth in character that the two general types of program have developed.

These assumptions, however, have significance not only for the basis on which Christian principles can be made effective in life, but also for the conception of the Christian life itself. By taking account more and more of the experience of the individual and of the factors conditioning his behavior—necessitated by the program adjustments in order to deal with the practical problems of the Christian life— the meaning of the Christian life has undergone a change. It has come to be conceived of as a determinant of conduct in emphasizing primarily the significance of personality and the obligation to seek its enrichment in the fullest sense; its specific program has become conditioned by developments in increased understanding of the factors controlling human response. In short, the Christian life has come to be thought of less in terms of a specific type of experience, or of one related to a particular time, or involving standardized forms of behavior; and more in terms of an inherently dynamic way of dealing with all the issues of life, with the immediate goals and processes in each case conditioned by the varying values and factors

[6] Bower, W. C., *op. cit.*, pp. 144-145.
[7] Elliott, H. S., *The Process of Group Thinking*, p. 5.

involved.   On this basis one is Christian to the degree that Jesus' valuation of personality dominates him, to the degree that there is inclusiveness and perspective in his approach to situations, and in proportion to the earnestness with which he seeks to find and utilize all resources from the past and present in dealing with the problems of life.

The issue is pertinent in view both of the disillusionment and confusion as to patterns of conduct in society, and of an intellectual atmosphere in the colleges and universities which is vastly different in many ways from that in which the Intercollegiate Y.M.C.A. started.   With the developments of science and stress upon its significance for all phases of human experience, a great many students are either not moved by the old "verities" or they are questioning their validity.   If religion is to become real for such students, it must be expressed in terms which are consonant with the new knowledge and the new experiences which they acquire.   Personal religion on such a basis becomes an effort to orient oneself to one's universe, one's cosmic and human environment, in search and expression of the most significant values in life.   Although there is a strong present-day emphasis in Christian circles which readily accepts this point of view,[8] there are other forces which stress anew individual Christian piety as expressed in the early days of the Intercollegiate Y.M.C.A.,[9] and the futility of human endeavor.[10]   Whether a vital religion can be developed with students which is wholly consonant with their present-day intellectual atmosphere, or whether it will become necessary to return to a type which is completely transcendent remains to be seen.   The experience, however, of the Intercollegiate Y.M.C.A. in its approach to the problem of the meaning and realization of the Christian life is pertinent.

[8] See A. Bruce Curry, "How Far May Christians Diverge from Jesus?" article in The Christian Century, Vol. XLVIII, No. 1, Jan. 7, 1931, p. 11.
[9] Cf. the "New Oxford Movement," also called "Buchmanism."
[10] Cf. the "Crisis Theology" movement.

These are some of the issues with which the Intercollegiate Y.M.C.A. has had to deal in its program of religious endeavor with students carried on during a period of more than half a century. The study is brought to a conclusion in a time of economic and social crisis, which will no doubt greatly influence the emphases of the Intercollegiate Y.M.C.A., no less than that of other movements and institutions. The problems with which the organization has labored, however, and its different types of response to them, with correspondingly different educational assumptions, are of such a character as to make its effort significant. It is suggestive of factors involved in a program of religious education with students today.

BIBLIOGRAPHY

Allen, F. L., *Only Yesterday,* Harper and Bros., New York, 1931.

Allport, F. H., "Social Psychology," Houghton, Boston, 1924.

Bergthold, J. W., *Christian Principles in Race Relations,* 1926.

Bickham, M. H., *Student Service Projects,* Association Press, New York, 1928.

Bower, William C., *Character Through Creative Experience,* University of Chicago Press, Chicago, 1930.

Brown, Arlo A., *A History of Religious Education in Recent Times,* Abingdon Press, New York, 1923.

Christian World Education Committee, leaflets on *Christian World Education Service,* Jan. 1929 (Council of Christian Associations, New York) ; *Scrap Book,* pamphlet, 1929, Council of Christian Associations, New York; *Student Opinion and the World Court,* Jan. 2, 1926. Council of Christian Associations, New York.

Coe, George Albert, *Motives of Men,* Scribners, New York, 1928; *Psychology of Religious Experience,* University of Chicago Press, Chicago, 1916. Report to the Faculty of Union Theological Seminary concerning the Student Volunteer Convention in 1920. Unpublished statement, January, 1920. Union Theological Seminary, New York.

Cooper, C. S., *Brief Historical Sketch of the Voluntary Bible Study Movement Among North American Students,* Y.M.C.A. Press, New York, 1908 (pamphlet) ; *The Training of Bible Teachers,* Y.M.C.A. Press, New York, 1910 (pamphlet).

Council of Christian Associations, *Education Adequate for Modern Times,* Association Press, New York, 1931.

Council of North American Student Movements, *The Denominations' Part in the College Voluntary Study Courses* (pamphlet). *Social Needs and the Colleges,* New York, 1914. *A Suggested Curriculum 'for Voluntary Study Groups in Colleges and Universities,* New York, 1913. *Voluntary Study Groups,* New York, 1913.

Curry, Bruce, *Facing Student Problems,* Association Press, New York, 1925. "How Far May Christians Diverge From Jesus?" *Christian Century,* Vol. xlviii, No. 1, p. 11, January 7, 1931. *Jesus and His Cause,* Association Press, New York, 1920, revised 1925.

Dartmouth College Senior Committee, *Report on Undergraduate Education,* Hanover, N. H., 1924.

Dewey, John, *Democracy and Education,* Macmillan, New York, 1916.

Eddy, Sherwood, *Religion and Social Justice,* Doran, New York, 1927. *Sex and Youth,* Tentative Edition, Doubleday, Doran & Co., New York, 1928.

Edwards, R. H., *Volunteer Social Service by College Men,* Association Press, 1914, New York.

Elliott, A. J., *Meetings for Christian Decision,* Association Press, New York, 1909.

Elliott, G. L., and Bone, H., *Sex Life of Youth,* Association Press, New York, 1929.

Elliott, H. S., "Christian Work in State Universities," *Report of Cleveland and Chicago Conferences,* 1918. National Council Y.M.C.A. Library, New York. "Historical Statement." (Concerning the development of the correlated voluntary studies.) MS, Library, National Council, Y.M.C.A., New York.

——*The Process of Group Thinking,* Association Press, New York, 1928; *Training an Adequate Leadership for Voluntary Study Groups,* Association Press, New York, 1918.

Exner, M. J., *Problems and Principles of Sex Education,* Association Press, New York, 1915; "Progress in Sex Education," *Journal of Social Hygiene,* Vol. 15, No. 7, Oct., 1929; *The Rational Sex Life of Men,* Association Press, New York, 1914.

Fisher, G. M., Ed., *Religion in the Colleges,* Association Press, New York, 1928.

Foster, John, *Decision of Character,* Student Volunteer Movement, New York. No date.

Galpin, C. J., Ed., *Church Work in State Universities,* Tracy, Gibbs & Co., Madison, Wis., 1910.

Goodspeed, Thomas W., *William Rainey Harper,* University of Chicago Press, 1928.

Gray, A. Herbert, *Men, Women and God,* Association Press, New York, 1923.

Hall, Thomas C., *The Religious Background of American Culture,* Little, Brown & Co., Boston, 1930.

Henson, Francis, Ed., *Toward a New Economic Society,* Council of Christian Associations, New York, 1931.

Hinckley, E. R., *et al., A Study of the Present Position of the Student Y.M.C.A. in Relation to Higher Education,* Association Press, New York, 1925.

't Hooft, W. A., Visser, *The Background of the Social Gospel in America,* H. D. Tjeenk Willink & Zoon, Haarlem, 1928.

Hopkins, L. B., "Personnel Procedure in Education," *The Educational Record,* Supplement No. 3, October, 1926.

Hurrey, C. D., *The Student General Secretary,* Association Press, New York, 1908.

Jenks, J. W., *Political and Social Significance of the Teachings of Jesus,* Y.M.C.A. Press, New York, 1906.

Kilpatrick, W. H., *Foundations of Method,* Macmillan, New York, 1925; "Life a Continual Novelty," *The Woman's Press,* Oct., 1931, pp. 597 ff.; "Statement of Position," *Twenty-sixth Year Book of National Society for the Study of Education,* Part II, p. 134.

King, H. C., *How to Make a Rational Fight for Character,* Y.M.C.A. Press, New York, 1901.

Loud, Grover C., *Evangelized America,* Longmans, Green & Co., Toronto, 1928.

Luccock, H. E., Ed., *Through the Eyes of Youth,* Abingdon Press.

McConaughy, James, *Christ Among Men,* Y.M.C.A. Press, New York, 1892.

McGiffert, Arthur C., *Rise of Modern Religious Ideas,* Macmillan, New York, 1915.

Miller, F. P., Ed., *Religion on the Campus,* Association Press, New York, 1927.

Moody, William R., *The Life of Dwight L. Moody,* Revell, New York, 1900.

Morse, Richard C., *History of the North American Young Men's Christian Associations,* Association Press, New York, 1913; *My Life with Young Men,* Association Press, New York, 1918.

Mott, J. R., *Bible Study for Personal Spiritual Growth,* Y.M.C.A. Press, New York. Not dated. *The Morning Watch,* Y.M.C.A. Press, New York, 1893. *Recent Developments in the Rela-*

tionships of the Student Young Men's Christian Association Movement to the Association Brotherhood. National Council Y.M.C.A's., New York, June 28, 1927.

Nevius, John, "The Student Volunteer Movement," *Missionary Review of the World,* Vol. 16, pp. 336 ff., May, 1923, Funk & Wagnalls, New York.

Ober, C. K., *Exploring a Continent,* Association Press, New York, 1929; *Luther D. Wishard,* Association Press, New York, 1927.

Pence, O. E., "A Report of a Vocational Emphasis in the 1927 Lake Geneva Student Conference," unpublished.

Porter, D. R., *The Necessity of the Student Christian Movement,* Student Division, National Council of Y.M.C.A's., New York, 1928.

Rauschenbusch, Walter, *Christianity and the Social Crisis,* Macmillan, New York, 1907.

Rouse, Ruth, *The Rebuilding of Europe.* Council of Christian Associations, New York, 1925.

Rowe, Henry K., *History of Religion in the United States,* Macmillan, New York, 1924.

Seldes, Gilbert, *The Stammering Century,* John Day Co., New York, 1928.

Shanks, T. J., *A College of Colleges,* Revell, New York, 1887.

Sharman, H. B., *Studies in the Life of Christ,* Y.M.C.A. Press, New York, 1896.

Shedd, C. P., "The Origin and Development of the Student Young Men's Christian Association Movement in North America." Unpublished. 1914. Library, National Council of Y.M.C.A's., New York.

Shotwell, James T., "Study of International Affairs in Colleges," *The New York Times,* Vol. 80, No. 26,860, Section 3, Aug. 9, 1931, p. 7.

Smith, Gerald B., Ed., *Religious Thought in the Last Quarter Century,* University of Chicago Press, 1927.

Strong, Frank, "The Problem of Religious Training in the Colleges and Universities," *Religious Education,* Vol. II, No. 6, Feb., 1908, pp. 211 ff.

Strong, Josiah, *The Challenge of the City,* Missionary Education Movement, New York, 1910.

Student Volunteer Movement, *An Appeal to the Churches from the*

Student Volunteers for Foreign Missions, Northfield, Mass., 1887.

Student Young Men's Christian Association, *The College Situation and Student Responsibility,* New York, 1924.

Sweet, William W., *The Story of Religions in America,* Harper & Bros., New York, 1930.

Tinker, W. H., *Life Work,* Association Press, New York, 1922.

Trawick, A. M., *College Men and Community Service,* Y.M.C.A. Press, New York.

Urbach, W. F., *A History of the University Pastor Movement in State Colleges and Universities of the United States.* M. A. Thesis, Yale University, 1915. Unpublished.

Weatherford, W. D., "The Secretaryship of the Student Y.M.C.A." *College Problems,* 1907, National Council Y.M.C.A. Library, New York; *Student Secretaries in Training,* Association Press, New York, 1909.

Weidensall, Robert, "Early History of the College Work of Young Men's Christian Associations," 1911. Library, National Council, Y.M.C.A., New York. Not published.

White, W. W., *Thirty Studies in Jeremiah,* International Committee Y.M.C.A., New York, 1896.

Wishard, Luther D., "Beginning of the Students' Era in Christian History," 1917. Library National Council Y.M.C.A., New York. Unpublished.

Wishard, Luther D., *et al., Outlines of Bible Study for the Training Class* (Editions for class members and for class leaders). International Committee Y.M.C.A., New York, 1886.

Wright, H. B. (Chairman), *Report of Commission on Student Voluntary Bible Study Texts.* Student Department, International Committee Y.M.C.A., New York. Undated.

Wright, H. B., *The Will of God and a Man's Life Work,* Association Press, New York, 1909.

World-Telegram, World Almanac, 1932, New York.

Y.M.C.A., *The Challenge of American Social Problems to College Men and Women,* Y.M.C.A. Press, New York, 1914; *College Y.M.C.A. Souvenir,* Summer School for Bible Study, Mt. Hermon, Mass., July, 1886; *Mr. Sayford's Work Among the Colleges,* 1889-94; 1898. Library, National Council Y.M.C.A., New York.

FILES OF PERIODICALS

The College Bulletin, November, 1878 to April, 1886, published monthly October to April.

The Intercollegian, bi-monthly from Jan., 1887, to May, 1889; monthly October, 1889 to June, 1891; monthly 1893 to 1912; monthly, except July, August, September, from October, 1918, to December, 1930.

Men, (successor to *Young Men's Era*), weekly Jan., 1896, to September, 1898; monthly October, 1898, to Sept., 1899.

The New Student, April 19, 1922, to June, 1929; at first a weekly, later a monthly.

The New York Times, Vol. 79, No. 26, 227, p. 29, Nov. 14, 1929.

The North American Student (successor to *The Intercollegian*), monthly October to June, Mar., 1913, to June, 1918.

The Student World, Quarterly of the World's Student Christian Federation. January, 1908, to 1930.

The Student Volunteer, monthly 1893-1898.

The Student Volunteer Movement Bulletin, 1915 to 1930.

The Watchman, monthly Nov., 1874, to Dec., 1878; semi-monthly Jan., 1879 to Dec., 1888; weekly Jan., 1889 to Dec., 1889.

Young Men's Era (successor to *The Watchman*), weekly Jan., 1889, to Dec., 1895.

YEAR BOOKS, AND REPORTS CONCERNING SPECIAL GATHERINGS, ETC.

"Cleveland Conference"—Minutes of Reference, New York, Mar. 14, 1916. Library, National Council, Y.M.C.A.; "Summary of the Cleveland Conference," 1915. Unpublished statement. Library, National Council, Y.M.C.A., New York.

Student Volunteer Movement: reports of Quadrennial conventions.

Y.M.C.A., *Report of Fifth Conference of Y.M.C.A's. of New England Colleges,* Feb. 18-20, 1887, Library, National Council, Y.M.C.A. *Report of the General Board of the Y.M.C.A. to the Meeting of the National Council of the Y.M.C.A.,* held at Chicago, 1929. *Report of the International Committee of Y.M.C.A's. to the International Convention of the Y.M.C.A's.,* 1922. *Reports of the International Conventions of Y.M.C.A's.,*

1870, 1881, 1883, 1899, 1901, 1907, 1913, 1916, 1919, 1922.
  *Reports of National Assemblies of Student Secretaries,
  Y.M.C.A.,* 1910 to 1930. *Reports of National Council Assemblies,* Y.M.C.A., 1924 to 1930. *Year Books,* 1877 to 1930.
Thirty-two Interview Documents, on file.
Eighteen Letter Documents, on file.
Eighty-three *Miscellaneous Reports* concerning staff reports, and
  staff conferences; reports of the Intercollegiate Y.M.C.A. and
  of the Student Volunteer Movement to the World's Student
  Christian Federation, and other miscellaneous statements.

INDEX OF NAMES

(For subjects consult the Table of Contents)

231